Hippocrene Lan

T0268834

UKRAINIAN
PHRASEBOOK
AND DICTIONARY

Hippocrene Language Studies

UKRAINIAN
PHRASEBOOK
AND DICTIONARY

Olesj P. Benyukh and Raisa I. Galushko

HIPPOCRENE BOOKS
New York

Sixth printing, 2008.

For information, address:
HIPPOCRENE BOOKS, INC.
171 Madison Avenue
New York, NY 10016
www.hippocrenebooks.com

ISBN-13: 978-0-7818-0188-1

Printed in the United States of America.

TABLE OF CONTENTS

A FEW WORDS ABOUT THIS BOOK

Ukraine is a very big country by any standards. Its territory is 601 square kilometers (that's bigger than France, Britain and Italy put together). Its population is over 55 million people. And now it's a free and independent state.

Interest is indeed great in the world about new Ukraine. Thousands of travellers - businessmen, students, sportsmen, working and retired people - go there in winter and summer, spring and fall. This book is meant to help them in their voyage of discovery of the ancient, and ever young, hospitable and beautiful Ненька-Україна (Mother Ukraine).

The first chapter will give you some initial information about the Ukrainian language. Each succesive chapter will lead you through customs and hotels, barbers and cinemas, doctors and post offices. When both the masculine and feminine forms are given, the masculine is presented first, followed by a slash and the feminine form.

The Ukrainian-English, English-Ukrainian dictionary at the end of the book with handy transliteration will also be of some help.

The situations described and the prices mentioned are true at the time of printing.

Transliteration Guide

а – a	ї – yee	у – u
б – b	й – y	ф – f
в – v	к – k	х – kh
г – g	л – l	ц – ts
д – d	м – m	ч – ch
е – e	н – n	ш – sh
є – ye	о – o	щ – shch
ж – zh	п – p	ю – yu
з – z	р – r	я – ya
и – i	с – s	ь – '
і – ee	т – t	' – "

1. THE LANGUAGE

The Cyrillic Alphabet

The Ukrainian language is written in Cyrillic, an alphabet developed from ancient Greek.

Ukrainian letter	English sound	Ukrainian letter	English sound
А/а	a h	Н/н	e h n
Б/б	b e h	О/о	o h
В/в	v e h	П/п	p e h
Г/г	g e h	Р/р	e h r
Д/д	d e h	С/с	e h s
Е/е	e h	Т/т	t e h
Є/є	y e h	У/у	o o
Ж/ж	z h e h	Ф/ф	e h f
З/з	z e h	Х/х	k h a
И/и	i h	Ц/ц	t s e h
I/i	e e	Ч/ч	c h a h
Ї/ї	y e e	Ш/ш	s h a h
Й/й	y	Щ/щ	s h c h a h
К/к	k a h	Ю/ю	y o o
Л/л	e h l	Я/я	y a h
М/м	e h m	Ь/ь	soft sign

Pronunciation

Like English, Ukrainian spelling is not strictly phonetic. One letter may have more than one sound value. That is why we use a system of transcription in which each symbol is assigned a constant value. The English transcription in this book will show you how to pronounce the Ukrainian words even if you do not know the Cyrillic alphabet. The transcription only approximates the Ukrainian sounds, however, since no sound is exactly like its Ukrainian counterpart.

Vowels

Ukrainian vowels are shorter and purer than the English vowel sounds they resemble. Depending on where the stress falls in a word, the sound value of some Ukrainian vowels may change. The following chart provides the approximate sounds of stressed vowels.

1

Ukrainian vowel	English approximation	English transcription
а	like the *a* in 'father'	a h
я	like *ya* in 'yard'	y a h
е	like *e* in 'bet'	e h
є	like *ye* in 'yet'	y e h
о	like *o* in 'note'	o h
і	like *ee* in 'beet'	e e
и	like *i* in 'pit'	i h
у	like *oo* in 'shoot'	o o
ю	like *ew* in 'pew'	y o o
ї	like *yi* in 'yield'	y e e

Consonants

Ukrainian consonants can be pronounced as either 'soft' or 'hard', voiced or voiceless. 'Softening', or palatalization occurs when the letter is pronounced closer to the front of the mouth or hard palate. In Ukrainian this occurs when consonants are followed by the vowels я, є, і, ї, ю or the 'soft sign' (Ь). Sometimes the palatalization of a letter can change the meaning of a word. For instance, 'пити' (pihtih) means 'to drink', whereas 'піти' means 'to go away'. Voiced consonants, those that make the vocal cords vibrate, become voiceless when they occur at the end of a word or before a voiceless consonant. For instance, 'вихід' is phonetically represented as 'vihkheet', not 'vihkheed' and 'вчора' becomes 'fchohrah', not 'vchohrah'. Likewise, voiceless consonants become voiced if they are placed before voiced consonants. Fortunately, you do not have to learn the rules for this; all of these distinctions will be made for you in the English transcription provided.

Ukrainian consonant	English approximation	English transcription
б	like the *b* in 'book'	b
в	like the *v* in 'vote'	v
г	like the *g* in 'goat'	g
д	like the *d* in 'dad'	d
ж	like the *s* in 'leisure'	zh
з	like the *z* in 'zebra'	z
к	like the *k* in 'cake'	k

2

л	like the *l* in 'lake'	l
м	like the *m* in 'mom'	m
н	like the *n* in 'nap'	n
п	like the *p* in 'pit'	p
р	like the *r* in 'red'	r
с	like the *s* in 'sail'	s
т	like the *t* in 'tail'	t
ф	like the *f* in 'fish'	f
х	like the *ch* in 'Bach'	kh
ц	like the *ts* in 'hats'	ts
ч	like the *ch* in 'chip'	ch
ш	like the *sh* in 'ship'	sh
щ	like *sh* followed by *ch*	shch

Diphthongs

When two vowels occur together in Ukrainian, they are both pronounced. The only diphthongs in Ukrainian are formed by a combination of a vowel and an ee-korotke (й).

Ukrainian diphthong	English approximation	English transcription
ой	like the *oy* in 'toy'	oy
ей	like the *ey* in 'hey'	ey
ай	like the *ye* in 'bye'	ay
яй	like the above sound with the *y* of 'yet' preceding it	yay
ий	like the *i* in 'pit' followed by the *y* of 'yet'	ihy
ій	like the long *e* in 'maybe'	eey
уй	like the *ooey* in 'phooey'	ooy
юй	like the above sound with the *y* of 'yet' preceding it	yooy

Other Letters

separative signs	English transcription	explanation
ь	'	The 'soft sign' is not pronounced. It simply shows that the preceding consonant is soft.

3

| ' | y | The 'apostrophe' is also not pro-nounced. It separates a prefix ending in a consonant from a stem beginning in a vowel. |

semi-vowel

| й | y | The 'ee-korotke' is a semi-vowel and always occurs with a full vowel as in diphthongs. |

Stress

Stress is very important in Ukrainian. Only one syllable in each word is stressed. Secondary stresses, commonly found in English pronunciation, should be avoided. The location of the stress in a word determines the pronunciation of certain vowels. Unstressed vowels are less distinct and slightly shorter than their stressed counterparts.

unstressed vowel	pronounced like Ukrainian vowel	example
о	y	*oo*dihn, not *oh*dihn
є	ï	*yee*dihnihy, not *yeh*dihnihy
я	ï	*yee*zihk, not *yah*zihk

Normally stress is not marked in Ukrainian texts. In this book the stressed syllable will be printed in capital letters in the transcription (ie: vohDA).

Commonly, in phrases of several short words, only one word will be stressed in the phrase (i.e.: Як вас звати? /yahk vahs ZVAHtih?)

Declension

Unlike English, Ukrainian expresses the relationship between words in a sentence by inflection. Nouns and adjectives take different endings depending on their function in a sentence. In Ukrainian these functions are grouped into six different categories called cases. Each case has its own endings. This explains why the same word may have different endings depending on its usage in a sentence.

4

II. ESSENTIAL EXPRESSIONS

The Basics

Yes./No	Так./Ні	tahk / nee
Maybe	Можливо	mohzhLIHvoh
Please	Будь ласка	bood' LAHSka
Thank you	Дякую	DYAHkooyoo
Thank you very much.	Дуже дякую/ Велике спасибі.	DOOzheh DYAHkooyoo/ veLIHkeh spahSIHbee
Thank you for the help /information.	Дякую за допомогу/ інформацію.	DYAHkooyoo zah dohpohMOH-goo/eenfor-MAHtseeyoo
You're welcome.	Нема за що/ Будь ласка.	nehMAH zah SHCHOH/ bood' LAHSkah
Ok.	Гаразд.	gahRAHZD
I beg your pardon.	Пробачте.	prohBAHCHteh
Excuse me.	Вибачте.	VIHbahchte
Why?	Чому?	chohMOO
Because.	Тому що.	tohMOOshchoh
That's the way it is.	Просто так.	PROHStoh tahk
Good.	Добре.	DOHBreh
Bad.	Погано.	pohGAHnoh
Can you tell me, please...	Скажіть, будь ласка...	skahZHEET' bood' LAHSkah
Help me.	Допоможіть мені.	dohpohmohZHEET' mehNEE
Is that right?	Правильно?	PRAHvihl'noh
Be so kind...	Будьте добрі...	BOOT'teh DOHBree
What?	Що?	shchoh
What's that?	Що це?	shchoh tseh
What does that mean?	Що це значить?	shchoh tseh ZNAHchiht'
Where?	Де?	deh
Where to?	Куди?	kooDIH
How?	Як?	yahk

5

How far?	Як далеко?	yahk dahLEHkoh
How long?	Як довго?	yahk DOHVgoh
When?	Коли?	kohLIH
Who?	Хто?	khtoh
Who is that?	Хто це?	khtoh tseh
I can't.	Я не можу	yah neh MOHzhoo
I want to	Я хочу	yah KHOHchoo
r e s t/	відпочити/	veedpohCHIHtih/
e a t/	їсти/	YEEstih
d r i n k/	пити/	PIHtih/
s l e e p.	спати.	SPAHtih

Greetings

Hello.	Добрий день.	DOHBrihy dehn'
Hi.	Привіт.	prihVEET
Good morning.	Доброго ранку.	DOHBrohgoh RAHNkoo
Good afternoon.	Добридень.	dohBRIHdehn'
Good evening.	Добрий вечір.	DOHBrihy VEHcheer
Good night.	Добраніч.	dohBRAHneech
Goodbye.	Допобачення.	dohpohBAHchehnyah
See you later.	До скорої зустрічі.	doh SKOHrohyee ZOOStreechee
Bye.	Бувай здоров.	booVAY zdohROHV
All the best.	Всього найкращого.	vsyohGOH nayKRAH-SHchohgoh

Introductions

Forms of address equivalent to Mr., Mrs., and Ms. do not exist in Ukraine. Instead, people usually address one another by their first name and patronym. To form the patronym they add a suffix - usually "-ovich" for men and "-ivna" for women to their father's first name. For example, if Ivan's father's first name is Petro, he would be called "Ivan Petrovych". Likewise, if Hanna's father's name is Mykhaylo, her patronymic would be "Hanna Mykhaylivna". If they know one another well or if they are talking to a child, Ukrainians may use a diminutive form like Halya or Vasya.

6

Male foreigners are sometimes addressed as "пан" and women as "пани" (p a h n, p a h n e e), but these are prerevolutionary terms and are never used when addressing citizens (except West Ukraine, where this old Polish tradition is still alive).

What's your name?	Як вас звати?	yahk vahs ZVAHtih
My name is...	Мене звати...	mehNEH ZVAHtih
Pleased to meet you.	Дуже приємно.	DOOzheh prihYEHMnoh
It's a pleasure to meet you.	Дуже приємно познайомитися з вами.	DOOzheh prihYEHMnoh pohznahYOH-mihtihsyah z VAHmih
May I introduce you to...	Дозвольте познайомити вас...	dohzVOHL'teh pohznahYOH-mihtih vahs...
my husband.	з моїм чоловіком.	z mohYEEM choh-lohVEEkohm
my wife.	з моєю дружиною.	z mohYEHyoo drooZHIHnohyoo
How are you?	Як життя?	yahk zhihTYAH
I'm fine, thanks.	Добре, дякую.	DOHBreh DYAHkooyoo
And you?	А у вас?	ah oo vahs
I'm ok.	Все гаразд.	vseh gahRAHZD
I'm not well.	Погано.	pohGAHnoh
How are things?	Як справи?	yahk SPRAHvih

Personal Information

Where are you from?	Звідки ви?	ZVEEDkih vih
I am from...	Я з...	yah z...
America.	Америки.	ahMEHrihkih
Canada.	Канади.	kahNADih
England.	Англії.	AHNgleeyee
What's your nationality?	Якої ви націо-нальності?	yahKOHyee vih nahtseeoh-NAHL'nohstee
I am...*	Я...	yah...

* Ukrainian does not have articles (a, the), nor does it have a present tense form of the verb "to be".

When there is a different word used for the masculine and feminine forms, both forms will be given, with the masculine form first, followed by the feminine (f) form.

7

American (m/f)	американець/ американка	ahmerihKAHnehts'/ ahmerih-KAHNkah
Canadian (m/f)	канадець/ка	kahNAHdehts'/kah
British (m/f)	англічанин/ка	ahngleeCHAHnihn/kah
What are you doing here?	Що ви тут робите?	shchoh vih toot ROHbihteh
I am a tourist (m/f)	Я турист/ туристка	yah tooRIHST/kah
I'm studying here.	Я вчуся тут.	yah VCHOOsyah toot
I'm here on business.	Я тут по справах.	yah toot poh SPRAHvahkh
What's your profession?	Хто ви за фахом/ по професії?	khtoh vih zah FAHkhohm/poh prohFEHseeyee
I'm a(n)...*	Я...	yah...
student (m/f)	студент/ка	stooDEHNT/kah
teacher (m/f)	вчитель/ка	VCHIHtel'/kah
professor	професор	prohFEHSsohr
businessman (m)	бізнесмен	beeznehsMEHN
journalist (m/f)	журналіст/ка	zhoornahLEEST/kah
nurse	медсестра	mehdsehsTRAH
housewife	домогосподарка	dohmohgohspoh-DAHRkah
doctor	лікар	LEEkahr
lawyer	адвокат	ahdvohKAHT
engineer	інженер	eenzhehNERH
chemist	хімік	KHEEmeek
How long have you been here?	Скільки часу ви вже тут?	SKEEL'kih CHAHsoo vih vzheh toot?
I have been here...	Я вже тут...	yah vzheh toot...
a day	день.	dehn'
a week	тиждень.	TIHZHdehn'
a month	місяць.	MEEsyahts'
Do you like it here?	Вам тут подобається?	vahm toot pohdoh-bahYET'syah

* Not all professions have a masculine and feminine form. Some, like professors, lawyers, and doctors, use one word for both male and female members of their professions.

8

English	Ukrainian	Pronunciation
Yes, very much.	Так, мені дуже подобається.	tahk, mehNEE DOOzheh pohdohbahYET'syah
No, not at all.	Ні, не подобається.	nee neh pohdohbahYET'syah
I'm having a wonderful time.	Я тут гарно проводжу час.	yah toot GAHRnoh prohVOHDzhoo chahs
Where are you staying?	Де ви зупинилися?	deh vih zoopihNIHlihsyah
At the hotel...	У готелі...	oo gohTEHlee
Are you married? (m/f)	Ви одружені?/ Ви заміжем?	vih ohDROOzhehnee/ vih ZAHmoozhehm
Yes, I am/ No, I am not. (men)	Так, одружений. Ні, не одружений.	tahk ohDROOzhehnihy/nee neh ohDROOzhehnihy
Yes, I am No, I am not (women)	Так, заміжем Ні, не заміжем	tahk ZAHmoozhehm/nee neh ZAHmoozhehm
Do you have children?	У вас є діти?	oo vahs yeh DEEtih

Making Oneself Understood

English	Ukrainian	Pronunciation
Do you speak...	Ви розмовляєте...	vih rohzmohvLYAHyehteh
English?	англійською/	ahngLEEYs'kohyoo/
Ukrainian?	українською/	ookrahYEEns'kohyoo/
Russian?	російською/	rohSEEYs'kohyoo/
German?	німецькою/	neeMEHTS'kohyoo/
French?	французькою/	frahnTSOOZ'kohyoo/
Spanish?	іспанською мовою?	eeSPAHNS'kohyoo MOHvohyoo
Only a little.	Тільки трохи.	TEEL'kih TROHkhih
Not at all.	Зовсім не розмовляю.	ZOHVseem neh rohzmohvLYAHyoo

9

I can understand Ukrainian, but I don't speak it very well.	Я розумію українську мову, але погано розмовляю.	yah rohzooMEEyoo ookrahYEENs'-koo MOHvoo ahLEH pohGAHnoh rohzmohv-LYAHyoo
Do you understand?	Ви розумієте?	vih rohzoo-MEEyehteh
I don't understand.	Я не розумію.	yah neh rohzooMEEyoo
Please speak more slowly.	Говоріть, будь ласка, повільніше.	gohvohREET' bood' LAHSkah pohVEEL'nee-sheh
Please repeat that.	Повторіть, будь ласка.	pohvtohREET' bood' LAHSkah
Please write it down for me.	Напишіть, будь ласка, це.	nahpihSHEET' bood' LAHSkah tseh
Translate this for me, please.	Перекладіть, будь ласка.	pehrehklahDEET' bood' LAHSkah
What does this/that mean?	Що це значить?	shchoh tseh ZNAHchiht'
What did he/she say?	Що він/вона сказав/ла?	shchoh veen/ vohNAH skahZAHV/lah

III. AT THE AIRPORT

Passport Control

When you arrive in Ukraine you will have to go through "Passport control" (Па́спортний контро́ль / PAHSpohrtnihy kohnTROHL') where they will check your passport and visa. Here they may ask you several questions to verify your identity. This is not the place to impress them with your knowledge of the country and its language.

Your passport, please.	Ваш па́спорт, будь ла́ска.	vahsh PAHSpohrt bood' LAHSkah
Here it is.	Ось він.	ohs' veen
How long are you staying?	Скі́льки ча́су ви тут бу́дете?	SKEEL'kih CHAHsoo vih toot BOOdehteh
A few days.	Де́кілька днів.	DEHkeel'kah dneev
A week.	Ти́ждень.	TIHZHdehn'
Two weeks.	Два ти́жні.	dvah TIHZHnee
A month.	Мі́сяць.	MEEsyahts'
Two months.	Два мі́сяці.	dvah MEEsyahtsee
I'm here...	Я тут...	yah toot
on vacation.	у відпу́стці.	oo veedPOOSTtsee
on business.	по спра́вах.	poh SPRAHvahkh
to study.	на навча́нні.	nah nahvchanNEE
I don't understand.	Я не розумі́ю.	yah neh rohzooMEEyoo
I don't know.	Я не зна́ю.	yah neh ZNAHyoo

Customs

You will have to fill out customs declarations upon entering and leaving the country. Be sure to declare all jewelry, photographic equipment and other valuables, so that you do not have to pay duty fees on them when you leave. Selling your personal possessions to Ukrainians (i.e., dealing on the black market) is illegal.

Customs.	Тамо́жня/ми́тниця	tahMOHZHnyah/ MIHTnihtsyah
To pass through customs.	Пройти́ ми́тний тамо́жений о́гляд.	prohyTIH MIHTnihy/tah- MOHZHehnnihy OHGlyahd

11

Customs Official.	Митник/ таможенник.	MIHTnikh/tah-MOHZHehnihk
Have you anything to declare?	Ви хочете щось обвявити?	vih KHOH-chehteh shchohs' ohbyahVIHtih
Open this suitcase.	Відкрийте цей чемодан.	veedKRIHYteh tsehy chehmoh-DAHN
What is this?	Що це?	shchoh tseh
You'll have to pay duty on this.	За це вам треба заплатити мито.	zah tseh vahm TREHbah zahplahTIHtih MIHtoh
It's for my personal use.	Це для особистого користування.	tseh dlya ohsoh-BIHStohgoh kohrihstoo-VAHNnyah
It's a gift.	Це подарунок.	tseh pohdah-ROOnohk
May I bring this in?	Можна це провезти?	MOHZHnah tseh prohVEHZtih
It's not new.	Це не нове.	tseh neh nohVEH
Do you have any more luggage?	Маєте ще багаж?	MAHyehteh shcheh bahGAHZH
Is that all?	Це все?	tseh vseh
I have...	Я маю...	yah MAHyoo...
a carton of cigarettes.	блок сигарет.	blohk sihgahREHT
a bottle of wine / whiskey.	пляшку вина/ віски.	PLYASHkoo vihNAH/ VEESkih
I don't understand.	Я не розумію.	yah neh rohzooMEEyoo
Does anyone here speak English?	Розмовляє тут хтось англій-ською мовою?	rohzmohVLYAHyeh toot khtohs' ahngLEEYS'-kohyoo MOHvohyoo

12

Baggage

English	Ukrainian	Pronunciation
Luggage claim.	Видача багажа.	VIHdahchah bahgahZHAH
Porter.	Носильник.	nohSIHL'nihk
Are there any luggage carts?	Візки є?	veezKIH yeh
Please carry this...	Будь ласка, візьміть...	bood' LAHSkah veez'MEET'
luggage.	багаж.	bahGAHZH
suitcase.	чемодан.	chehmohDAHN
That's mine, (too).	Це моє/теж/.	tseh mohYEH (tehzh)
There's a suitcase missing.	Не вистачає одного чемодана.	neh vihstah-CHAHyeh ohdNOHgoh chehmoh-DAHnah
Take these things to the...	Віднесіть ці речі до...	veednehSEET' tsee REHchee doh...
bus.	автобусу.	ahvTOHboosoo
taxi.	таксі.	tahkSEE
customs.	таможні.	tahMOHZHnee
baggage room.	камери зберігання.	KAHmehrih zbehree-GAHNnyah
How much do I owe you?	Скільки я вам винен/винна?	SKEEL'kih yah vahm VIHNehn/ VIHNnah
My luggage is lost.	Мій багаж загублено.	meey bahGAHZH zahGOOB-lehnoh

Currency Exchange

It is best to change money at the airport or in your hotel. Hours of operation are often irregular, however, so you should plan ahead. Try not to exchange more than you need because the reexchange rate is less than the exchange rate and you will lose money. You will have to present your passport and currency declaration form each time you change money. You may bring in as much foreign currency as you like, but Ukrainian money is not allowed out of the country.

Currency exchange.	Обмін валюти.	OHBmeen vahLYOOtih
Where can I change some money?	Де можна обміняти валюту?	deh MOHZHnah ohbmee-NYAHtih vahLYOOtoo
I'd like to change some dollars.	Я хотів/ла би обміняти долари.	yah khohTEEV/lah bih ohbmee-NYAHtih DOHlahrih
Can you cash these traveller's checks?	Можете обміняти ці дорожні чеки?	MOHzhehteh ohbmee-NYAHtih tsee dohROHZHnee CHEHkih
Can you change this for Ukrainian money?	Можете обміняти це на україн-ські гроші?	MOHzhehteh ohbmee-NYAHtih tseh nah ookrahYEEN-s'kee GROHshee
What's the exchange rate?	Який валютний курс?	yahKIHY vahLYOOTnihy koors
Can you give me smaller bills?	Можете дати мені дрібними купюрами?	MOHzhehteh DAHtih mehNEE dreebNIHmih kooPYOO-rahmih

Car Rental

Driving in the Ukraine is only for the very brave at heart. Gas stations are scarce and gas is even scarcer. Road regulations are complex and strictly enforced, even on foreigners, who are subject to the full severity of Ukrainian law. You can rent cars at the airport or through some Intourist hotels, but you must have an international driver's license. Insurance premiums are usually included in the rental fee and gas is bought with coupons sold by Intourist, the Ukrainian tourism agency, which is called Ukrintour.

Car rental.	Прокат машин.	prohKAHT mahSHIHN
I'd like to rent a car.	Я хотів/ла би взяти напрокат машину.	yah khohTEEV/lah bih VZYAtih nahprohKAHT mahSHIHnoo
What's the rate...	Скільки це коштує...	SKEEL'kih tseh KOHSHtooyeh
per day?	на день?	nah dehn'
per week?	на тиждень?	nah TIHZHdehn'
What's the charge per kilometer?	Скільки коштує кілометр?	SKEEL'kih KOHSHtooyeh keelohMEHTR
Are the prices of gas and oil included?	Бензин і масло включені в ціну?	behnZIHN ee MAHSloh VKLYOO- chehnee v tseeNOO
I need it for...	Вона потрібна мені на...	vohNAH pohTREEBnah mehnee...
a day.	день.	nah dehn'.
3 days.	три дні.	nah trih dnee.
a week.	тиждень.	nah TIHZHdehn'.
2 weeks.	два тижні.	nah dvah TIHZHnee.
Here's my (international driver's) license.	Ось мої міжна- родні права водія.	ohs' mohYEE meezhnah- ROHDnee prahVAH vohdeeYAH
Here's my credit card.	Ось моя кредитна картка.	ohs' mohYAH krehDIHTnah KAHRTkah
I am not familiar with this car.	Ця машина мені не відома.	tsyah mahSHIHnah mehNEE neh veeDOHmah
What is this?	Що це?	shchoh tseh
Explain this to me.	Поясніть мені це.	pohyasNEET' mehNEE tseh

English	Ukrainian	Pronunciation
Show me how this mechanism works.	Покажіть мені, як цей механізм працює.	pohkahZHEET' mehNEE yahk tsey mehkhah-NEEZM prahTSYOOyeh
Where can I buy gas?	Де я можу купити бензин?	deh yah MOHZHoo kooPIHtih behnZIHN
Where can I buy gas coupons?	Де можна купити талони на бензин?	deh MOHZHnah kooPIHtih tahLOHnih nah behnZIHN
Gas pump.	Бензоколонка.	behnzohkoh-LOHNkah
Service station.	Автозаправочна станція.	ahvtohzahPRAH-vohchnah STAHNtseeyah
Parking lot.	Стоянка для машин.	stohYAHNkah dlyah mahSHIHN

16

IV. AT THE HOTEL

Hotel arrangements must be made before you arrive in the Ukraine and payment is expected in advance. Many hotels in this country open to foreign tourists are run by Ukrainian Intourist. A variety of services are usually available at your hotel, depending on its size. The larger ones will have a post office, currency exchange office, gift shop, restaurant, bar, dry cleaner, laundry, hair dresser and barbershop. The hotels also usually have an information or service office (бюро́ обслуго́вування /byooROH ohbslooGOHvoovahnnyah), where the staff knows English and can answer your questions, give advice and book tours.

Check In

Upon checking in at your hotel, you will be given something resembling a temporary visa, called a пере́пустка (pehREHpoostkah), which you will be expected to show at the door to gain entry to the hotel and again to the hall monitor to get your keys each time you return to your room.

Do you speak English?	Ви розмовля́єте англі́йською мо́вою?	vih rohzmohv-LYAHyehteh ahngLEEYs'kohyoo MOHvohyoo
My name is...	Моє́ прі́звище...	mohYEH PREEZvihshcheh...
I have a reservation.	Я замо́вив/ла зазда́легідь.	yah zahMOHvihv/lah zahzdahlehGEED'
Here are my documents.	Ось мої́ докуме́нти.	ohs' mohYEE dohkooMEHNtih
I'd like a single/ double room.	Я хоті́в би но́мер на одно́го/ на двох.	yah khohTEEV/lah bih NOHmehr nah ohdNOHgoh/ nah dvohkh
I'd like a room with...	Я хоті́в/ла би но́мер з...	yah khohTEEV/lah bih NOHmehr z...
a double bed.	двоспа́льним лі́жком.	dvohSPAHL'nihm LEEZHkohm
two twin beds.	двома́ лі́жками.	dvohMAH LEEZHkahmih

a bath.	ванною.	VAHNnohyoo
a shower.	душем.	DOOSHehm
a private toilet.	особистим туалетом.	ohsohBIHStihm tooahLEHTohm
a telephone.	телефоном.	tehlehFOHnohm
a television.	телевізором.	tehlehVEEzohrohm
a balcony.	балконом.	bahlKOHnohm
a view.	краєвидом.	krahyehVIHdohm
Is there...	Чи є у вас...	chih yeh oo vahs
room service?	обслуговування у номері?	ohbslooGOHvoovahnnyah oo NOHmehree
a dining room?	їдальня?	yeeDAHL'nyah
a restaurant?	ресторан?	rehstohRAHN
air conditioning?	кондиціонер?	kohndihtseeohNEHR
heating?	опалення?	ohPAHlehnnyah
hot water?	гаряча вода?	gahRYAHchah vohDAH
a garage?	гараж?	gahRAHZH
May I see the room?	Можна подивитися номер?	MOHZHnah pohdihVIHtihsyah NOHmehr
Yes, I'll take it.	Так, це підійде.	tahk tseh peeDEEYdeh
No, I don't like it.	Ні, мені не подобається.	nee mehNEE neh pohDOHbahyeht'syah
Do you have anything else?	Чи є у вас інший номер?	chih yeh oo vahs EENshihy NOHmer
I asked for a room with a bath.	Я просив/ла номер з ванною.	yah prohSIHV(lah) NOHmehr z VAHNnohyoo

Registration

Once your reservation has been confirmed, you will be asked to present your passport and fill out a registration form. Your passport may be kept overnight for processing, but you should be able to pick it up the next day. If you plan to exchange money, be sure you do it before you register, since you'll need your passport to carry out the transaction.

Registration.	Реєстрація	rehyehSTRAHtseeyah
Registration form.	Анкета для приїжджих.	ahnKEHtah dlyah prihYIHZHdzhihkh
Fill out this form.	Заповніть цю анкету.	zahPOHVneet' tsyoo ahnKEHtoo
Sign here.	Підпишіться тут.	peedpihSHEET'syah toot

18

Your passport, please.	Будь ласка, ваш паспорт.	bood' LAHSkah vahsh PAHSpohrt
How long will you be here?	Як довго ви тут пробудете?	yahk DOHVgoh vih toot prohBOOdete
What does this mean?	Що це означає?	shchoh tseh ohznahCHAHyeh
What's my room number?	Який у мене номер?	yahKIHY oo MEHneh NOHmehr
My key, please.	Мій ключ, будь ласка.	meey klyooch bood' LAHSkah
Take my luggage to my room, please.	Віднесіть, будь ласка, багаж до мого номеру.	veednehSEET' bood' LAHSkah bahGAHZH doh mohGOH NOHmehroo
Is there an elevator?	Чи є ліфт?	chih yeh leeft

The Staff

You will find that the most important person at your hotel will be the hall monitor. It is a good idea to be polite and friendly to her, because she can make your stay much more pleasant.

Hall/Floor monitor.	Чергова	chehrGOHvah
Doorman.	Швейпар	shveyTSAHR
Porter.	Носильник	nohSIHL'nihk
Maid.	Покоївка	pohkohYEEVkah
Receptionist.	Секретарка	sehkrehTAHRkah
Switchboard operator.	Телефоністка	tehlehfohNEESTkah
Waiter.	Офіціант	ohfeetseeAHNT
Waitress.	Офіціантка	ohfeetseeAHNTkah
Manager.	Директор	dihREHKtohr

Questions

The voltage in the Ukraine is 220 A.C. The plugs and sockets are like those used in Europe, so Americans should bring electrical adaptors and converters for their electrical appliances.

Can you please bring me...	Принесіть мені, будь ласка...	prihnehSEET' mehNEE bood' LAHSkah
a towel.	рушник	rooshNIHK
a blanket.	ковдру	KOHVDroo

19

a pillow.	подушку	pohDOOSHkoo
a pillowcase.	наволочку	NAHvohlohchkoo
an ashtray.	попільничку	pohpeel'NIHCHkoo
some hangers	декілька вішалок	DEHkeel'kah VEEshahlohk
some soap	мило	MIHloh
Where are the toilets?	Де туалет?	deh tooahLEHT
Where is the...	Де...	deh
restaurant?	ресторан?	rehstohRAHN
bar?	бар?	bahr
post office?	пошта?	POHSHtah
information office?	бюро обслу- говування?	byooROH ohbsloo- GOHvoovahnnyah
hair dresser/ barber?	перукарня?	pehrooKAHRnyah
currency ex- change office?	обмін валюти?	OHBmeen vahLYOOtih
light switch?	вимикач?	vihmihKAHCH
electrical outlet?	розетка?	rohZEHTkah

Problems

You should be aware that hot water is routinely shut off for several weeks at a time in the Ukraine during the summer for annual repairs.

The ... doesn't work.	...не працює	...neh prahTSYOOyeh
shower	душ	doosh
faucet	кран	krahn
toilet	туалет	tooahLEHT
heating	опалення	ohPAHlehnnyah
air conditioning	кондиціонер	kohndihtseeohNEHR
radio	радіо	RAHdeeoh
television	телевізор	tehlehVEEzohr
telephone	телефон	tehlehFOHN
electrical socket	розетка	rohZEHTkah
There is no...	Немає...	nehMAHyeh
(hot) water.	/гарячої/ води	(gahRYAHchoyee) vohDIH
lamp	лампи	LAHMpih
light	світла	SVEETlah
fan	вентилятора	vehntihLYAHtohrah
The sink is clogged.	раковина забита	RAHkohvihnah zahBIHtah

20

The door/window is jammed.	Двéрі/вікнó не зачиняються	DVEHree/veekNOH neh zahchih-NYAHyoot'syah
The door doesn't lock.	Двéрі не замикаються	DVEHree neh zahmihKAHyoot'syah
Can it be repaired?	Мóжна це відремонтувáти?	MOHZHnah tseh veedreh-mohntooVAHtih

Check Out

I'm leaving	Я від'їжджáю	yah veedyeezhd-ZHAHyoo
today/ tomorrow morning.	сьогóдні/ зáвтра врáнці	syohGOHDnee/ ZAHVtrah VRAHNtsee
Please prepare my bill.	Приготýйте, будь лáска, мій рахýнок	prihgohTOOYteh bood' LAHSkah meey rahKHOOnohk
Do you accept credit cards?	Мóжна оплатúти кредúтною кáрткою?	MOHZHnah ohplahTIHtih krehDIHTnohyoo KAHRTkohyoo
I think there's a mistake.	Менí здаéться, що ви помилúлися	mehNEE zdahYEHT'syah shchoh vih pohmihLIHlihsyah
Could you please send someone to get my bags?	Пришлíть, будь лáска, кого-небудь вúнести мій багáж.	prihSHLEET' bood' LAHSkah kohGOH-NEHbood' VIHnestih meey bahGAHZH
Where can I get a cab?	Де мóжна піймáти таксí?	deh MOHZHnah peeyMAHtih tahkSEE

V. AT THE RESTAURANT

Eating out in Ukraine can be fun and interesting, but do not expect it to be like at home as it is in the West. Restaurants are generally inexpensive, but with the exception of some of the regional dining establishments, the food is mediocre at best. Usually restaurant staff are not known for their eagerness to please and service can be quite slow. Do not be surprised to be seated at a table with people you don't know; it is a common practice in Eastern Europe, particularly in smaller restaurants. Dishes that don't have prices on the menu are not available. Your best bet is to ask your waiter for his suggestions and then choose accordingly.

Types of Establishments

Ресторáн (rehstohRAHN)
Restaurants generally have a broad choice of dishes, as well as orchestras and dancing. People usually go early and make a leisurely evening of it. Reservations are strongly recommended and can usually be made through your hotel. Restaurants typically close by 11 pm.

Кафé (kahfEH)
Cafés can vary quite a bit, but in general the better ones resemble restaurants, except for a slightly more limited menu. They usually close between 9 and 10 pm.

Кооперати́вне кафé (kohohpehrahTIHVneh kahFEH)
Like its name suggests, *cooperative cafes* are privately run dining establishments. The quality of food and service should be higher due to the profit motive, but be prepared for higher prices, as well.

Їдáльня (yeeDAHL'nyah)
As in the US, *cafeterias* can be found in most institutions like universities, libraries and factories. They are selfserve and inexpensive. Alcohol is prohibited.

Закýсочна/Буфéт (zahKOOsohchnah / booFEHT)
Snack bars are found virtually everywhere in Ukraine from train stations to music conservatories. Here one can get a variety of light

snacks such as open-faced sandwiches, fruit, cookies, bottled water and juices.

Варени́чна (vahrehNIHCHnah)

These are small cafés specializing in вареники - dumplings filled with pot cheese, vegetables (potatoes, cabbage) or fruits (in summer). Many of these specially food places do not have seats; instead, customers eat side-by-side, standing up at counters.

Млинці́ (mlihnTSEE)

Another type of specialty café, the Млинці, offers paper-thin Ukrainian pancakes, filled with meat, pot cheese, jam or apples, called млинці (mlihnTSEE) or налисники (nahLIHSnihkih). They are commonly ordered as hors d'oeuvres in larger restaurants, but can also be enjoyed as a meal onto themselves.

Пиріжко́ва (pihreezhKOHvah)

Similar to the Варенична and Млинці, these small establishments specialize in пиріжки (pihreezhKIH) - large dumplings filled with meat, rice, cabbage, jam or fruits.

Шашли́чна (shahshLIHCHnah)

For those who want to try dishes from the Caucasus and Central Asia, this type of restaurant specializes in шашлик (shahshLIHK), a shish kebob usually made with lamb and vegetables.

Кафе́-кондитерська (kahFEH - kohnDIHtehrs'kah)

Closer to what we normally think of as a café, this type of establishment serves tea, cookies, cake and other sweets.

Кафе́-моро́зиво (kahFEH - mohROHzihvoh)

Similar to Western-style ice cream parlors, these cafés offer ice cream, cookies, and other sweets.

Ча́йна (CHAYnah)

This small tea shop offers a variety of teas, coffee, cookies and pastries.

Бар (bahr)

These days almost all existing bars are found in Intourist hotels. Patronage is usually limited to hotel guests and only foreign currency is accepted.

23

I'm hungry (m/f)	Я голодний./ Я голодна	yah gohLOHDnihy./ yah gohLOHDnah.
I'd like to eat/drink.	Мені хочеться їсти/пити	mehNEE KHOHcheht'syah YEEStih/PIHtih
Can you recommend a good restaurant?	Чи можете ви порекоменду- вати гарний ресторан?	chih MOHzhehteh vih pohrehkohmehndoo- VAHtih GAHRnihy rehstohRAHN
Do you serve breakfast/ lunch/ dinner?	Ви накриваєте сніданок/ обід/ вечерю?	vih nahkrihVAHyehteh sneeDAHnohk/ ohBEED/ vehCHEHryoo
I'd like to make a reservation.	Я хотів/ла би замовити столик.	yah khohTEEV/lah bih zahMOHvihtih STOHlihk
There are 2/3/4 of us.	Нас двоє/ трoє/ четверо.	nahs DVOHyeh/ TROHyeh/ CHEHTvehroh
We'll come at six.	Ми прийдемо о шостій.	mih prihyDEHmoh oh SHOHSteey
Where is the coat check?	Де гардероб/ роздягальня?	deh gahrdehROHB/ rohzdyahGAHL'nya
Coat check number.	Номерок	nohmehROHK
Where are the bathrooms?	Де туалет?	deh tooahLEHT
Is this place taken/ reserved/ free?	Чи це місце зайняте/ замовлене/ вільне?	chih tseh MEEStseh ZAHYnyateh/ zahMOHVlehneh/ VEEL'neh
It's taken/ reserved/ free.	Воно зайняте/ замовлене/ вільне.	vohNOH ZAHYnyahteh/ zahMOHVlehneh/ VEEL'neh
Have a seat!	Сідайте!	seeDAHYteh
We'd prefer a table...	Ми воліємо столик...	mih vohLEEyehmoh STOHlihk...
in the corner.	у закутку	oo ZAHkootkoo
by the window.	біля вікна	BEElyah veekNAH
outside.	на свіжому повітрі	nah SVEEzhohmoo pohVEETree
May we have another table?	Дайте нам, будь ласка, інший столик	DAHYteh nahm bood' LAHSkah EENshihy STOHlihk

24

Is smoking permitted here?	Чи тут можна курити/ палити?	chih toot MOHZHnah kooRIHtih/ pahLIHtih

Ordering

Waiter./ Waitress.	Офіціант/ Офіціантка	ohfeetseeAHNT/ ohfeetseeAHNTkah
This way please.	Сюди, будь ласка.	syooDIH bood' LAHSkah
May I have a menu, please.	Принесіть, будь ласка, меню.	prihnehSEET' bood' LAHSkah mehNYOO
Have you decided?	Чи ви вже вибрали?	chih vih vzheh VIHBrahlih
What do you recommend?	Що ви порадите?	shchoh vih pohRAHdihteh
Unfortunately, we don't have...	На жаль, у нас немає...	nah zhahl' oo nahs nehMAHyeh...
Why not take this instead.	Краще візьміть ось це.	KRAHshcheh veez'MEET' ohs' tseh...
What would you like?	Що би ви хотіли?	shchoh bih vih khohTEElih
Go ahead.	Слухаю вас.	SLOOkhahyoo vahs
I'll have...	Я хочу...	yah KHOHchoo...
for appetizers...	на закуску...	nah zahKOOSkoo...
for the first course...	на перше...	nah PEHRsheh...
for the second course...	на друге...	nah DROOgeh...
for the third course/ desert...	на третє/ на солодке/ на десерт...	nah TREHTyeh/ nah sohLOHDkeh/ nah dehSEHRT...
A small portion.	Маленьку порцію	mahLEHN'koo POHRtseeyoo
What would you like to drink?	Що би ви хотіли випити?	shchoh bih vih khohTEElih VIHpihtih
I recommend...	Раджу...	RAHDzhoo
That's all, thank you.	Це все, дякую.	tseh vseh DYAHkooyoo

The Meal

Enjoy your meal!	Смачного!	smahchNOHgoh
How is it?	Як воно вам, подобається?	yahk vohNOH vahm pohDOHbahyeht'syah

It's very tasty.	Дуже смачне.	DOOzheh smahchNEH
Please	Передайте,	pehrehDAHYteh
pass me...	будь ласка...	bood' LAHSkah
Please	Принесіть мені,	prihnehSEET' mehNEE
bring me...	будь ласка...	bood' LAHSkah
a cup	чашку	CHASHkoo
a glass	склянку	SKLYAHNkoo
a fork	виделку	vihDEHLkoo
a knife	ніж	neezh
a spoon	ложку	LOHZHkoo
a plate	тарілку	tahREELkoo
a napkin	серветку	sehrVEHTkoo
an ashtray	попільничку	pohpeel'NIHCHkoo
some salt	сіль	seel'
some pepper	перець	PEHrehts'
sugar	цукор	TSOOkohr
water	воду	VOHdoo
bread and	бутерброд/	bootehrBROHD/
butter	канапку	kahNAHPkoo
Can I have	Можна мені	MOHZHnah mehNEE
some more	ще трохи	shcheh TROHkhih
of this?	цього?	tsyohGOH
Would you like	Подати вам	pohDAHtih vahm
anything else?	ще щось?	shcheh shchohs'

Complaints

I have a	Я хочу	yah KHOHchoo
complaint.	поскаржитися.	pohSKAHRzhihtihsyah
This is...	Це...	tseh...
cold	холодне	khohLOHDneh
hot	гаряче	gahRYAHcheh
too spicy	занадто гостре	zahNAHDtoh GOHSTreh
too sweet/ salty	Занадто солодке/	zahNAHDtoh sohLOHDkeh/
	пересолене	pehrehSOHlehneh
sour	кисле	KIHSleh
stale	не свіже	neh SVEEzheh
tough	тверде	TVEHRdeh
overdone	пересмажене	pehrehSMAHzhehneh
underdone	недосмажене	nehdohSMAHzhehneh
This is dirty	Це брудне	tseh broodNEH
I don't like this	Це мені не	tseh mehNEE neh
	подобається.	pohDOHbahyeht'syah

You can take this away	Можете забрати це.	MOHzhehteh zahBRAHtih tseh
There's been a mistake	Ви помилилися.	vih pohmih-LIHlihsyah
This isn't what I ordered	Це не те, що я замовляв/ла.	tseh neh teh shchoh yah zahmohvLYAHV/lah
I ordered...	Я замовляв/ла...	yah zahmohvLYAHV/lah
I don't want it	Я цього не хочу.	yah tsyohGOH neh KHOHchoo

The Check

Although tipping is officially discouraged, it is still appreciated and often expected when serving foreigners. Between five and ten percent is about average for waiters. More than extra money, people welcome small gifts and souvenirs such as a pack of cigarettes or chewing gum, perfume, cigarette lighters or key chains. Ukrainians are very hospitable and like to make presents too. Most of all they present Ukrainian-style things such as needlework, handicraft wares made of wood and so on.

We're finished.	Ми закінчили.	mih zahKEENchihlih
I have had enough.	Мені досить.	mehNEE DOHsiht'
Bring me the check, please.	Принесіть мені, будь ласка, рахунок.	prihnehSEET' mehNEE bood' LAHSkah rahKHOOnohk
There's been a mistake.	Ви не помилилися?	vih neh pohmihLIHlihsyah
How did you get this total?	Що входить у цю суму?	shchoh VHOHdiht' oo tsyoo SOOmoo
Is a tip included?	Чи чайові включені в рахунок?	chih chahyohVEE VKLYOOchehnee v rahKHOOnohk
Pay the cashier.	Платіть до каси.	plahTEET' doh KAHsih
We'd like to pay separately.	Ми хотіли б розплатитися окремо.	mih khohTEElih b rohzplahTIHtihsya ohKREHmoh
Do you accept...	Ви берете...	vih behREHteh
traveler's checks?	подорожні чеки?	pohdohROHZHnee CHEHkih
credit cards?	кредитні картки?	krehDIHTnee KAHRTkih
Intourist food vouchers?	інтуристівські талони на обід?	eentooRIHSteevs'kee tahLOHnih nah ohBEED

27

| Thank you, this is for you. | Дякую, це для вас. | DYAHkooyoo tseh dlyah vahs |

Snack Bars and Cafeterias

At Ukrainian snack bars, just like in the US, you usually pick up what you want yourself or else ask someone behind the counter for it. Ukrainian cafeterias are a bit more complex. First, you decide what you want from a printed menu at the cashier's window. Then, you tell the cashier what you want, pay her and receive food coupons for the desired items. Next, you either take the coupons to the serving line and pick up your meal, or you take a seat and someone collects your coupons and brings you your food. Be sure to carry small bills with you because the cashiers very often will not accept anything larger than a ten-coupon note. Since people tend to hang on to their fifteen-kopeck pieces to use on public phones, do not be surprised to receive candy as small change.

What's this?	Що це таке?	shchoh tseh tahKEH
Please give me one of those.	Дайте, будь ласка, мені один з них.	DAHYteh bood' LAHSkah mehNEE ohDIHN z nihkh
I'd like (that) please.	Мені б хотілося цього, будь ласка.	mehNEE b khohTEElohsyah tsyohGOH bood' LAHSkah
Please give me a piece of that.	Дайте мені, будь ласка, шматок цього.	DAHYteh mehNEE bood' LAHSkah shmahTOHK tsyohGOH
May I help myself?	Чи можу я взяти сам/ма?	chih MOHzhoo yah VZYAHtih sahm/mah
Just a little.	Тільки трошки.	TEEL'kih TROHSHkih
A little more, please.	Трохи більше, будь ласка.	TROHkhih BEEL'sheh bood' LAHSkah
Enough?	Досить?	DOHsiht'
Anything else?	Що-небудь ще?	shchoh-NEHbood' shcheh
That's all, thank you.	Це все, дякую.	tseh vseh DYAHkooyoo
How much is it?	Скільки це коштує?	SKEEL'kih tseh KOHSHtooyeh
Is that to go?	Візьмете зі собою?	veez'MEHteh zee sohBOHyoo

28

VI. FOOD AND DRINK

The main thing to keep in mind with regard to the various foods and drinks listed in this chapter is their limited availability. Not everything will be available everywhere you go, so be prepared to experience new foods and methods of preparation. Most Ukrainian national dishes are very delicious.

Breakfast

Where can I have breakfast?	Де можна поснідати?	deh MOHZHnah pohSNEEdahtih
What time is breakfast served?	О котрій годині сніданок?	oh KOHTreey gohDIHnee sneeDAHnohk
How late is breakfast served?	До котрої години можна снідати?	doh kohtROHyee goh-DIHnih MOHZHnah SNEEdahtih
I'd like...	Я хотів/ла би...	yah khohTEEV/lah bih
(black)	/чорну/	CHOHRnoo
coffee	каву	KAHvoo
with milk	з молоком	z mohlohKOHM
with sugar	з цукром	z TSOOKrohm
without sugar	без цукру	behz TSOOKroo
tea	чай	chay
with lemon	з лимоном/ цитриною	z lihMOHnohm/ tsihTRIHnohyoo
with milk	з молоком	z mohlohKOHM
with honey	з медом	z MEHdohm
with sugar	з цукром	z TSOOKrohm
cocoa	какао	kahKAHoh
milk	молоко	mohlohKOH
juice	сік	seek
orange	апельсиновий	ahpehl'SIHnohvihy
grapefruit	грейпфрутовий	greypFROOtohvihy
tomato	томатний	tohMAHTnihy
kefir (a yogurt drink)	кефір	kehFEER
bread	хліб	khleeb
toast	грінки	GREENkih
a roll	булочку	BOOlohchkoo
butter	масло	MAHSloh

29

cheese	сир	sihr
pot cheese	сир	sihr
jam	повидло	pohVIHDloh
honey	мед	mehd
hot cereal	кашу	KAHshoo
hot buckwheat cereal	гречану кашу	grehCHAHnoo KAHshoo
hot rice cereal	рисову кашу	RIHsohvoo KAHshoo
farina	манну кашу	MAHNnoo KAHshoo
oatmeal	вівсяну кашу	veevSYAHnoo KAHshoo
eggs	яйця	YAYtsyah
scrambled eggs	омлет	ohmLEHT
a fried egg	яєшню	yaYEHSHnyoo
a boiled egg	варене яйце	vahREHneh YAYtseh
a hard boiled egg	круте яйце	krooTEH YAYtseh
salt/pepper	сіль/перець	seel'/PEHrehts'.

Appetizers

Ukrainian appetizers are quite hearty and may often seem like an entire meal onto themselves.

Appetizers	Закуски	zahKOOSkih
For an appetizer I want....	На закуску я хочу...	nah zahKOOSkoo yah KHOHchoo
(black/red) caviar	чорну/червону ікру	CHOHRnoo/chehrVOHnoo eekROO
cold, boiled pork with vegetables	буженину/ шинку з гарніром	boozhehNIHnoo/ SHIHNkoo z gahrNEErohm
cold roast beef with vegetables	ростбиф з гарніром	ROHSTbihf z gahrNEErohm
assorted meat/fish plate	асорті м'ясне/ рибне	ahsohrTEE myahsNEH/ RIHBneh
smoked/ pickled herring	копченого/ маринованого оселедця.	kohpCHEHnohgoh/ mahrihNOHvahnohgoh ohsehLEHDtsyah
meat/fish in aspic	заливне/ну м'ясо/рибу	zahlihvNEH/noo MYAHsoh/RIHboo
sausage	ковбасу	kohvbahSOO
sturgeon	осетрину	ohsehtRIHnoo

lox	сьомгу	SYOHMgoo
pancakes with...	млинці...	mlihnTSEE
caviar	з ікрою	z eekROHyoo
herring	з оселедцем	z ohsehLEHDtsehm
sour cream	зі сметаною	zee smehTAHnohyoo
jam	з варенням	z vahREHNnyahm
small pies filled with...	пиріжки...	pihreezhKIH
meat	з м'ясом	z MYAHsohm
cabbage	з капустою	z kahPOOStohyoo
rice	з рисом	z RIHsohm
potatoes	з картоплею	z kahrTOHPlehyoo
meat-filled dumplings	пельмені/вареники з м'ясом	pehlMEHnee/vahREH-nihkih z MYAHsohm
marinated/salted mushrooms	мариновані/солені гриби	mahrihNOHvahnee/ sohLEHnee grihBIH
mushrooms baked in a sour cream sauce	жульєн з грибів	zhool'YEHN z grihBEEV
chicken baked in a sour cream sauce	жульєн з курчат	zhool'YEHN z koorCHAHT
Russian vege-table salad	вінігрет	veeneeGREHT
cucumber salad	салат з огірків	sahLAHT z ohgeerKEEV
tomato salad	салат з помідорів	sahLAHT z pohmeeDOHreev
cabbage salad	салат з капусти	sahLAHT z kahPOOStih
radish salad	салат з редиски	sahLAHT z rehDIHSkih
potato salad	картопляний салат	kahrtohpLYAHnihy sahLAHT
meat salad	м'ясний салат	myahsNIHY sahLAHT
saurkraut	квашену капусту	KVAHshehnoo kahPOOStoo
liver pate	паштет з печінки	pahshtTEHT z pehCHEENkih
olives	маслини	mahsLIHnih
radishes	редиску	rehDIHSkoo

Soups

For the first course I want...	На перше я хочу...	nah PEHRsheh yah KHOHchoo

31

English	Ukrainian	Pronunciation
Please bring me some...	Принесіть мені, будь ласка...	prihnehSEET' mehNEE bood'LAHSkah
borscht	борщ	bohrshch
boullion	бульйон	bool'YOHN
cabbage soup	капусняк	kahPOOSnyahk
chicken soup...	курячий суп...	KOOryachihy soop...
with noodles	з локшиною	z LOHKshihnohyoo
with rice	з рисом	z RIHsohm
cold kvas soup	окрошку	ohKROHSHkoo
cold vegetable soup	холодний борщ	khohLOHDnihy bohrshch
fish soup	рибна юшка	RIHBnah YOOSHkah
mushroom soup	грибний суп	grihbNIHY soop
pea soup	гороховий суп	gohROHkhohvihy soop
pickled cucumber soup	розсольник	rohzSOHL'nihk
potato soup	картопляний суп	kahrtohpLYAHnihy soop
spicy Georgian beef soup	харчо	khahrCHOH
tart meat/ fish soup	м'ясна/рибна солянка	myahsNAH/RIHBnah sohLYAHNkah
vegetable soup	овочевий суп	ohvohCHEHvihy soop

Grains and Cereals

English	Ukrainian	Pronunciation
I'd like...	Я хотів/ла би...	yah khohTEEV/lah bih
rice	рис	rihs
pilaf	плов	plohv
pasta	макарони	mahkahROHnih
potatoes	картоплю	kahrTOHPlyoo
fried	смажену	SMAHzhehnoo
boiled	варену	vahREHnoo
mashed	пюре	pyooREH
baked	печену	pehCHEHnoo
buckwheat	гречану кашу	grehCHAHnoo KAHshoo

Vegetables

English	Ukrainian	Pronunciation
What kind of vegetables are available?	Які у вас є овочі?	yahKEE oo vahs yeh OHvohchee
Cabbage	Капуста	kahPOOStah

Red cabbage	Брюссельська капуста	bryoosSEHL's'kah kahPOOStah
Beets	Буряки	booryahKIH
Tomatoes	Помідори	pohmeeDOHrih
Potatoes	Картопля	kahrTOHPlyah
Radishes	Редиска	rehDIHSkah
Cucumbers	Огірки	ohgeerKIH
Eggplant	Баклажани	bahklahZHAHnih
Mushrooms	Гриби	grihBIH
Peas	Горох	gohROHKH
Green beans	Квасоля	kvahSOHlyah
Wax beans	Спаржа	SPAHRzhah
Carrots	Морква	MOHRKvah
Onions	Цибуля	tsihBOOlyah
Leeks	Зелена цибуля	zehLehnah tsihBOOlyah
Corn	Кукурудза	kookooROODzah
Green peppers	Солодкий перець	sohLOHDkihy PEHrehts'
Red peppers	Червоний перець	chehrVOHnihy PEHrehts'
Parsley	Петрушка	pehtROOSHkah
Turnips	Ріпа	REEpah
Garlic	Часник	chahsNIHK
Cauliflower	Цвітна капуста	tsveetNAH kahPOOStah
Horseradish	Хрін	khreen

Preparations

How is this dish prepared?	Як готують цю страву?	yahk gohTOOyoot' tsyoo STRAHvoo
It's...	Вона...	vohNAH
baked	печена	pehCHEHnah
boiled	варена	vahREHnah
braised	тушкована	tooshKOHvahnah
breaded	запанірована	zahpahneeROHvahnah
chopped	посічена	pohSEEchehnah
fried	підсмажена	peedSMAHzhehnah
ground	перемелена	pehrehMEHlehnah
marinated	маринована	mahrihNOHvahnah
poached	відварена	veedVAHrehnah
raw	сира	sihRAH
roasted	засмажена	zahSMAHzhehnah
smoked	копчена	kohpCHEHnah
steamed	парова	pahrohVAH
stuffed	нафарширована	nahfahrshihROHvahnah

33

Meat and Meat Dishes

For the second course I want...	На друге я хочу...	nah DROOgeh yah KHOHchoo
What kind of meat do you have?	Яке у вас є м'ясо?	yahKEH oo vahs yeh MYAHsoh
What kind of meat dishes do you have?	Які у вас є м'ясні страви?	yahKEE oo vahs yeh myahsNEE STRAHvih
Mutton	Баранина	bahRAHnihnah
Lamb	Молода баранина	mohlohDAH bahRAHnihnah
Lamb chop	Бараняча відбивна	bahRAHnyahchah veedbihvNAH
Beef	Яловичина	yahlohVIHchihnah
Pork	Свинина	svihNIHnah
Pork chop	Свиняча відбивна	svihNYAHchah veedbihvNAH
Veal	Телятина	tehLYAHtihnah
Veal cutlet	Теляча відбивна	tehLYAHCHAH veedbihvNAH
Ham	Шинка	SHIHNkah
Roast beef	Ростбиф	ROHSTbihf
Pot roast	Тушкована яловичина	tooshKOHvahnah yahlohVIHchihnah
Meat patties	Битки	BIHTkih
Beefsteak	Біфштекс	beefSHTEHKS
Bacon	Корейка	kohREYkah
Meatloaf	М'ясний рулет	myahsNIHY rooLEHT
Meatballs	Тюфтелі	tyoofTEHlee
Sausages	Сосиски	sohSIHSkih
Shnitzel	Шніцель	SHNIHtsehl'
Meat stew	Рагу	rahGOO
Liver	Печінка	pehCHEENkah
Kidneys	Нирки	NIHRkih
Cutlet	Котлета відбивна	kohtLEHtah veedbihvNAH
Tongue	Язик	yahZIHK
Shish kebob	Шашлик	shahshLIHK
Ground lamb kebob	Люля-кебаб	lyooLYAH kehBAHB
Goulash	Гуляш	gooLYAHSH

Beef casserole	Душенина	dooshehNIHnah
Lamb stew	Азу	ahZOO
Chopped meat in a sauce	Смаженина	smahzhehNIHnah
Beef Stroganoff	Біфстроганов	beefSTROHgahnohv
Cabbage rolls with meat	Голубці	gohloobTSEE

Poultry and Game

What kind of poultry/ wild game dishes do you have?	Які у вас є страви з птицею і дичиною?	yahKEE oo vahs yeh STRAHvih z PTIHtsehyoo ee dihchihNOHyoo
Chicken	Курка	KOORkah
Duck	Качка	KAHCHkah
Goose	Гуска	GOOSkah
Turkey	Індик	eenDIHK
Woodcock	Вальдшнеп	vahl'dSHNEHP
Pigeon	Голуб	GOHloob
Hazel grouse	Рябчик	RYAHBchihk
Rabbit	Крілик	KREElihk
Hare	Заяць	ZAHyahts'
Venison	Оленина	ohlehNIHnah
Chicken Kiev	Котлети по-київськи	kohtLEHtih poh-KIHyihvs'kih
Georgian fried chicken	Курчата табака	koorCHAHtah tahbahKAH
Chicken cutlets	Пожарські котлети	pohZHAHRs'kee kohtLEHtih

Fish and Seafood

What kind of fish do you have?	Яка у вас є риба?	yahkah oo vahs yeh RIHbah
I'll take...	Я візьму...	yah veez'MOO
sturgeon	осетрину	ohsehtRIHnoo
pike-perch	судак	sooDAHK
trout	форель	fohREHL'
pike	щуку	SHCHOOkoo
flounder	камбалу	KAHMbahloo
carp	коропа	KOHrohpah
halibut	палтуса	PAHLtoosah

35

cod	тріску	treesKOO
salmon	лососину	lohsohSIHnoo
tuna	тунця	toonTSYAH
herring	оселедця	ohsehLEHDtsyah
seafood	пасту "Океан"	PAHStoo "OhkehAHN"
prawns	креветки	krehVEHTkih
crayfish	раки	RAHkih
oysters	устриці	OOStrihtsee

Fruit

Some restaurants do not offer fresh fruit on their menus, but you may buy it at public markets, snack bars and kiosks.

What kind of fruit do you have?	Які у вас є фрукти?	yahKEE oo vahs yeh FROOKtih
Is it fresh?	Вони свіжі?	vohnih SVEEzhee
Apples	Яблоки	YAHBlohkih
Oranges	Апельсини	ahpehl'SIHnih
Tangerines	Мандарини	mahndahRIHnih
Pears	Груші	GROOshee
Peaches	Персики	PEHRsihkih
Plums	Сливи	SLIHvih
Melon	Диня	DIHnyah
Watermelon	Кавун	kahVOON
Bananas	Банани	bahNAHnih
Apricots	Абрикоси	abrihKOHsih
Pineapple	Ананаси	ahnahNAHsih
Grapes	Виноград	vihnohGRAHD
Raisins	Родзинки	rohDZIHNkih
Figs	інжир	eenZHIHR
Dates	Фініки	FEEneekih
Lemon	Лимони	lihMOHnih
Grapefruit	Грейпфрути	greypFROOtih
Prunes	Чорнослив	chohrnohSLIHV
Currants	Порічки	pohREEchkih
Strawberries	Полуниці	pohlooNIHtsee
Wild strawberries	Суниці	sooNIHTsee
Cherries	Черешня	chehREHSHnyah
Blackberries	Ожина	ohZHIHnah
Cranberries	Клюква	KLYOOKvah
Raspberries	Малина	mahLIHnah
Blueberries	Чорниці	chohrNIHTsee

Dessert

Ukrainians claim that their ice cream, sold at kiosks year round, is the best in the world. Whether you agree or not, it is certainly worth a taste.

English	Ukrainian	Pronunciation
What do you have for dessert?	Що у вас є на десерт?	shchoh oo vahs yeh nah dehSEHRT
I'd like...	Я хотів/ла би...	yah khohTEEV/lah bih
ice cream	морозиво	mohROHzihvoh
a cookie	печиво	PEHchihvoh
pie	пиріг	pihREEG
pastry	тістечко	TEEStehchkoh
honey cake	медівник	mehdeevNIHK
cake	торт	tohrt
stewed fruit	компот	kohmPOHT
thin pancakes with jam	млинці з варенням	mlihnTSEE z vahREHNnyahm
thin fruit jelly	фруктове желе	frookTOHveh zhehLYEH
marzipan pastry	марципан	mahrtsihPAHN
filled doughnuts	пончики	POHNchihkih
an eclair	еклер	ehkLYEHR
chocolate	шоколад	shohkohLAHD
baked pudding	запіканку	zahpeeKAHNkoo

Drinks

Ukrainians are a tea-drinking people. Tea is usually served pre-sweetened with honey, jam or sugar. Although coffee has gained in popularity, it is still much more expensive and harder to find than tea. Bottled fruit juices and waters are also very popular, but iced and cold drinks are not. Drinking tap water is not a good idea.

English	Ukrainian	Pronunciation
What do you have to drink?	Що у вас є пити?	shchoh oo vahs yeh PIHtih
Please bring me...	Принесіть мені, будь ласка...	prihnehSEET' mehNEE bood' LAHSkah
(black) coffee	(чорну) каву	CHOHRnoo KAHvoo
with milk	з молоком	z mohlohKOHM
with sugar	з цукром	z TSOOKrohm
without sugar	без цукру	behz TSOOKroo
tea	чай	chay
with lemon	з лимоном	z lihMOHnohm
with milk	з молоком	z mohlohKOHM
with honey	з медом	z MEHdohm

with jam	з варенням	z vahREHNnyahm
a soft drink	безалкогольний	behzahlkohGOHL'nihy
I'd like a glass of...	Я хотів/ла би склянку...	yah khohTEEV/lah bih SKLYAHNkoo
milk	молока	mohlohKAH
lemonade	лимонаду	lihmohNAHdoo
I'd like a bottle of...	Я хотів/ла би пляшку...	yah khohTEEV/lah bih PLYAHSHkoo
mineral water	мінеральної води	meenehRAHL'nohyee vohDIH
I'd like a bottle of juice...	Я хотів/ла би пляшку... соку	yah khohTEEV/lah bih PLYAHSHkoo SOHkoo
apple	яблочного	YAHBlohchnohgoh
cherry	вишневого	vihshNEHvohgoh
grape	виноградного	vihnohGRAHDnohgoh
grapefruit	грейпфрутового	greypFROOtohvohgoh
orange	апельсинового	ahpehl'SIHnohvohgoh
plum	сливового	slihVOHvohgoh
tangerine	мандаринового	mahndahRIHnohvohgoh

Alcoholic Drinks

The most popular Ukrainian wines come from the Crimea. Sweet, and similar to a sparkling wine, native champagne is a good choice with dessert. Gorilka* comes in a variety of flavors and is most often served chilled in 50 gram shot glasses.

Do you serve alcohol?	У вас є алкогольні напої?	oo vahs yeh ahlkohGOHL'-nee nahPOHyee
Which wine would you recommend?	Яке вино ви пропонуєте?	yahKEH vihNOH vih prohpohNOOyehteh
How much is a bottle of...	Скільки коштує пляшка...	SKEEL'kih KOHSHtooyeh PLYASHkah
I'd like a glass/ bottle of...	Я хотів/ла би склянку/ пляшку...	yah khohTEEV/lah bih SKLYAHNkoo/ PLYAHSHkoo
wine	вина	vihNAH
red wine	червоного вина	chehrVOHnohgoh vihNAH
white wine	білого вина	BEElohgoh vihNAH

---

* Gorilka is the name of Ukrainian vodka.

dry wine	сухого виня	sooKHOHGOH vihNAH
sweet wine	солодкого виня	sohLOHDkohgoh vihNAH
Georgian wine	грузинського вина	grooZIHNs'kohgoh vihNAH
Champagne (sparkling wine)	шампанського	shahmPAHNs'kohgoh
beer	пива	PIHvah
kvas	квасу	KVAHsoo
vodka	горілки	gohREELkih
pepper-flavored vodka	горілки з перцем	gohREELkih z PEHRtsehm
lemon-flavored vodka	лимонової горілки	lihMOHnohvohyee gohREELkih
cherry-flavored vodka	вишньовки	vihshNYOHVkih
dark, smooth, old vodka	старки	STAHRkih
whiskey straight up	віски чистого	VEESkih CHIHStohgoh
with ice	зі льдом	zee l'dohm
with soda	зі содовою	zee SOHdohvohyoo
Azerbaijani/ Armenian brandy	азербайджанського/ вірменського коньяку	ahzehrbayDZHAHNs'kohgoh/ veerMEHNs'kohgoh kohnYAHkoo
a gin (and tonic)	джину (з тоніком)	DZHIHnoo z TOHneekohm
a scotch	шотландського віски	shohtLAHNDs'kogoh VEESkih

Toasts

To your health!	За ваше здоров'я!	zah VAHsheh zdohROHVyah
To peace and friendship!	За мир і дружбу!	zah mihr ee DROOZHboo
I wish you happiness/ health/ success!	Бажаю вам щастя/ здоров'я/ успіхів!	bahZHAHyoo vahm SHCHAHStyah/ zdohROHVyah/ OOSpeekheev
Congratulations!	Вітаю вас!	veeTAHyoo vahs

39

VII. SERVICES

Currency Exchange

If you do not exchange your money upon arrival at the airport or in your hotel, you may also exchange it at exchange offices or banks. Be forewarned, however, that they are less common than in the west. The karbovanets (coupon) is the equivalent of 100 kopecks. Trading or exchanging money with individual people is illegal.

English	Ukrainian	Pronunciation
Currency exchange	Обмін валюти	OHBmeen vahLYOOtih
Where can I exchange money?	Де можна обміняти валюту?	deh MOHZHnah ohbmeeNYAHtih vahLYOOtoo
Where can I find the nearest foreign-trade bank?	Де знаходиться найближчий зовнішторг банк?	deh znahKHOHdiht'syah nayBLIHZHchihy zohvneeshTOHRG bahnk
When does the bank open?	Коли відчиняється банк?	kohLIH veedchih-NYAHyeht'syah bahnk
How late is the bank open?	О котрій годині банк зачиняється?	oh kohtREEY gohDIHnee bahnk zahchihNYAHyeht'syah
The bank is open from 9:30 am to 1 pm.	Банк працює з 9.30 до 1.	bahnk prahTSYOOyeh z dehvyahTIH trihd-tsyahTIH doh PEHRshohyee
What is the exchange rate for dollars (today?)	Який сьогодні обмінний курс долара?	yahKIHY syohGOHDnee ohbMEENnihy koors DOHlahrah
I'd like to cash some traveler's checks	Я хотів/ла би поміняти подорожні чеки/долари.	yah khohTEEV/lah bih pohmeeNYAHtih pohdohROHZHnee CHEHkih/DOHlahrih
Can I purchase an international money order here?	Можна одержати тут міжнародний поштовий переказ?	MOHZHnah ohDEHRzhahtih toot meezhnahROHDnihy pohshTOHvihy pehREHkahz
What's the charge?	Скільки це коштує?	SKEEL'kih tseh KOHSHtooyeh

40

I'm expecting money from America.	Я чекаю на грошовий переказ з Америки.	yah chehKAHyoo nah grohshohVIHY pehREHkahz z ahMEHrihkih
Has it arrived?	Чи він вже прийшов?	chih veen vzheh prihySHOHV
Go to the cashier's office.	Ідіть до каси.	eeDEET' doh KAHsih
Where is the cashier's office?	Де знаходиться каса?	deh znahKHOHdiht'syah KAHsah
When is the cashier open?	Коли каса відчинена?	kohLIH KAHsah veedCHIHnehnah
Are you the cashier?(f)	Ви касир/ка?	vih kahSIHR/kah
Here's my identification.	Ось моє посвідчення.	ohs' mohYEH pohsVEEDchehnnyah
Here's my passport.	Ось мій паспорт.	ohs' meey PAHSpohrt
Where do I sign?	Де мені підписатися?	deh mehNEE peedpihSAHtihsyah
May I please have large bills?	Дайте мені, будь ласка, крупними купюрами.	DAYteh mehNEE bood' LAHSkah KROOPnihmih kooPYOOrahmih
May I please have small bills?	Дайте мені, будь ласка, дрібними купюрами.	DAYteh mehNEE bood' LAHSkah dreebNIHmih kooPYOOrahmih
Can you give me small change?	Дайте мені, будь ласка, дрібними монетами.	DAYteh mehNEE bood' LAHSkah dreebNIHmih mohNEHtahmih
I think you've made a mistake.	Мені здається, що ви помилилися.	mehNEE zdahYEHT'syah shchoh vih pohmihLIHlihsyah

Mail

In addition to the regular postal services, the main branch post office provides international telegram and telephone services, as well. In Kiev the main post office is open twenty-four hours. Packages to be sent out of Ukraine must be brought to a post office unwrapped. There they will be weighed, inspected, wrapped and stamped.

41

English	Ukrainian	Pronunciation
Post office	Пошта	POHSHtah
Letter/ Letters	Лист/ листи	lihst/ lihsTIH
Where's the nearest post office?	Де найближча пошта?	deh nayBLIHZHchah POHSHtah
Where's the main post office?	Де поштамт?	deh pohshTAHMT
When does the post office open/ close?	Коли пошта відчиняється/ зачиняється?	kohLIH POHSHtah veedchihNYAHyeht'syah/ zahchihNYAHyeht'syah
The post office is open from 9 to 6.	Пошта працює з 9 до 6.	POHSHtah prahTSYOOyeh z dehvYAHtohyee doh SHOHStoyee
Where can I find a mailbox?	Де можна знайти поштову скриньку?	deh MOHZHnah znayTIH pohshTOHvoo SKRIHN'koo
Can I buy... here?	Можна тут купити...	MOHZHnah toot kooPIHtih
envelopes.	конверти	kohnVEHRtih
post cards	поштові картки	pohshTOHvee KAHRTkih
stamps	марки	MAHRkih
Please give me ten airmail stamps for letters/ post cards to the USA.	Дайте мені, будь ласка, де- сять марок для авіалистів/ авіакарток до США.	DAYteh mehNEE bood' LAHSkah DEHsyaht' MAHrohk dlyah ahveeahlihsTEEV/ ahveeahKAHRtohk doh sshah
I'd like to send this letter/post card by...	Я хотів/ла би надіслати цей лист/поштову картку...	yah khohTEEV/lah bih nahdeeSLAHtih tsey lihst/pohshTOHvoo KAHRTkoo
surface mail	простою поштою	prohsTOHyoo POHSHtohyoo
airmail	авіапоштою	ahveeahPOHSHtohyoo
registered mail	рекомен- дованою поштою	rehcohmehn- DOHvahnohyoo POHSHtohyoo
special delivery	терміновою поштою	tehrmeeNOHvohyoo POHSHtohyoo
Will this go out today?	Чи це піде сьогодні?	chih tseh peeDEH syohGOHDnee

I'd like to send this to...	Я хотів/ла би надіслати це до...	yah khohTEEV/lah bih nahdeeSLAHtih tseh doh
America	Америки	ahMEHrihkih
Canada	Канади	kahNAHdih
England	Англії	AHNGleeyee
Germany	Німеччини	neeMEHCHchihnih
France	Франції	FRAHNtseeyee
I'd like to send this parcel	Я хотів/ла би відправити цю посилку	yah khohTEEV/lah bih veedPRAHvihtih tsyoo pohSIHLkoo
It contains books/ souvenirs/ fragile material	В ній книги/ сувеніри/ крихкий матеріал	v neey KNIHgih/ soovehNEErih/ krihkhKIHY mahtehreeAHL
Wrap it up, please.	Загорніть, будь ласка.	zahgohrNEET' bood' LAHSkah
Write the address here.	Напишіть адресу ось тут.	nahpihSHEET' ahdREHsoo ohs' toot
Return address.	Зворотна адреса.	zvohROHTnah ahdREHsah
Have I received any mail?	Чи є для мене листи?	chih yeh dlyah MEHneh lihsTIH
My name is...	Моє прізвище...	mohYEH PREEZvihshcheh
Here's my passport.	Ось мій паспорт.	ohs' meey PAHSpohrt

Telegrams

Most larger post offices have a telegraph department.

I'd like to send a telegram.	Я хочу надіслати телеграму	yah KHOHchoo nahdeeSLAHtih tehlehGRAHmoo
Where can I send a telegram?	Де можна надіслати телеграму?	deh MOHZHnah nahdeeSLAHtih tehlehGRAHmoo
May I have an international form?	Дайте мені, будь ласка, міжнародний бланк.	DAYteh mehNEE bood' LAHSkah meezhnahROHDnihy blahnk
What is the rate per word?	Скільки коштує слово?	SKEEL'kih KOHSHtooyeh SLOHvoh

43

What will the total cost be?	Скільки буде коштувати телеграма?	SKEEL'kih BOOdeh KOHSHtoovahtih tehlehGRAHmah
How long will it take to reach the USA/ England?	Скільки часу йде телеграма до США/ Англії?	SKEEL'kih CHAHsoo yDEH tehlehGRAHmah doh sshah/ AHNGleeyee

Telephones

Phonebooks exist in Ukraine, but they are not available in every hotel room. Local calls can be made at any time from any phone. International calls, however, can only be made by reservation at the telephone office of the main post office or through your hotel. They must be booked in advance. To make a local call from a phone booth you first drop in fifteen-kopeck piece, pick up the phone, wait for a long, continuous buzz, then dial. Long signals mean the phone is ringing; shorter ones mean the line is busy.

Public phone	Телефон-автомат	tehlehFOHN ahvtohMAHT
Where's the nearest telephone?	Де найближчий телефон?	deh nayBLIHZHchihy tehlehFOHN
May I use your phone?	Можна від вас подзвонити?	MOHZHnah veed vahs pohdzvohNIHtih
Hello (on the phone).	Алло/ Слухаю.	ahlLOH/SLOOkhahyoo
Who is this?	Хто це?	khtoh tseh
This is...	Це...	tseh
My name is...	Мене звати...	mehNEH ZVAHtih
I'd like to speak to...	Я хотів/ла би порозмовляти з...	yah khohTEEV/lah bih pohrohzmohvLYAHtih z...
He/She isn't in.	Його/ її нема.	yohGOH/yeeYEE nehMAH
When will he/she return?	Коли він/вона повернеться?	kohLIH veen/vohNAH pohVEHRneht'syah
Tell him/her that I called.	Передайте йому/ їй, що я дзвонив/ла.	pehrehDAYteh yohMOO/ YEEy shchoh yah dzvohNIHV/lah
Take a message, please.	Передайте, будь ласка, що...	pehrehDAYteh bood' LAHSkah shchoh
My number is...	Мій номер телефону...	meey NOHmehr tehlehFOHnoo
Ask him/her to call me back.	Попросіть його/ її подзвонити мені.	pohprohSEET" yohGOH/ yeeYEE pohdzvohNIHtih mehNEE

44

English	Ukrainian	Pronunciation
I don't understand.	Я не розумію.	yah neh rohzooMEEyoo
Do you speak English?	Ви розмовляєте англійською мовою?	vih rohzmohvLYAHyehteh ahngLEEYS'kohyoo MOHvohyoo
I can't hear you.	Не чути.	neh CHOOtih
Can you speak slowly/ louder?	Говоріть повільніше/ голосніше, будь ласка.	gohvohREET' pohVEEL'neesheh/ gohlohsNEEsheh bood' LAHSkah
With whom do you want to speak?	З ким ви хочете розмовляти?	z kihm vih KHOHchehteh rohzmohvLYAHtih
You've got the wrong number.	Ви помилилися номером.	vih pohmihLIHlihsyah NOHmehrohm
Dial again.	Наберіть ще раз.	nahbehREET' shcheh rahz
The number has been changed.	Номер телефону змінився.	NOHmehr tehlehFOHnoo zmeeNIHVsyah
The phone is broken.	Телефон не працює.	tehlehFOHN neh prahTSYOOyeh
Long-distance phone call.	Міжміська розмова.	meezhmees'KAH rohzMOHvah
International phone call.	Міжнародна розмова.	meezhnahROHDnah rohzMOHvah
Can I dial direct?	Чи можу я сам/ сама набрати?	chih MOHzhoo yah sahm/ sahMAH nahBRAHtih
Operator, please get me this number.	Телефоністка, з'єднайте мене, будь ласка, з цим номером.	tehlehfohNEESTkah zyehdNAYteh mehNEH bood' LAHSkah z tsihm NOHmehrohm
I'd like to order a phone call to the USA.	Я хотів/ла би замовити розмову з США.	yah khohTEEV/lah bih zahMOHvihtih rohzMOHvoo z sshah
How much does a call to New-York cost?	Скільки коштує телефонна розмова з Нью-Йорком?	SKEEL'kih KOHSHtooyeh tehlehFOHNnah rohzMOHvah z n'yoo-YOHRkohm
What number are you calling?	Який номер ви набираєте?	yahKIHY NOHmehr vih nahbihRAHyehteh
Do I have to wait long?	Мені довго чекати?	mehNEE DOHVgoh chehKAHtih

45

English	Ukrainian	Pronunciation
How long do you want to speak?	Скільки хвилин ви хочете говорити?	SKEEL'kih khvihLIHN vih KHOHchehteh gohvohRIHtih
Wait a minute.	Почекайте!/ Хвилинку!	pohchehKAYteh/ khvihLIHNkoo
Your call is in booth No.2.	Ваша розмова у кабіні номер два.	VAHshah rohzMOHvah oo kahBEEnee NOHmehr dvah
Your time is up.	Ваш час закінчився.	vahsh chahs zahKEENchihvsyah
How much did the call cost?	Скільки коштувала розмова?	SKEEL'kih KOHSHtoovahlah rohzMOHvah
There's a call for you.	Вас викликають по телефону.	vahs vihklihKAHyoot' poh tehlehFOHnoo
Hold on, please.	Не вішайте трубку.	neh VEEshayteh TROOBkoo
It's busy.	Лінія зайнята.	LEEneeyah ZAYnyahtah
There's no answer.	Не відповідають.	neh veedpohveeDAHyoot'
I can't get through.	Я не можу додзвонитися.	yah neh MOHzhoo dohdzvohNIHtihsyah
We've been cut off.	Нас роз'єднали.	nahs rohzyedNAHlih

Dry Cleaning and Laundry

Laundry and dry cleaning services are often available in your hotel. Ask your floor monitor (чергова) for details and assistance.

English	Ukrainian	Pronunciation
Where can I get my laundry washed?	Де мені можуть випрати білизну?	deh mehNEE MOHzhoot' VIHPrahtih beeLIHZnoo
Where is the nearest dry cleaner?	Де найближча хімчистка?	deh nayBLIHZHchah kheemCHIHSTkah
I need these things...	Мені потрібно ці речі...	mehNEE pohtREEBnoh tsee REHchee...
dry cleaned	почистити	pohCHIHStihtih
washed	випрати	VIHPrahtih
ironed	випрасувати	VIHPrahsoovahtih
No starch, please.	Не крохмальте, будь ласка.	neh krohkhMAHL'teh bood' LAHSkah
Can you get this stain out?	Можна вивести цю пляму?	MOHZHnah VIHvehstih tsyoo PLYAHmoo

English	Ukrainian	Pronunciation
Can you mend/ sew this?	Можете ви це заштопати/ зашити?	MOHzhehteh vih tseh zahSHTOHpahtih/ zahSHIHtih
Sew on this button, please.	Пришийте, будь ласка, цього ґудзика.	prihSHIHYteh bood' LAHSkah tsyohGOH GOODzihkah
When will it be ready?	Коли воно буде готове?	kohLIH vohNOH BOOdeh gohTOHveh
Is my laundry ready?	Чи моя білизна готова?	chih mohYAH beeLIHZnah gohTOHvah
How much do I owe you? (f)	Скільки я вам винен/на?	SKEEL'kih yah vahm VIHnehn/nah
This isn't mine.	Це не моє.	tseh neh mohYEH
I'm missing something.	Чогось не вистачає.	chohGOHS' neh vihstahCHAHyeh
This is torn.	Це розірване.	tseh rohZEERvahneh
Can I borrow...	Можна попросити на хвилину...	MOHZHnah pohprohSIHtih nah khvihLIHnoo
a needle and thread?	голку з ниткою?	GOHLkoo z NIHTkohyoo
scissors?	ножиці?	NOHzhihtsee

Optician

English	Ukrainian	Pronunciation
Optician	Оптика	OHPtihkah
Where can I find an optician?	Де можна знайти оптику?	deh MOHZHnah znayTIH OHPtihkoo
I have broken my glasses.	У мене розбилися окуляри.	oo MEHneh rohzBIHlihsyah ohkooLYAHrih
The frame is broken.	Оправа зломана.	ohPRAHvah ZLOHmahnah
The lenses are broken.	Стекла розбиті.	STEHKlah rohzBIHtee
Can you fix them?	Чи можна їх полагодити?	chih MOHZHnah yeekh pohLAHgohdihtih
How long will it take?	Скільки це займе часу?	SKEEL'kih tseh ZAYmeh CHAHsoo
Here's my prescription.	Ось мій рецепт.	ohs' meey rehTSEHPT

I've lost/ ripped a contact lense.	Я загубив/ла зірвав/ла свою кон-тактну лінзу.	yah zahgooBIHV/lah zeerVAHV/lah svohYOO kohn-TAHKTnoo LEENzoo
Can you replace it?	Чи у вас є такі лінзи?	chih oo vahs yeh tahKEE LEENzih
I have hard/soft lenses.	У мене тверді/ м'які лінзи.	oo MEHneh tvehrDEE/ myahKEE LEENzih
Do you sell contact lens fluid?	У вас є рідина для контакт-них лінз?	oo vahs yeh reedihNAH dlyah kohn-TAHKTnihkh leenz

Shoe Repair

Shoe repair.	Ремонт взуття.	rehMOHNT vzootTYAH
Shine my shoes, please.	Почистіть, будь ласка, мої черевики.	pohCHIHSteet' bood' LAHSkah mohYEE chehrehVIHkih
Can these shoes be repaired?	Чи можна полагодити ці черевики?	chih MOHZHnah pohLAHgohdihtih tsee chehrehVIHkih
I need new soles/ heels.	Мені потрібні нові підмет-ки/ каблуки.	mehNEE pohtREEBnee nohVEE peedMEHTkih/ kahblooKIH
The heel/ strap broke.	Каблук/ ремінець зломаний.	kahbLOOK/ rehmeeNEHTS' ZLOHmahnihy
Can this be sewn up?	Можна це зашити?	MOHZHnah tseh zahSHIHtih
How much will it cost?	Скільки це буде коштувати?	SKEEL'kih tseh BOOdeh KOHSHtoovahtih
When will they be ready?	Коли вони будуть готові?	kohLIH vohNIH BOOdoot' gohTOHvee

Barber/Hairdresser

Barber/Hair-dresser.	Перукарня.	pehrooKAHRnyah
Where is the nearest barber?	Де найближча перукарня?	deh nayBLIHZHchah pehrooKAHRnyah
Is there a hair-dresser in the hotel?	Чи в цьому готелі є перукарня?	chih v TSYOHmoo gohTEHlee yeh pehrooKAHRnyah

Can I make an appointment for Monday?	Можна записатися на понеділок?	MOHZHnah zahpihSAHtihsyah nah pohnehDEElohk
Have a seat	Сідайте	seeDAYteh
Haircut	Стрижка	STRIHZHkah
Hair style	Зачіска	ZAHcheeskah
Part (hair)	Проділ	PROHdeel
Dye	Фарбування	fahrbooVAHNnyah
A hair cut, please.	Підстрижіть мене, будь ласка.	peedstrihZHEET' mehNEH bood' LAHSkah
Just a trim.	Тільки підрівняйте.	TEEL'kih peedreevNYAYteh
Take a little off the sides, please.	Зніміть трохи з боків, будь ласка.	zneeMEET' TROHkhih z bohKEEV bood' LAHSkah
Not too short.	Не занадто коротко.	neh zahNAHDtoh KOHrohtkoh
Just a little more, please.	Трохи більше, будь ласка.	TROHkhih BEEL'sheh bood' LAHSkah
Shampoo and set, please.	Вимийте і укладіть волосся, будь ласка.	VIHmihyteh ee ooklahDEET' vohLOHSsyah bood' LAHSkah
Blow-dry my hair.	Укладіть моє волосся феном.	ooklahDEET' mohYEH vohLOHSsyah FEHnohm
A shave, please.	Побрийте мене, будь ласка.	pohBRIHYteh mehNEH bood' LAHSkah
Trim my beard/ mustache/ sideburns.	Підстрижіть мою бороду/ мої вуса/мої бакенбарди.	peedstrihZHEET' mohyoo BOHrohdoo/ mohYEE VOOsah/ mohYEE bahkehnBAHRdih
Dye my hair in this color.	Пофарбуйте моє волосся в цей колір.	pohfahrBOOYteh mohYEH vohLOHSsyah v tsey KOHleer
I would like a facial/ manicure/ permanent.	Я хотіла б чистку/ масаж обличчя/ манікюр/ перманент.	yah khohTEElah b CHIHSTkoo/ mahSAHZH ohbLIHCHchyah/ mahneeKYOOR pehrmahNEHNT

49

Thank you.	Дякую	DYAHkooyoo
How much do I owe you? (f)	Скільки я вам винен /винна?	SKEEL'kih yah vahm VIHnehn /VIHNnah

Film Development

It is best to bring enough film and photography supplies from home to supply you for your entire trip. If you do purchase Ukrainian film, be sure to have it developed at a "photo-laboratory" (фотолабораторія) before you leave, as their processing procedure differs from ours. The list of things which are off-limits to photographers in Ukraine includes train stations, airports, military installations and much more. It is impolite to photograph people without their permission.

Photography	Фотографія	fohtohGRAHfeeyah
Camera	Фотоапарат	fohtohahpahRAHT
Film	Плівка	PLEEVkah
Black and white film	Чорно-біла плівка	CHOHRnoh-BEElah PLEEVkah
Color film	Кольорова плівка	kohlyohROHvah PLEEVkah
Thirty-six exposure	Тридцять шість кадрів	TRIHDtsyaht' sheest' KAHDreev
How much does processing cost?	Скільки коштує проявити плівку?	SKEEL'kih KOHSHtooyeh prohyahVIHtih PLEEVkoo
I'd like this enlarged.	Я хотів/ла би збільшити це.	yah khohTEEV/lah bih ZBEEL'shihtih tseh
I'd like another copy of this print.	Я хотів/ла би ще одну копію.	yah khohTEEV/lah bih shcheh ohdNOO KOHpeeyoo
When will they be ready?	Коли фотографії будуть готові?	kohLIH fohtohGRAHfeeyee BOOdoot' gohTOHvee

50

VIII. TRANSPORTATION

Public transportation in Ukraine is cheap, clean and efficient. Buses, street cars and trolleys all cost ten coupons per ride and run from 6 am until 1 am. Tickets are usually purchased on board or at the bus stops, shops and other places. If the bus or trolley is crowded, it is common practice to merely pass the money towards the direction of the driver who sells tickets and your ticket will be passed back to you. Spot checks are done occasionally and passengers without tickets are fined. Stops are marked with an 'A' for buses, 'T' for trolleys and a different capital 'T' for street cars. These signs also carry the name of the stop, the name of the terminal stop, and time table or interval between buses. The routes are denoted by numbers. If a passenger asks you if you are getting off and you are not, it is expected that you will move out of the way for him to get by.

Buses, Street Cars and Trolleys

Bus	Автобус	ahvTOHboos
Street car	Трамвай	trahmVAY
Trolley	Тролейбус	trohLEYboos
Where is the bus/ street car/ trolley stop?	Де зупинка автобуса/ трамвая/ тролейбуса	deh zooPIHNkah ahvTOHboosah/ trahmVAYoo/ trohLEYboosah
How often does the bus/street car/trolley run?	Як часто зупиняється автобус/ трамвай/ тролейбус?	yahk CHAHStoh zoopihNYAHyeht'syah ahvTOHboos/ trahmVAY/ trohLEYboos
When's the next bus?	Коли буде наступний автобус?	kohLIH BOOdeh nahsTOOPnihy ahvTOHboos
Bus driver	Водій	vohDEEY
Fare	Проїзд	prohYEEZD
Monthly pass	Щомісячний квиток	shchohMEEsyahchnihy kvihTOHK
Five-kopeck piece	П'ятикопієчна монета	pyahtihkohPEEyehchnah mohNEHtah
Cash box	Каса	KAHsah
Pass me a ticket, please.	Передайте, будь ласка, мені квиток.	pehrehDAHYteh bood' LAHSkah mehNEE kvihTOHK

51

What bus do I take to get to Khreshchatyk?	Який автобус іде до Хрещатика?	yahKIHY ahvTOHboos eeDEH doh khrehSHCHAHtihkah
Do I have to transfer?	Чи треба мені пересісти?	chih TREHbah mehNEE pehrehSEEStih
Does this bus go near Kyyiv State University?	Чи пройде цей автобус біля Київського державного університету?	chih PROHYdeh tsehy ahvTOHboos BEElyah KIHyeevs'kohgoh dehrZHAHVnohgoh ooneevehrsihTEHtoo
How many stops until we reach the center of town?	Скільки зупинок до центру міста?	SKEEL'kih zooPIHnohk doh TSEHNtroo MEEStah
You've gotten on the wrong bus.	Ви сіли не на той автобус.	vih SEElih neh nah tohy ahvTOHboos
Can you tell me where to get off?	Ви не скажете, де мені треба вийти?	vih neh SKAHzhehteh deh mehNEE TREHbah VIHYtih
You've missed your stop.	Ви проїхали свою зупинку.	vih prohYEEkhahlih svohYOO zooPIHNkoo
Are you getting off?	Ви зараз виходите?	vih ZAHrahz vihKHOHdihteh
I want to get off here/at the next stop.	Я хочу вийти тут/на наступній зупинці.	yah KHOHchoo VIHYtih toot/ nah nahsTOOPneey zooPIHNtsee
Excuse me, can I get through?	Пробачте, можна пройти?	prohBAHCHteh MOHZHnah prohyTIH
Excuse me, I'm getting off at the next stop.	Пробачте, я виходжу на наступній зупинці.	prohBAHCHteh yah vihKHOHDzhoo nah nahsTOOPneey zooPIHNtsee
Just a minute!	Хвилиночку!	KHVIHlihnohchkoo
I'm getting off now.	Я зараз виходжу.	yah ZAHrahz vihKHOHDzhoo

Subway

Ukrainian subways are clean, quick and efficient. The stations are marked by a large red 'M,' which is illuminated at night. The kyyiv system is not as old as the Moscow one. In order to get to the trains,

you must buy a special counter (it costs 10 coupons) and drop it into
a turnstile. Trains run from 6 am till 1 am. Smoking is prohibited.

Subway	Метро́	mehtROH
Entrance	Вхід	vkheed
Exit	Ви́хід	VIHkheed
No entrance	Нема́ вхо́ду	nehMAH VKHOHdoo
No exit	Нема́ ви́ходу	nehMAH VIHkhohdoo
Way out	Ви́хід до мі́ста	VIHkheed doh MEEStah
To the trains	До поїздів	doh pohyeezDEEV
Transfer	Перехі́д	pehrehHEED
Keep to the left/	Трима́йтеся	trihMAHYtehsyah
right	лі́вої/пра́вої	LEEvohyee
	сторони́	PRAHvohyee
		stohrohNIH
Change machines	Ка́си-автома́ти	KAHsih ahvtohMAHtih
May I have	Розмі́няйте,	rohzmeeNYAHYteh
change, please.	будь ла́ска	bood' LAHSkah
Where's the	Де найбли́жча	deh nahyBLIHZHchah
nearest	ста́нція	STAHNtseeyah
subway stop?	метро́?	mehtROH
Does this line go	Чи ця лі́нія іде́	chih tsyah LEEneeyah
to...	до...,	eeDEH doh
What line should	По які́й лі́нії я	poh yahKEEY LEEneeyee
I take to...	дої́ду до...	yah dohYEEdoo doh
Do I have to	Чи тре́ба бу́де	chih TREHbah BOOdeh
transfer?	пересі́сти?	pehrehSEEStih
Can you tell me	Скажі́ть, будь	skahZHEET' bood'
what the next	ла́ска, яка́	LAHSkah yahkah
station is?	насту́пна	nahsTOOPnah
	ста́нція?	STAHNtseeyah
The next station	Насту́пна	nahsTOOPnah
is...	ста́нція...	STAHNtseeyah
Can you tell me	Ви ска́жете	vih SKAHzhehteh
where to get	мені́, коли́	mehNEE kohLIH
off?	тре́ба ви́йти?	TREHbah VIHYtih
Careful, the doors	Обере́жно,	ohbehREHZHnoh
are closing.	две́рі	DVEHree
	зачиня́ються.	zahchihNYAHyoot'sya
The train goes as	По́їзд іде́ до	POHyeezd eeDEH doh
far as...	ста́нції...	STAHNtseeyee
This is the last	По́їзд да́лі не	POHyeezd DAHlee neh
stop.	піде́.	PEEdeh

Taxi

In addition to being ordered by phone, taxis can be found in front of major hotels and at taxi stands. A small, green light in the front window means that the cab is available. It is common to share a cab with strangers.

Taxi	Таксі	tahkSEE
Taxi stand	Стоянка таксі	stohYAHNkah tahkSEE
Where can I get a taxi?	Де можна піймати таксі?	deh MOZHnah peeyMAHtih tahkSEE
Where is the nearest taxi stand?	Де найближча стоянка таксі?	deh nahyBLIHZHchah stohYAHNkah tahkSEE
Please call me a taxi.	Викличте, будь ласка, для мене таксі.	VIHKlihchteh bood' LAHSkah dlyah MEHneh tahkSEE
Are you free?	Чи ви вільні?	chih vih VEEL'nee
Where do you want to go?	Куди вам?	kooDIH vahm
Here's the address	Ось адреса	ohs' ahdREHsah
To the Opera Theater, please.	До оперного театру, будь ласка.	doh OHpehrnohgoh tehAHTRoo bood' LAHSkah
How much will the ride cost?	Скільки цей проїзд буде коштувати?	SKEEL'kih tsehy prohYEEZD BOOdeh KOHSHtoovahtih
Can you get my bags, please.	Візьміть, будь ласка, мої сумки.	veez'MEET' bood' LAHSkah mohYEE SOOMkih
I'm (not) in a hurry.	Я /не/ поспішаю.	yah neh pohspeeSHAHyoo
Stop here.	Зупиніться тут.	zoopihNEET'syah toot
Wait for me here.	Почекайте мене.	pohchehKAHYteh mehNEH
I'll be back in a couple of minutes.	Я повернуся через кілька хвилин.	yah pohvehrNOOsyah CHEHrehz KEEL'kah khvihLIHN
Keep the change.	Здачу залишите собі	ZDAHchoo zahLISHteh sohBEE
Thank you.	Дякую.	DYAHkooyoo
Goodbye.	До побачення.	doh pohBAHchehnnyah

Boats

Boat/Motor boat	Човен/Моторний човен	CHOHvehn/mohTOHR-nihy CHOHvehn
Ship/Steamship	Корабель/ Пароплав	kohrahBEHL'/ pahrohPLAHV
Hydrofoil	Судно на підводних крилах.	SOODnoh nah peedVOHDnihkh KRIHlahkh
Ferry	Паром	pahROHM
Cruise	Круїз	krooEEZ
Tour	Екскурсія	ehksKOORseeyah
When does the next ship leave?	Коли відходить наступний пароплав?	kohLIH veedKHOHdiht' nahsTOOPnihy pahrohPLAHV
Where do we get tickets?	Де можна придбати квитки?	deh MOHZHnah prihdBAHtih kvihtKIH
How much are the tickets?	Скільки коштують квитки?	SKEEL'kih KOHSHtooyoot' kvihtKIH
Where is the pier?	Де пристань?	deh PRIHStahn'
How long is the trip?	Скільки часу триває подорож?	SKEEL'kih CHAHsoo trihVAHyeh POHdohrohzh
Where do we stop?	Де ми зупиняємося?	deh mih zoopihNYAHyehmohsyah
Deck	Палуба	PAHloobah
Cabin	Каюта	kahYOOtah
Life jacket	Рятунковий пояс	ryahtoonKOHvihy POHyahs
Lifeboat	Рятунковий човен	ryahtoonKOHvihy CHOHvehn
I feel seasick	Мене нудить	mehNEH NOOdiht'

Trains

Like all long-distance travel in Ukraine, train trips must be reserved in advance. You can usually make reservations through your hotel.

Train	Поїзд	POHyeezd
Train station	Вокзал	vohkZAHL
Ticket office	Квиткова каса	kvihtKOHvah KAHsah

When does the ticket office open?	Коли відчиниться квиткова каса?	kohLIH veedCHIHniht'syah kvihtKOHvah KAHsah
Reservation office	Попередній продаж квитків	pohpehREHDneey PROHdahzh kvihtKEEV
Information office	Довідкове бюро	dohveedKOHveh byooROH
Express long-distance train	Експрес-поїзд	ehksPREHS-POHyeezd
Standard long-distance train	Швидкий поїзд	shvihdKIHY POHyeezd
Local train	Електричка	ehlehkTRIHCHkah
Deluxe class	Вагон міжнародного класу.	vahGOHN meezhnah-ROHDnohgoh KLAHsoo
First class	М'який вагон.	myahKIHY vahGOHN
Second class	Купейний вагон	kooPEHYnihy vahGOHN
Third class	Плацкартний вагон	plahtsKAHRTnihy vahGOHN
One-way ticket	Квиток в одну сторону	kvihTOHK v ohdNOO STOHrohnoo
Round-trip ticket	Квиток туди й назад	kvihTOHK tooDIH y nahZAHD
Time table	Розклад руху поїздів	ROHZklahd ROOkhoo pohyeezDEEV
Departure time	Час відправлення	chahs veedPRAHVlehnnyah
Arrival time	Час прибуття	chahs prihbootTYAH
When is the next train to Lviv?	Коли відходить наступний поїзд до Львова?	kohLIH veedKHOHdiht' nahsTOOPnihy POHyeezd doh L'VOHvah
Is it a direct train?	Чи це прямий поїзд?	chih tseh pryahMIHY POHyeezd
Do I have to change trains?	Чи мені треба робити пересадку?	chih mehNEE TREHbah rohBIHtih pehrehSAHDkoo
What's the fare to Tbilisi?	Скільки коштує квиток до Тбілісі?	SKEEL'kih KOHSHtooyeh kvihTOHK doh TbeeLEEsee

English	Ukrainian	Pronunciation
I'd like to reserve a seat.	Я хотів/ла би замовити плацкарту.	yah khohTEEV/lah bih zahMOHvihtih plahtsKAHRtoo
I'd like to reserve a berth in the sleeping car.	Я хотів/ла би замовити квиток до спального вагону.	yah khohTEEV/lah bih zahMOHvihtih kvihTOHK doh SPAHL'nohgoh vahGOHnoo
From what platform does the train to Kharkov leave?	З якої платформи відходить поїзд до Харкова?	z yahKOHyee plahtFOHRmih veedKHOHdiht' POHyeezd doh KHAHRkohvah
When does the train arrive in Odesa?	О котрій годині поїзд прибуває до Одеси?	oh KOHTreey gohDIHnee POHyeezd prihbooVAHyeh doh ohDEHsih
Are we on time?	Чи поїзд іде по розкладу?	chih POHyeezd eeDEH poh ROHZklahdoo
The train is twenty minutes late.	Поїзд запізнюється на двадцять хвилин.	POHyeezd zahPEEZnyooyeht'syah nah DVAHDtsyat' khvihLIHN
Where are we now?	Де ми зараз?	deh mih ZAHrahz
How long do we stop here?	Скільки поїзд стоїть тут?	SKEEL'kih POHyeezd stohYEET' toot.
Is there time to get off?	Чи я встигну вийти?	chih yah VSTIHGnoo VIHYtih
Is this seat taken?	Чи це місце зайняте?	chih tseh MEEStseh ZAHYnyahteh
This is my seat.	Це моє місце.	tseh mohYEH MEEStseh
Am I bothering you?	Я вам заваджаю?	yah vahm zahvahdZHAHyoo
Can I open/shut the window?	Чи можна відчинити/зачинити вікно?	chih MOHZHnah veedchihNIHtih/zahchihNIHtih veekNOH
Can I turn out/on the light?	Можна виключити/включати світло?	MOHZHnah VIHKluoochihtih/vklyooCHIHtih SVEETloh
I'd like the top/bottom bunk.	Я хотів/ла би верхню/нижню лавку.	yah khohTEEV/lah bih VEHRKHnyoo/NIHZHnyoo LAHVkoo

English	Ukrainian	Pronunciation
We'd like some tea.	Принесіть нам чаю.	prihnehSEET' nahm CHAHyoo
Two glasses, please.	Дві склянки, будь ласка.	dvee SKLYAHNkih bood' LAHSkah
Where is the...	Де знаходиться...	deh znahKHOHdiht'syah
baggage check?	багажний відділ?	bahGAHZHnihy VEEDdeel
lost and found?	бюро знахідок?	byooROH ZNAHkheedohk
baggage room?	камера зберігання?	KAHmehrah zbehreeGAHNnyah
snack bar?	буфет?	booFEHT
bathroom?	туалет?	tooahLEHT
conductor?	кондуктор?	kohnDOOKtohr
ticket taker? (m/f)	провідник/ провідниця?	prohveedNIHK/ prohveedNIHtsyah
ticket checker?	контролер?	kohntrohLEHR
porter?	носильник?	nohSIHL'nihk
platform?	платформа?	plahtFOHRmah
gate?	вхід?	vkheed
waiting room?	зала для чекання?	ZAHlah dlyah chehKAHNnyah
sleeping car?	спальний вагон?	SPAHL'nihy vahGOHN
dining car?	вагон-ресторан?	vahGOHN rehstohRAHN
smoking car?	вагон для курців?	vahGOHN dlyah koorTSEEV
my sleeping compartment?	моє купе?	mohYEH kooPEH
Have a good trip!	Щасливої дороги!	shchahsLIHvohyee dohROHgih

Planes

Ukrintourist can help you make domestic plane reservations on the Ukrainian airline.

English	Ukrainian	Pronunciation
Plane	Літак	leeTAHK
Airport	Аеропорт	ahehrohPOHRT
Arrival	Прибуття	prihbootTYAH
Departure	Виліт	VIHleet
Boarding pass	Посадочний талон	pohSAHdohchnihy tahLOHN
I'd like to make a reservation.	Я хочу замовити квиток	yah KHOHchoo zahMOHvihtih kvihTOHK

58

English	Ukrainian	Pronunciation
I'd like a flight to Kyyiv.	Дайте мені квиток до Києва.	DAHYteh mehNEE kvihTOHK doh KIHyehvah
Is there a direct flight?	Чи є прямий політ?	chih yeh pryahMIHY pohLEET
How long is the lay-over?	На який час затримується виліт?	nah yahKIHY chahs zahTRIHmooyeht'syah VIHleet
When is the next flight?	Коли наступний рейс?	kohLIH nahSTOPnihy rehys
Is there a connection to Lviv?	Чи є зв'язок зі Львовом?	chih yeh zvyahZOHK zee L'VOHvohm
One-way ticket	Квиток в одну сторону.	kvihTOHK v ohdNOO STOHrohnoo
Round-trip ticket	Квиток туди й назад.	kvihTOHK tooDIH y nahZAHD
Is flight (N° 5) on time?	Чи рейс (номер п'ять) іде по розкладу?	chih rehys /NOHmehr pyaht'/ eeDEH poh ROHZklahdoo
I'd like to change/ confirm my flight.	Я хотів/ла би поміняти/ підтвердити свій рейс	yah khohTEEV/lah bih pohmeeNYAHtih/ peedTVEHRdihtih sveey rehys
I'd like to cancel my reservation.	Я хотів/ла би відмовитися від свого замовлення.	yah khohTEEV/lah bih veedMOHvihtihsyah veed SVOHgoh zahMOHVlehnnyah
How much luggage am I allowed?	Якої ваги багаж дозволяється провозити?	yahKOHyee vahGIH bahGAHZH dohzvohLYAHyeht'syah prohVOHzihtih
What's the flight number?	Який номер рейсу?	yahKIHY NOHmer REHYsoo
What gate do we leave from?	З якого виходу посадка на наш рейс?	z yahKOHgoh VIHkhohdoo pohSAHDkah nah nash rehys
Boarding gate	Вихід на посадку.	VIHkheed nah pohSAHDkoo
What time do we leave/ arrive?	Коли виліт/ приземлення?	kohLIH VIHleet/ prihZEHMlehnnyah

English	Ukrainian	Pronunciation
What time should I check in?	Коли́ я пови́нен/на́ реєструва́ти бага́ж?	kohLIH yah pohVIHnehn/nah rehyehstrooVAHtih bahGAHZH
Call the stewardess	Ви́кличте стюарде́су.	VIHKlihchteh styooahrDEHsoo
Fasten your seat belts.	Пристебні́ть ремні́	prihstehbNEET' rehmNEE
Will there be food served?	Чи нас бу́дуть годува́ти в літаку́?	chih nahs BOOdoot' gohdooVAHtih v leetahKOO
Can I smoke on board?	Мо́жна кури́ти?	MOHZHnah kooRIHtih
Is there a bus from the airport into the city?	Чи є автобус від аеропо́рту до мі́ста?	chih yeh ahvTOHboos veed ahehrohPOHRtoo doh MEEStah

IX. SIGHTSEEING AND RELAXING

Asking Directions

If the locals can not help you get where you want to go, you can always ask directions at special kiosks marked Довідки (Information). For ten coupons (karbovanetses) you will be given a small slip of paper with directions, street names, subway stops or bus numbers to direct you to your desired destination.

English	Ukrainian	Pronunciation
I'm lost (m/f)	Я заблудився/ заблудилася.	yah zahblooDIHVsyah/ zahblooDIHlahsyah
Excuse me	Пробачте/ Вибачте	prohBAHCHteh/ VIHbahchteh
Can you tell me how to get to... Khreshchatyk Street?	Скажіть, будь ласка, як потрапити... на Хрещатик	skahZHEET' bood' LAHSkah yahk pohTRAHpihtih nah khrehSHCHAHtihk
the center of town?	до центру міста	doh TSEHNTroo MEEStah
I'm looking for...	Я шукаю...	yah shooKAHyoo
Am I going in the right direction?	Чи я йду у правильному напрямі?	chih yah yhdoo oo PRAHvihl'nohmoo NAHPryahmee
Do you know where ... is?	Ви не знаєте, де знахо- диться...?	vih neh ZNAHyehteh deh znahKHOH- diht'syah
Is it far?	Це далеко?	tseh dahLEHkoh
Is it close?	Це не далеко?	tseh neh dahLEHkoh
Can I walk there?	Можна дійти туди пішки?	MOHZHnah deeyTIH tooDIH PEESHkih
It would be best to take a bus or the metro.	Вам краще, скористатися автобусом або метро.	vahm KRAHSHcheh skohrihsTAHtihsyah ahvTOHboosohm ahBOH mehtROH
What bus can I take to get to...?	Яким автобусом можна доїхати до...?	yahKIHM ahvTOHboosohm MOHZHnah dohYEEkhahtih doh
What street is this?	Яка це вулиця?	yahKAH tseh VOOlihtsyah

61

English	Ukrainian	Pronunciation
Please show me on the map where I am.	Покажіть мені, будь ласка, на карті, де я знаходжуся?	pohkahZHEET' mehNEE bood' LAHSkah nah KAHRtee deh yah znahKHOHDzhoosyah
Go straight ahead.	ідіть прямо.	eeDEET' PRYAHmoh
Go in this/ that direction.	ідіть у цей/той бік.	eeDEET' oo tsehy/tohy beek
Turn left/ right...	Поверніть наліво/ направо...	pohvehrNEET' nahLEEvoh/ nahPRAHvoh
at the next corner	на найближчому розі.	nah nahyBLIHZHchohmoo ROHzee
at the light	біля світлофора.	BEElyah sveetlohFOHrah
Take this road.	ідьте по цій вулиці.	YEED'teh poh tseey VOOlihtsee
You have to go back	Вам треба повернутися.	vahm TREHbah pohvehrNOOtihsyah
You're on the wrong bus.	Ви сіли не на той автобус.	vih SEElih neh nah tohy ahvTOHboos
Do I have to transfer?	Чи мені треба пересісти?	chih mehNEE TREHbah pehrehSEEStih
North/South	Північ/Південь	PEEVneech/PEEVdehn'
East/West	Схід/Захід	skheed/ZAHkheed
It's there...	Це там...	tseh tahm
on the right/left	направо/наліво	nahPRAHvoh/ nahLEEvoh
after/behind...	після/позаду...	PEESlyah/pohZAHdoo
next to/opposite...	поряд/напроти...	POHryahd/nahPROHtih
There it is (m/f/n)	Ось він/вона/воно	ohs' veen/vohNAH/vohNOH
This/That way	Сюди/Туди	syooDIH/tooDIH

Taking a Bus Trip

The Ukrintour representative of your hotel can help you sign up for the bus tours available in that city.

English	Ukrainian	Pronunciation
What sights should we see?	Які тут визначні пам'ятки?	yahKEE toot vihznahchNEE PAHMyahtkih
Where can I sign up for an excursion?	Де можна записатися на екскурсію?	deh MOHZHnah zahpih-SAHtihsyah nah ehksKOORseeyoo

English	Ukrainian	Pronunciation
What excursion do you suggest?	Яку екскурсію ви мені порадите?	yahKOO ehksKOORseeyoo vih mehNEE pohRAHdihteh
I want to take a bus trip around the city.	Я хочу записатися на автобусну екскурсію по місту.	yah KHOHchoo zahpihSAHtihsyah nah ahvTOHboosnoo ehksKOORseeyoo poh MEEStoo
I'd like to sign up for this excursion.	Я хотів/ла би записатися на цю екскурсію.	yah khohTEEV/lah bih zahpihSAHtihsyah nah tsyoo ehksKOORseeyoo
Do I have to sign up in advance?	Чи мені треба заздалегідь замовити?	chih mehNEE TREHbah zahzdahlehGEED' zahMOHvihtih
What does a ticket cost?	Скільки коштує квиток?	SKEEL'kih KOHSH-tooyeh kvihTOHK
When does it leave?	Коли відправляється екскурсія?	kohLIH veedprahv-LYAHyeht'syah ehksKOORseeyah
How long does it last?	Скільки часу триває екскурсія?	SKEEL'kih CHAHsoo trihVAHyeh ehksKOORseeyah
When do we get back?	Коли ми повернемося?	kohLIH mih pohVEHRnehmohsyah
Will we stop somewhere for lunch?	Чи ми будемо де-небудь обідати?	chih mih BOOdehmoh deh-NEHbood' ohBEEdahtih
From where does the excursion leave?	Звідки відправляється екскурсія?	ZVEEDkih veedprahv-LYAHyeht'syah ehksKOORseeyah
Tour guide.	Екскурсовод	ehkskoorsohVOHD
Is there an English-speaking guide?	Чи є екскурсовод, що розмовляє англійською мовою?	chih yeh ehkskoorsohVOHD shchoh rohzmohv-LYAHyeh ahngLEEYS'-kohyoo MOHvohyoo
Will we have free time there?	Чи буде у вас там вільний час?	chih BOOdeh oo nahs tahm VEEL'nihy chahs
When should we be back on the bus?	Коли ми повинні повернутися до автобусу?	kohLIH mih pohVIHNnee pohvehrNOOtihsyah doh ahvTOHboosoo

Taking a Walking Tour

Guided walking tours are available in most larger museums.

When does it open/ close?	Коли там, відчиняється/ зачиняється?	kohLIH tahm veedchih-NYAHyeht'syah/ zahchihNYAHyeht'syah
I want to sign up for a tour.	Я хочу записа-тися на екскурсію	yah KHOHchoo zahpih-SAHtihsyah nah ehksKOORseeyoo
When does it start/end?	Коли вона почінається/ завершається?	kohLIH vohNAH pohchihNAHyeht'syah/ zahvehrSHAHyeht'syah
What is the cost?	Скільки кош-тує квиток?	SKEEL'kih KOHSH-tooyeh kvihTOHK
Free admission	Вхід безкоштовний	vkheed behzkohshTOHVnihy
Do you sell guidebooks in English?	У вас є путівник англійською мовою?	oo vahs yeh pooteevNIHK ahngLEEYS'kohyoo MOHvohyoo
Is there a map?	У вас є план/ карта?	oo vahs yeh plahn/ KAHRtah
In front of...	Перед...	PEHrehd
To the rear of...	Позаду...	pohZAHdoo
In the middle of...	Посередині...	pohsehREHdihnee
On the left of...	Зліва...	ZLEEvah
On the right of...	Справа...	SPRAHvah
Where can I buy post cards?	Де можна купи-ти поштові картки?	deh MOHZHnah kooPIH-tih pohSHTOHvee KAHRTkih
May I see what post cards you have for sale?	Можна подиви-тись, які у вас є поштові картки?	MOHZHnah pohdihVIH-tihs' yahkee oo vahs yeh pohSHTOHvee KAHRTkih
I'd like to buy this set.	Я куплю цей комплект.	yah koopLYOO tsehy kohmPLEHKT
How much is it?	Скільки це коштує?	SKEEL'kih tseh KOHSHtooyeh
Can I take pictures?	Можна тут фо-тографувати?	MOHZHnah toot fohtohgrahfooVAHtih
No cameras allowed.	Фотографувати заборо-няється	fohtohgrahfooVAHtih zahbohroh-NYAHyeht'syah

64

I want to see the sights.	Я хочу оглянути визначні пам'ятки	yah KHOHchoo ohGLYAH-nootih vihznahchNEE PAHmyahtkih
Let's go for a walk.	Давайте прогуляємося	dahVAHYteh prohgooLYAHyehmohsyah
What kind of ... is that?	Що це за...?	shchoh tseh zah
animal/	тварина/	tvahRIHnah/
bird/	пташка/	PTAHSHkah/
fish/	риба/	RIHbah/
flower/	квітка/	KVEETkah/
tree	дерево	DEHrehvoh
We don't have those at home.	У нас таких немає.	oo nahs tahKIH nehMAHyeh
What a beautiful view!	Який чарівний краєвид!	yahKIHY chahREEV-nihy krahyehVIHD
What's that building?	Що це за будинок?	shchoh tseh zah booDIHnohk
When was it built?	Коли він був збудований?	kohLIH veen boov zbooDOHvahnihy
Who built it?	Хто його побудував?	khtoh yohGOH pohboodooVAHV
Who was the architect/ artist?	Хто був архітектором/ художником?	khtoh boov ahrkhee-TEHKtohrohm/ khooDOHZHnihkohm
When did he/she live?	Коли він/вона жив/ла?	kohLIH veen/vohNAH zhihv/LAH
Where's the house where... lived?	Де знаходиться будинок, в якому... жив/ла?	deh znaKHOHdiht'syah booDIHnohk v yahKOHmoo zhihv/LAH
Can we go in?	Можна зайти?	MOHZHnah zahyTIH
Very interesting.	Дуже цікаво.	DOOzheh tseeKAHvoh
It's...	Це...	tseh
beautiful	гарно	GAHRnoh
ugly	бридко	BRIHDkoh
wonderful	чудово	chooDOHvoh
horrible	жахливо	zhahkhLIHvoh
great	розкішно	rohzKEESHnoh
terrible	страшно	STRAHSHnoh

65

amazing	дивно	DIHVnoh
strange	дивовижно	dihvohVIHZHnoh
cute	мило	MIHloh
foreboding	страхітливо	strahkheetLIHvoh
Let's rest	Давайте відпочинемо	dahVAHYteh veedpohCHIHnehmoh
I'm tired	Я стомився/ лася/	yah stohMIHVsyah/ lahsyah
I'm bored	Мені нудно	mehNEE NOODnoh

Worship Services

Most places of worship do not mind visitors, as long as you observe their customs and do not disturb their services. Orthodox churches demand that women cover their heads with a kerchief or hat. Taking pictures inside churches is usually not permitted.

Worship services	Служба божа	SLOOZHbah BOHzhah
Monastery	Монастир	mohnahSTIHR
Cathedral	Собор	sohBOHR
Church	Церква	TSEHRKvah
Synagogue	Синагога	sihnahGOHgah
Temple	Храм	khrahm
Mosque	Мечеть	mehCHEHT'
Orthodox	Православний	prahvohSLAHVnihy
Old-Believers	Старо-обрядці	STAHroh-ohbRYAHDtsee
Saint	Святий	svyahTIHY
Altar	Алтар	ahlTAHR
Iconostasis	Іконостас	eekohnohSTAHS
Icons	Ікони	eeKOHnih
Incense	Ладан	LAHdahn
Candle	Свічка	SVEECHkah
Contribution	Пожертвування	pohZHEHRTvoovahnnyah
Prayers	Молитви	mohLIHTvih
Prayer book	Молитвеник	mohLIHTvehnnihk
Rabbi	Равін	rahVEEN
Priest	Священик	svyahSHCHEHnihk
When's the service?	Коли служба?	kohLIH SLOOZHbah
I want to look around the church.	Я хочу оглянути церкву	yah KHOHchoo ohGLYAHnootih TSEHRKvoo
You must cover your head.	Вам треба покрити голову	vahm TREHbah pohKRIHtih GOHlohvoo

Are women allowed?	Чи жінки допускаються?	chih zheenKIH dohpoosKAHyoot'syah
May I take a picture?	Чи можна тут фотографувати?	chih MOHZHnah toot fohtohgrahfooVAHtih
No cameras allowed.	Фотографувати забороняється	fohtohgrahfooVAHtih zahbohrohNYAHyehtsyah
Cemetary	Кладовище/ Цвинтар	klahDOHvihshcheh TSVIHntahr
Grave	Могила	mohGIHlah
Tombstone	Пам'ятник	PAHmyahtnihk

Outdoor Recreation

I enjoy...	Мені подобається...	mehNEE pohDOHbahyeht'syah
running	бігати	BEEgahtih
cycling	велоспорт	vehlohSPOHRT
tennis	теніс	TEHnees
horseback riding	їздити верхи	YEEZdihtih VEHRkhih
swimming	плавання	PLAHvahnnyah
sailing	парусний спорт	PAHroosnihy spohrt
mountain climbing	альпінізм	ahl'peeNEEZM
skiing	лижний спорт	LIHZHnihy spohrt
skating	ковзання	KOHVzahnnyah
I want to play tennis.	Я хочу грати в теніс	yah KHOHchoo GRAHtih v TEHnees
Can we rent rackets?	Можна взяти ракетки напрокат?	MOHZHnah VZYAHtih rahKEHTkih nahprohKAHT
Are there courts here?	Чи тут є корти?	chih toot yeh KOHRtih
Is there a swimming pool here?	Чи тут є басейн?	chih toot yeh bahSEHYN
Can one go swimming here?	Можна тут плавати?	MOHZHnah toot PLAHvahtih
Is it safe to swim here?	Тут безпечно плавати?	toot behzPEHCHnoh PLAHvahtih
Is the water here deep?	Тут глибоко?	toot glihBOHkoh
Is the water cold?	Чи вода холодна?	chih vohDAH khohLOHDnah
No swimming.	Купатися заборонено	kooPAHtihsyah zahbohROHnehnoh

67

I want to lie on the beach.	Я хочу лежати на пляжі	yah KHOHchoo lehZHAHtih nah PLYAHzhee
I want to sun-bathe.	Я хочу загорати	yah KHOHchoo zahgohRAHtih
Can I rent...	Можна взяти напрокат...	MOHZHnah VZYAHtih nahprohKAHT
a beach chair?	шезлонг?	shehzLOHNG
a sun umbrella?	парасолю від сонця?	pahrahSOHlyoo veed SOHNtsyah
a row boat?	човен?	CHOHvehn
water skis?	водяні лижі?	vohdyahNEE LIHzhee
skiing equipment?	лижне спорядження?	LIHZHneh spohRYAHDzhehnnyah
skates?	ковзани?	kohvzahNIH
What's the charge per hour/per day?	Скільки коштує на годину/ день?	SKEEL'kih KOHSHtooyeh nah gohDIHnoo/ dehn'
Is there a skating rink here?	Чи тут є ковзанка?	chih toot yeh KOHVzahnkah
Where can I go skiing?	Де можна кататися на лижах?	deh MOHZHnah kahTAHtihsyah nah LIHzhahkh

Camping

Camping	Кемпінг	KEHMpeeng
Camping equipment	Обладнання для кемпінга	ohbLAHDnahnnyah dlyah KEHMpeengah
Is swimming allowed?	Чи можна тут купатися?	chih MOHZHnah toot kooPAHtihsyah
Camping permit	Дозвіл на кемпінг	DOHZveel nah KEHMpeeng
Can we camp here?	Можна влаштувати тут стоянку?	MOHZHnah vlahshtooVAHtih toot stohYAHNkoo
What's the charge per day?/per person?	Скільки коштує день/на особу?	SKEEL'kih KOHSHtooyeh dehn'/ nah ohSOHboo
Are there show-ers/toilets?	Чи тут є душ/ туалет?	chih toot yeh doosh/ tooahLEHT
Where are the toilets?	Де знаходиться туалет?	deh znahKHOHdiht'syah tooaLEHT

Can we light a fire here?	Мо́жна тут зроби́ти вогни́ще?	MOHZHnah toot zrohBIHtih VOHGnihshcheh
Is there electricity?	Чи тут є еле́ктрика?	chih toot yeh ehLEHKtrihkah
Can we fish here?	Тут мо́жна лови́ти ри́бу?	toot MOHZHnah lohVIHtih RIHboo
Do we need a license to fish?	Чи потрі́бен до́звіл на ло́влю ри́би?	chih pohTREEbehn DOHZveel nah LOHVlyoo RIHbih
Can we rent equipment?	Мо́жна взя́ти напрока́т обла́днання для ке́мпінга?	MOHZHnah VZYAHtih nahprohKAHT ohbLAHDnahnnyah dlyah KEHMpeengah
Where can we get (a)...	Де мо́жна діста́ти...	deh MOHZHnah deesTAHtih
corkscrew?	што́пор?	SHTOHpohr
candles?	сві́чки?	SVEECHkih
can opener?	консе́рвний ніж?	kohnSEHRVnihy neezh
charcoal?	вугі́лля?	vooGEEL'lyah
compass?	ко́мпас?	KOHMpahs
cooking utensils?	кухо́нні ре́чі?	kooKHOHNnee REHchee
cooler?	су́мку-те́рмос?	SOOMkoo-TEHRmohs
fire wood?	дро́ва?	DROHvah
first-aid kit?	апте́чку?	ahpTEHCHkoo
flashlight?	кишенько́вий лі́хтар?	kihshehn' KOHvihy leekhTAHR
groundsheet?	підсти́лку під пала́тку?	peedSTIHLkoo peed pahLAHTkoo
kerosene?	гас?	gahs
lantern?	лі́хтар?	leekhTAHR
mattress?	матра́ц?	mahtRAHTS
sleeping bag?	спа́льний мішо́к?	SPAHL'nihy meeSHOHK
tent?	наме́т?	nahMEHT
thermos?	те́рмос?	TEHRmohs

Public Baths

Ukrainian public baths usually have saunas and pools where you can relax Ukrainian-style. After sitting for a while in the sauna, it is an Ukrainian custom to beat oneself lightly with dried birch or oak switches.

Public bath	Баня/Лазня	BAHnyah/LAHZnyah
Men	Чоловіки	chohlohveeKIH
Women	Жінки	zheenKIH
What's the admission?	Скільки коштує вхід?	SKEEL'kih KOHSH-tooyeh vkheed
I'd like to rent...	Я хотів/ла би взяти напрокат...	yah khohTEEV/lah bih VZYAHtih nahprohKAHT
a towel	Рушник	rooshNIHK
a sheet	Простирадло	prohstihRAHDloh
It's too hot/cold here.	Тут занадто гаряче/ холодно	toot zahNAHDtoh GAHryahcheh/ KHOHlohdnoh
Shower	Душ	doosh
Pool	Басейн	bahSEHYN
Bathing cap	Шапочка для купання	SHAHpohchkah dlyah kooPAHNnyah
Bathing suit	Купальний костюм	kooPAHL'nihy kohsTYOOM
Soap	Мило	MIHloh
Bucket	Відро	veedROH
Steam room	Парилка	pahRIHLkah
Birch switches	Березовий віник	behREHzohvihy VEEnihk
Massage	Масаж	mahSAHZH

X. ENTERTAINMENT

Tickets

Tickets can be purchased most easily from Ukrintour for dollars. You can also try your luck at buying tickets from kiosks on the street, but do not expect to get your first choice. Ukrainians are avid theater-goers and most performances sell out quickly. If you really want to see a particular performance, you can go down to the theater a little early and try to buy spare tickets (зайві квитки) from people outside the theater. This is not only accepted behavior, it is actually quite common.

Tickets.	Квитки.	kvihtKIH
(Theater) box office.	Театральна каса.	tehahtRAHL'nah KAHsah
Ticket window.	Квиткова каса.	kvihtKOHvah KAHsah
Can you recommend a(n) opera/ concert/ play?	Чи можете ви порадити оперу/ кон- церт/ п'єсу?	chih MOHzhehteh vih pohRAHdihtih OHpehroo/ kohn- TSEHRT PYEHsoo
Have you any tickets for tonight's performance?	У вас є квитки на сьогод- нішню виставу?	oo vahs yeh kvihtKIH nah s'ohGOHD- neeshnyoo vihsTAHvoo
How much are they?	Скільки вони коштують?	SKEEL'kih vohNIH KOHSHtooyoot'
I'd like two for...	Я хотів/ла би два на...	yah khohTEEV/lah bih dvah nah
We're sold out.	Всі квитки продані.	vsee kvihtKIH PROHdahnee
What time does it begin?	Коли починаєть- ся виставa?	kohLIH pohchihNAHyeht'- syah vihsTAHvah
How do I get to this theater?	Як мені доїхати до цього театру?	yahk mehNEE dohYEE- khahtih doh TS'OHgoh tehAHTroo
The Shevchenko Opera Theater.	Оперний театр імені Шевченка.	OHpehrnihy tehAHTR EEmehnee shehvCHEHNkah
The I. Franko Drama Theater.	Драматичний театр імені I. Франка	drahmahTIHCHnihy tehAHTR EEmehnee EE. frahnKAH
The "Ukraina" Concert Hall.	Концертний зал "Україна".	kohnTSEHRTnihy zahl "ookrahYEEnah"

Lysenko Conservatory.	Консерваторія імені Лисенка.	kohnsehrvahTOHreeyah EEmehnee LIHsehnkah
No admittance after the third bell.	Після третього дзвінка вхід до зали глядачів заборонено.	PEESlyah TREHt'ohgoh dzveenKAH vkheed doh ZAHlih glyahdahCHEEV zahbohROHnehnoh
Orchestra stalls.	Партер.	pahrTEHR
Amphitheater.	Амфітеатр.	ahmfeetehAHTR
Balcony.	Балкон.	bahlKOHN
Box.	Ложа.	LOHzhah
Left side.	Ліва сторона.	LEEvah stohrohNAH
Right side.	Права сторона.	PRAHvah stohrohNAH
Middle.	Середина.	sehrehDIHnah
Lobby.	Фойе.	fohYEH
Snack bar.	Буфет.	booFEHT
Smoking room.	Кімната для куріння.	keemNAHtah dlyah kooREEN'nyah
Cloakroom.	Гардероб.	gahrdehROHB
Cloakroom attendant. (m/f)	Гардеробник/ Гардеробниця.	gahrdehROHBnihk/ gahrdehROHBnihtsyah
Entrance to auditorium.	Вхід до зали глядачів.	vkheed doh ZAHlih glyahdahCHEEV
Exit.	Вихід.	VIHkheed

Theater and Movies

Movies are shown all day long . No one is admitted after the lights are turned off.

Play.	П'єса.	PYEHsah
Performance.	Вистава.	vihsTAHvah
Movie.	Кіно.	keeNOH
Theater.	Театр.	tehAHTR
What's at the...?	Що іде в...?	shchoh eeDEH v
What kind of play/ movie is it?	Що це за п'єса/ фільм?	shchoh tseh zah PYEHsah/ feel'm
It's a...	Це...	tseh
cartoon.	мультфільм.	mool'tFEEL'M
comedy.	комедія.	kohMEHdeeyah
documentary.	документальний фільм.	dohkoomehnTAHL'nihy feel'm

drama.	драмати́чний фільм.	drahmahTIHCHnihy feel'm
Who's the director?	Хто режисе́р?	khtoh rehzhihSEHR
Who's playing the lead?	Хто гра́є головну́ роль?	khtoh GRAHyeh gohlohvNOO rohl'
Are there any tickets left?	Чи є ще квитки́?	chih yeh shcheh kvihtKIH
Is there a matinee?	Це де́нна виста́ва?	tseh DEHNnah vihsTAHvah
When does the show begin?	Коли́ почина́ється виста́ва?	kohLIH pohchihNAHyeht' syah vihsTAHvah
Do you have any extra tickets?	У вас є за́йві квитки́?	oo vahs yeh ZAYvee kvihtKIH

Opera, Concerts and Ballet

Opera.	О́пера.	OHpehrah
Concert.	Конце́рт.	kohnTSEHRT
Ballet.	Бале́т.	bahLEHT
Orchestra.	Орке́стр.	ohrKEHSTR
Folk songs/ dances.	Наро́дні пісні́/ та́нці.	nahROHDnee peesNEE TAHNtsee
Here is my ticket.	Ось мій квито́к.	ohs' meey kvihTOHK
Where is my seat?	Де моє́ мі́сце?	deh mohYEH MEEStseh
Follow me.	Іді́ть слі́дом за мно́ю.	eeDEET' SLEEdohm zah MNOyoo
How much for a program?	Скі́льки ко́штує програ́ма?	SKEEL'kih KOHSHtooyeh prohGRAHmah
May I have a program, please?	Да́йте, будь ла́ска, програ́му.	DAYteh bood' LAHSkah prohGRAHmoo
Want to rent opera glasses?	Біно́кль вам не потрі́бен?	beeNOHKL' vahm neh pohtREEbehn
No, thank you.	Ні, дя́кую.	nee DYAkooyoo
I don't need them.	Він мені́ не потрі́бен.	veen mehNEE neh pohtREEbehn
Who is the conductor?	Хто дириге́нт?	khtoh dihrihGEHNT
Who is dancing the lead?	Хто танцю́є головну́ па́ртію?	khtoh tahnTSYOOyeh gohlohvNOO PAHRteeyoo
Who is the soloist? (f)	Хто солі́ст/ка?	khtoh sohLEEST/kah

When is the intermission?	Коли́ антра́кт?	kohLIH ahnTRAHKT
How long is the intermission?	Скі́льки ча́су трива́є антра́кт?	SKEEL'kih CHAHsoo trihVAHyeh ahnTRAHKT
Pardon me, can I get by?	Проба́чте, мо́жна пройти́?	prohBAHCHteh MOHZHnah proyTIH
That's my seat.	Це моє́ мі́сце.	tseh mohYEH MEEStseh

Circus and Puppet Show

Circus.	Цирк.	tsihrk
Puppet theater.	Лялько́вий теа́тр.	lyahl'KOHvihy tehAHTR
Do you have tickets for the circus/ puppet theater?	Ви ма́єте квитки́ до ци́рку/, лялько́вого теа́тру?	vih MAHyehteh kvihtkih doh TSIHRkoo/ lyahl'KOHvohgoh tehAHTroo
How do I get to the circus?	Як мені́ ді́йти́ до ци́рку?	yahk mehNEE deeyTIH doh TSIHRkoo
Is there a matinee today?	Чи сього́дні є де́нна виста́ва?	chih syohGOHDnee yeh DEHNnah vihsTAHvah
Do you have a spare ticket?	Ви не ма́єте за́йвого квитка́?	vih neh MAHyehteh ZAYvohgoh kvihtKAH
Give me a program, please.	Да́йте мені́, будь ла́ска, програ́му.	DAYteh mehNEE bood' LAHSkah prohgRAHmoo

Sporting Events

Sporting events.	Спорти́вні змага́ння.	spohrTIHVnee zmahGAHNnyah
Sports fan.	Болі́льник.	bohLEEL'nihk
I want to see a hockey/ soccer game.	Я хо́чу подиви́тися хокей́ний/футбо́льний матч.	yah KHOHchoo pohdihVIHtihsyah khohKEYnihy/ footBOHL'nihy mahtch
How much are the tickets?	Скі́льки ко́штують квитки́?	SKEEL'kih KOHSHtooyoot' kvihtKIH
Are there any tickets for today's game?	Чи є квитки́ на сього́днішній матч?	chih yeh kvihtKIH nah syohGOHDneeshneey mahtch

English	Ukrainian	Pronunciation
How do I get to Central Stadium?	Як мені доїхати до Централь-ного стадіону?	yahk mehNEE dohYEEkhah-tih doh tsehnTRAHL'-nohgoh stahdeeOHnoo
Who is playing?	Які команди грають?	yahKEE kohMAHNdih GRAHyoot'
Scoreboard.	Табло.	tahbLOH
Who is winning?	Хто виграє?	khtoh vihGRAHyeh
What's the score?	Який рахунок?	yahKIHY rahKHOOnohk
Dynamos are ahead 3-1.	Три один на ко-ристь Динамо.	trih ohDIHN nah KOH-rihst' dihNAHmoh
It's scoreless.	Нічия.	neechihYAH
Score a point.	Виграти очко.	VIHGrahtih ohchKOH
Score a goal.	Забити гол.	zahBIHtih gohl
Who won?	Хто виграв?	khtoh VIHGrahv
Scoreless tie.	Нічия.	neechihYAH
Do you want to play chess?	Ви хочете гра-ти в шахи?	vih KHOHchehteh GRAH-tih v SHAHkhih
Check mate.	Мат.	maht

XI. STORES

Kyyiv has one large department store, known as TSUM (Central Department Store), which is open from 9 am to 8 pm. Food stores typically open at 8 am and close at 7 pm. Other shops, like bookstores and souvenir shops, are open from 10 am to 7 pm. Most stores, except those selling food, are closed on Sundays.

Finding the Right Store

The easiest and most convenient, although also the most expensive, stores for foreigners are the hard currency stores or Kashtans. Specifically set aside for foreigners, these stores accept only foreign currency and credit cards. The staff usually speaks some English.

Where can I buy...?	Де можна купити...?	deh MOHZNnah kooPIHtih
Where can I find a...?	Де можна знайти...?	deh MOHZHnah znayTIH
Is there a... near here?	Чи є поблизу...	chih yeh pohBLIHzoo
bakery.	булочна.	BOOlochnah
bookstore.	книжковий магазин.	knihzhKOHvihy mahgahZIHN
candy shop.	кондитерська.	kohnDIHtehrs'kah
clothes store.	одяг/будинок моди.	OHdyahg/booDIHnohk MOHdih
dairy.	молочарня.	mohlohCHAHRnyah
department store.	універмаг.	ooneevehrMAHG
drug store.	аптека.	ahpTEHkah
farmer's market.	базар.	bahZAHR
fish market.	рибний магазин.	RIHBnihy mahgahZIHN
fruit and vege-table store.	фрукти і овочі.	FROOKtih ee OHvohchee
furrier.	хутро.	KHOOTroh
gift shop.	подарунки.	pohdahROONkih
greengrocer.	зелень.	ZEHlehn'
grocery.	продукти.	prohDOOKtih
Kashtan.	Каштан.	kahshTAHN
hat shop.	магазин голов-них уборів.	mahgahZIHN gohlohv-NIHKH ooBOHreev

76

jeweler.	ювелірний магазин.	yoovehLEERnihy mahgahZIHN
liquor store.	вино.	vihNOH
newsstand.	преса.	PREHsah
record store.	грампластинки.	grahmplahsTIHNkih
secondhand bookstore.	букіністична крамниця.	bookeeneesTIHCHnah krahmNIHtsyah
secondhand store.	комісійний магазин.	kohmeeSEEYnihy mahgahZIHN
shoe store.	взуття.	vzootTYAH
souvenirs.	сувеніри.	soovehNEErih
stationary.	канцтовари.	kahntstohVAHrih
tobacconist.	тютюн.	tyooTYOON
toy store.	магазин іграшок.	mahgahZIHN EEGrahshohk

Looking Around

Service.	Обслуговування.	ohbslooGOHvoovahnnyah
Can you help me...	Допоможіть, будь ласка...	dohpohmohZHEET' bood' LAHSkah
Where's the ... department?	Де знаходиться відділ...	deh zhahKHOH-diht'syah VEEDdeel
Can I help you?	Слухаю вас.	SLOOkhahyoo vahs
Do you have...	Чи є у вас...	chih yeh oo vahs
What kind of ... would you like?	Який... ви бажаєте?	yahKIHY...vih bahZHAHyehteh
I'd like...	Я хотів/ла б...	yah khohTEEV/lah b
I'm sorry, we don't have any.	Пробачте, цього у нас немає...	prohBAHCHteh tsyohGOH oo nahs nehMAHyeh
We're sold out.	Все розпродано.	vseh rohzPROHdahnoh
Anything else?	Що-небудь ще?	shchohNEHbood' shcheh
Show me (this/ that), please.	Покажіть мені це/то, будь ласка.	pohkahZHEET' mehNEE tseh/toh bood' LAHSkah
No, not that, but that there ... next to it.	Ні, не це, а он те...що поряд з ним.	nee neh tseh ah ohn teh...shchoh POHryahd z nihm
It's not what I want.	Це не то, що я хочу.	tseh neh teh shchoh yah KHOHchoo
I don't like it.	Це мені не подобається.	tseh mehNEE neh pohDOHbahyeht'syah

I'm just looking.	Я тільки оглядаю.	yah TEEL'kih ohglyahDAHyoo
I prefer...	Я волію...	yah vohLEEyoo
Something not too expensive.	Що-небудь не дуже дороге.	shchohNEHbood' neh DOOzheh dohrohGEH
How much is it?	Скільки це коштує?	SKEEL'kih tseh KOHSHtooyeh
Repeat that, please.	Повторіть, будь ласка.	pohvtohREET' bood' LAHSkah
Please write it down.	Напишіть це, будь ласка.	nahpihSHEET' tseh bood' LAHSkah

Making a Purchase

Shopping in Ukraine is an adventure. There are usually several steps involved in making a purchase. First, you choose your merchandise and take note of the price. Next, you go to the register and pay for it, receiving a чек (receipt) in return. Finally, you take this receipt to another counter where you receive your purchase.

Have you decided?	Чи ви вже вирішили?	chih vih vzheh VIHreeshihlih
Yes, I want this.	Так, хочу взяти.	tahk KHOHchoo VZYAHtih
I'll take it.	Я візьму це.	yah veeZ'MOO tseh
Will I have problems with customs?	Я не буду мати ускладнень на таможні?	yah neh BOOdoo MAHtih ooSKLAHDnehn' nah tahMOHZHnee
Pay at the cashier.	Платіть до каси.	plahTEET' doh KAHsih
Do you accept traveler's checks/ credit cards/ dollars?	Чи ви берете подорожні чеки/ кредитні картки/ долари?	chih vih behREHteh pohdohROHZHnee CHEHkih/ krehDIHTnee KAHRTkih/ DOHlahrih
Can I have a receipt, please.	Дайте, будь ласка, квитанцію.	DAYteh bood' LAHSkah kvihTAHNtseeyoo
Wrap it up for me, please.	Загорніть, будь ласка.	zahgohrNEET' bood' LAHSkah
Please give me a bag.	Дайте мені, будь ласка, сумку.	DAYteh mehNEE bood' LAHSkah SOOMkoo

XII. SHOPPING

Gifts and Souvenirs

Before buying gifts for hard currency at the Kashtans, you might try shopping in a Подарунки or Сувеніри store, where you can often find the same merchandise at cheaper prices in Ukrainian money.

Amber	Бурштин	boorSHTIHN
Balalaika	Балалайка	bahlahLAYkah
Books	Книги	KNIHgih
Box of candy	Коробка цукерок	kohROHBkah tsooKEHrohk
Caviar	Ікра	eekRAH
Ceramics	Кераміка	kehRAHmeekah
Chess set	Шахи	SHAHkhih
Chocolate	Шоколад	shohkohLAHD
Cigarettes	Сигарети	sihgahREHtih
Cigarette case	Портсигар	pohrtsihGAHR
Cigarette lighter	Запальничка	zahpahl'NIHCHkah
Coins	Монети	mohNEHtih
Fur hat	Хутряна шапка	khootRYAHnah SHAHPkah
Icon	Ікона	eeKOHnah
Jewelry	Дорогоцінності	dohrohgohTSEENnohstee
Lace	Мереживо	mehrehZHIHvoh
Nested wooden doll	Матрьошка	mahtRYOHSHkah
Palekh boxes	Палехські скриньки	PAHlehkhskee SKRIHN'kih
Perfume	Парфума	pahrFOOmah
Postcards	Листівки	lihsTEEVkih
Posters	Плакати	plahKAHtih
Records	Пластинки	plahSTIHNkih
Samovar	Самовар	sahmohVAHR
Scarf	Шарф/Шалик	shahrf/shahLIHK
Shawl	Хустка	KHOOSTkah
Stamps	Марки	MAHRkih
Tapes	Касети	kahSEHtih
Tea caddy	Чайниця	CHAYnihtsyah
Toys	Іграшки	EEGrahshkih
Vodka	Горілка	gohREELkah
Wine	Вино	vihNOH
Wood carvings	Різьба по дереву	reez'BAH poh DEHrehvoo
Wooden spoons and bowls	Дерев'яні ложки та миски	dehrehvYAHnee LOHZHkih tah MIHSkih

79

Jewelry

Jewelry depart- ment	Ювелірні вироби	yoovehLEERnee VIHrohbih
Jewelry	Дорогоцінності	dohrohgohTSEENnohstee
Bracelet	Браслет	brahsLEHT
Brooch	Брошка	BROHSHkah
Chain	Ланцюжок	lahntsyooZHOHK
Charm	Брелок	brehLOHK
Clips	Кліпси	KLEEPsih
Cufflinks	Запонки	ZAHpohnkih
Earrings	Серги	SEHRgih
Money clip	Скріпка для грошей	SKREEPkah dlyah grohSHEY
Necklace	Намисто	nahMIHStoh
Pendant	Кулон	kooLOHN
Ring	Перстень	PEHRstehn'
Tie pin	Шпилька для краватки	SHPIHL'kah dlyah krahVAHTkih
Watch	Годинник	gohDIHNnihk

Stones and Metals

What's it made of?	З чого це зроблено?	z CHOHgoh tseh ZROHBlehnoh
Is it real silver/ gold?	Чи це справжнє срібло/золото?	chih tseh SPRAHVZHnyeh SREEBloh/ZOHlohtoh
How many carats is this?	Скільки тут каратів?	SKEEL'kih toot kahRAHteev
What kind of me- tal/ stone is it?	Що це за ме- тал/ камінь?	shchoh tseh zah mehTAHL/ KAHmeen'
Amber	Бурштин	boorshTIHN
Amethyst	Аметист	ahmehTIHST
Copper	Мідь	meed'
Coral	Корал	kohRAHL
Crystal	Кришталь	krihshTAHL'
Diamond	Діамант	deeahMAHNT
Ebony	Чорне дерево	CHOHRneh DEHrehvoh
Emerald	Смарагд	smahRAHGD
Garnet	Гранат	grahNAHT
Gilded	Позолочений	pohzohLOHchehnihy
Glass	Скло	skloh
Gold	Золото	ZOHlohtoh

Ivory	Слонова кістка	slohNOHvah KEESTkah
Jade	Нефрит	nehFRIHT
Onyx	Онікс	OHneeks
Pearl	Перлина	pehrLIHnah
Pewter	Олово	OHlohvoh
Platinum	Платина	PLAHtihnah
Ruby	Рубін	rooBEEN
Sapphire	Сапфір	sahpFEER
Silver	Срібло	SREEBloh
Silver plated	Срібний	SREEBnihy
Topaz	Топаз	tohPAHZ
Turquoise	Бірюза	beeryooZAH

Books and Stationary Supplies

Bookstore	Книгарня	knihGAHRnyah
Newsstand	Газетний кіоск	gahZEHTnihy keeOHSK
Secondhand bookstore	Букіністична крамниця	bookeeneesTIHCHnah krahmNIHtsyah
Stationary store	Канцтовари	kahntstohVAHrih
Do you have any books in English?	Чи є у вас книги англійською мовою?	chih yeh oo vahs KNIHgih ahngLEEYS'kohyoo MOHvohyoo
Do you have any children's books /art books?	Чи є у вас дитячі книги/книги з мистецтва?	chih yeh oo vahs dihTYAHchee KNIHgih /KNIHgih z mihsTEHTStvah
Where are the guidebooks/ dictionaries?	Де знаходяться путівники/ словники?	deh znahKHOHdyaht'syah pooteevnihKIH/ slohvnihKIH
How much is this book?	Скільки коштує ця книга?	SKEEL'kih KOHSHtooyeh tsyah KNIHgah
Where do I pay?	Де мені платити?	deh mehNEE plahTIHtih
Have you got...	Чи у вас є...	chih oo vahs yeh
calendars?	календарі?	kahlehndahREE
envelopes?	конверти?	kohnVEHRtih
magazines in English?	журнали англій- ською мовою?	zhoorNAHlih ahngLEEYS'- kohyoo MOHvohyoo
maps?	плани/карти?	PLAHnih/KAHRtih
notebooks?	блокноти?	blohkNOHtih
paper?	папір?	pahPEER
pens?	ручки?	ROOCHkih
pencils?	олівці?	ohleevTSEE

81

post cards?	листівки?	lihsTEEVkih
stationary?	поштовий	pohshTOHvihy
	папір?	pahPEER

Records

Records	Пластинки	plahsTIHNkih
Cassettes	Касети	kahSEHtih
Have you got any recording by...	Чи є у вас пластинки...	chih yeh oo vahs plahsTIHNkih
Do you have any...	Чи є у вас...	chih yeh oo vahs
Russian folk songs?	російські народні пісні?	rohSEEYS'kee nahROHDnee peesNEE
Ukrainian folk songs?	українські народні пісні?	ookrahYEENs'kee nahROHDnee peesNEE
music of the peoples of the former USSR?	музика народів колишнього СРСР?	MOOzihkah nahROHdeev kohLISHnyohgoh ehsEHRehsEHR
poets reading their work?	поети, які читають свої вірші?	pohEHtih yahKEE chihTAHyoot' svohYEE VEERshee
classical music?	класична музика?	klahSIHCHnah MOOzihkah
popular music?	естрадна музика?	ehsTRAHDnah MOOzihkah
recordings of operas and plays?	записи опер і драматичних вистав?	ZAHpihsih OHpehr ee drahmahTIHCHnihkh vihsTAHV
rock?	рок-музика?	rohk-MOOzihkah
Can I listen to this record?	Можна прослухати цю пластинку?	MOHZHnah prohSLOOkhahtih tsyoo plahsTIHNkoo

Toys

Toys/Games	Іграшки/Ігри	EEGrahshkih/EEGrih
For a boy	Для хлопчика	dlyah KHLOHPchihkah
For a girl	Для дівчинки	dlyah DEEVchihnkih
Ball	М'яч	myahch
Blocks	Кубики	KOObihkih
Cards	Ігральні карти	eegRAHL'nee KAHRtih
Checkers	Шашки	SHAHSHkih
Chess	Шахи	SHAHkhih

Doll	Лялька	LYAL'kah
Electronic game	Електронна гра	ehlehkTROHNnah grah
Stuffed animal	Чучело	CHOOchehloh
Teddy bear	Ведмедик	vehdMEHdihk
Wooden toys	Дерев'яні іграшки	dehrehvYAHnee EEGrahshkih

Clothes

Clothes	Одяг	OHdyahg
Where can I find a...	Де можна знайти...	deh MOHZHnah znay-TIH
bathing cap?	шапочку для купання?	SHAHpohchkoo dlyah kooPAHNnyah
bathing suit?	купальник?	kooPAHL'nihk
bathrobe?	халат?	khahLAHT
belt?	пояс?	POHyahs
blouse?	блузку?	BLOOZkoo
bra?	бюстгальтер?	byoostGAHL'tehr
children's clothes?	дитячий одяг?	dihTYAHchihy OHdyahg
coat?	пальто?	pahl'TOH
dress?	сукню?	SOOKnyoo
fur coat?	шубу?	SHOOboo
fur hat?	хутряну шапку?	khootryahNOO SHAHPkoo
gloves?	рукавички?	rookahVIHCHkih
handkerchief?	хусточку для носа?	KHOOStohchkoo dlyah NOHsah
hat?	капелюха?	kahpehLYOOkhah
jacket?	куртку?	KOORTkoo
panties?	трусики?	TROOsihkih
pants?	брюки?	BRYOOkih
pajamas?	піжаму?	peeZHAHmoo
raincoat?	плащ?	plahshch
scarf?	шарф?	shahrf
shirt?	сорочку?	sohROHCHkoo
shorts?	шорти?	SHOHRtih
skirt?	спідницю?	speedNIHtsyoo
slip?	комбінацію?	kohmbeeNAHtseeyoo
socks?	шкарпетки?	shkahrPEHTkih
stockings?	панчохи?	pahnCHOHkhih
suit?	костюм?	kohsTYOOM
sweater?	светер?	SVEHtehr

English	Ukrainian	Pronunciation
sweatsuit?	спортивний костюм?	spohrTIHVnihy kohsTYOOM
swimming trunks?	плавки?	PLAHVkih
tie?	краватку?	krahVAHTkoo
t-shirt?	майку?	MAYkoo
underwear?	білизну?	beeLIHZnoo

F i t

I don't know my size.	Я не знаю свого розміру	yah neh ZNAHyoo svohGOH ROHZmeeroo
I take a size...	Мій розмір...	meey ROHZmeer
Is there a mirror?	Чи є у вас дзеркало?	chih yeh oo vahs DZEHRkahloh
Can I try it on?	Можна поміряти?	MOHZHnah pohMEEryahtih
Where is the fitting room?	Де примірочна?	deh prihMEErohchnah
Does it fit?	Гарно сидить?/ Воно пасує мені?	GAHRnoh sihDIHT'/ vohNOH pah-SOOyeh mehNEE
It fits well.	Дуже гарно сидить	DOOzheh GAHRnoh sihDIHT'
It doesn't suit me.	Це мені не підходить	tseh mehNEE neh peedKHOHdiht'
It's too...	Воно занадто...	vohNOH zahNAHDtoh
big/small	велике/мале	vehLIHkeh/mahLEH
long/short	довге/коротке	DOHVgeh/kohROHTkeh
loose/tight	широке/вузьке	shihROHkeh/vooz'KEH

C o l o r s

Color	Колір	KOHleer
What color is it?	Якого це кольору?	yahKOHgoh tseh KOHl'ohroo
I don't like the color	Мені не подобається цей колір	mehNEE neh pohDOHbahyeht'syah tsey KOHleer
Do you have other colors?	Чи у вас є інші кольори?	chih oo vahs yeh EENshee kohl'ohRIH
I'd like something bright	Я хотів/ла би щось яскраве	yah khohTEEV/lah bih shchohs' yahsKRAHveh

84

English	Ukrainian	Pronunciation
Do you have anything in red?	У вас є що-небудь черво-ного кольору?	oo vahs yeh shchoh-NEHbood' chehrVOH-nohgoh KOHl'ohroo
Red	Червоний	chehrVOHnihy
Pink	Рожевий	rohZHEHvihy
Violet	Фіолетовий	feeoLEHtohvihy
Purple	Пурпуровий	poorpooROHvihy
Blue	Синій	SIHneey
Light blue	Блакитний	blahKIHTnihy
Green	Зелений	zehLEHnihy
Orange	Оранжевий	ohRAHNzhohvihy
Yellow	Жовтий	ZHOHVtihy
Brown	Коричневий	kohRIHCHnehvihy
Beige	Бежевий	BEHzhehvihy
Grey	Сірий	SEErihy
Black	Чорний	CHOHRnihy
White	Білий	BEElihy
Light (+color)	Світло-...	SVEETloh
Dark (+color)	Темно-...	TEHMnoh

Materials and Fabrics

English	Ukrainian	Pronunciation
Aluminum	Алюміній	ahlyooMEEneey
Brass	Латунь	lahTOON'
Canvas	Полотно (льняне)	pohlohtNOH (l'nyahNEH)
Ceramics	Кераміка	kehRAHmeekah
Chiffon	Шифон	shihFOHN
China	Порцеляна	pohrtsehLYAHnah
Copper	Мідь	meed'
Corduroy	Вельвет	vehl'VEHT
Cotton	Бавовняний	bahvohvNYAHnihy
Crepe	Креп	krehp
Crystal	Кришталь	krihshTAHL'
Fabric	Тканина	tkahNIHnah
Felt	Фетр	fehtr
Flannel	Фланель	flahNEHL'
Fur	Хутро	KHOOTroh
Glass	Скло	skloh
Gold	Золото	ZOHlohtoh
Iron	Залізо	zahLEEzoh
Lace	Мереживо	mehREHzhihvoh
Leather	Шкіра	SHKEErah

Linen	Полотно́	pohlohtNOH
Metal	Мета́л	mehTAHL
Nylon	Нейло́н	neyLOHN
Plastic	Пластма́са	plahstMAHsah
Satin	Атла́с	ahtLAHS
Silk	Шовк	shohvk
Silver	Срі́бло	SREEBloh
Steel	Сталь	stahl'
Stone	Ка́мінь	KAHmeen'
Suede	За́мша	ZAHMshah
Synthetic	Синте́тика	sihnTEHtihkah
Terrycloth	Мохна́та	mohkhNAHtah
	ткани́на	tkahNIHnah
Velvet	Оксами́т	ohksahMIHT
Wood	Де́рево	DEHrehvoh
Wool	Шерсть	shehrst'

S h o e s

Shoes	Взуття́	vzootTYAH
Boots	Чо́боти	CHOHbohtih
Felt boots	Валянки	VAHlyahnkih
Sandals	Босоні́жки	bohsohNEEZHkih
Slippers	Та́почки	TAHpohchkih
Children's shoes	Дитя́че взуття́	dihTYAHcheh vzootTYAH
Shoelaces	Шнурки	shnoorKIH
Are these made of cloth/ suede/ leather/ rubber?	Чи вони зро́блені з ткани́ни/ за́мші/шкі́ри/ гуми?	chih vohNIH ZROHBlehnee z tkahNIHnih/ ZAHMshee/ SHKEErih/GOOmih
Can I try these on in a size...	Мо́жна поміря́ти ро́змір...	MOHZHnah pohMEEryahtih ROHZmeer
These are too big/ small/ narrow/ wide	Вони́ зана́дто вели́кі/ малі́/ вузькі́/широкі.	vohNIH zahNAHDtoh vehLIHkee/ mahLEE/ vooz'KEE/shihROHkee

G r o c e r i e s

Groceries	Проду́кти	prohDOOKtih
I'd like...	Я хотів/ла би...	yah khohTEEV/lah bih
a piece of that	шмато́к цього	shmahTOHK TSYOHgoh
a half kilo...	півкіло́...	peevkeeLOH
a kilo...	кілогра́м...	keelohGRAHM

one-and-a-half kilos...	півтора кіло...	peevtohRAH keeLOH
50 grams...	п'ятдесят грамів...	pyahtdehSYAHT GRAHmeev
100 grams...	сто грамів...	stoh GRAHmeev
a liter of...	літр...	leetr
a bottle of...	пляшку...	PLYAHSHkoo
ten eggs	десяток яєць	dehSYAHtohk yahYEHTS'
a packet of cookies/tea	пачку печива/ чаю	PAHCHkoo PEH- chihvah/ CHAHyoo
a can of pears	банку груш	BAHNkoo groosh
a jar of sour cream	банку сметани	BAHNkoo smehTAHnih
a loaf of bread	буханець хліба	bookhahNEHTS' KHLEEbah
a box of candy	коробку цукерок	kohROHBkoo tsooKEHrohk
a bar of chocolate	плитку шоколаду	PLIHTkoo shohkohLAHdoo

Health and Beauty Aides

Absorbent cotton	Вата	VAHtah
Antiseptic	Антисептична мазь	ahntihsehpTIHCHnah mahz'
Aspirin	Аспірин	ahspeeRIHN
Ace-bandage	Еластичний бинт	ehlahsTIHCHnihy bihnt
Adhesive Bandage	Пластир	PLAHStihr
Bobby-pins	Шпильки	SHPIHL'kih
Comb	Гребінь	GREHbeen'
Condoms	Презервативи	prehzehrvahTIHvih
Contraceptives	Протизачаточні засоби	prohtihzahCHAHtohchnee ZAHsohbih
Cough drops	Таблетки від кашлю	tahbLEHTkih veed KAHSHloo
Curlers	Бігуді	beegooDEE
Deodorant	Дезодорант	dehzohdohRAHNT
Diapers	Пелюшки	pehlyooshKIH
Disinfectant	Дезинфікуючий засіб	dehzihnfeeKOOyoochihy ZAHseeb
Ear drops	Вушні каплі	vooshNEE KAHPlee
Eye drops	Каплі для очей	KAHPlee dlyah ohCHEY
Eye liner	Туш для вій	toosh dlyah veey

Eye shadow	Тіні для вій	TEEnee dlyah veey
Hair brush	Щітка для волосся	SHCHEETkah dlyah vohLOHSsyah
Hair dye	Фарба	FAHRbah
Hair spray	Лак	lahk
Hand cream	Крем для рук	krehm dlyah rook
Insect repellent	Засіб від комарів	ZAHseeb veed kohmahREEV
Iodine	Йод	yohd
Laxative	Послаблююче	pohsLAHBlyooyoocheh
Lipstick	Губна помада	goobNAH pohMAHdah
Make-up	Косметика	kohsMEHtihkah
Mascara	Туш для вій	toosh dlyah veey
Nail clipper	Ножиці для ногтей	NOHzhihtsee dlyah nohgTEHY
Nail file	Пилочка	PIHlohchkah
Nail polish	Лак для ногтей	lahk dlyah nohgTEHY
Nail polish remover	Ацетон	ahtsehTOHN
Pacifier	Соска	SOHSkah
Perfume	Парфума	pahrFOOmah
Razor	Бритва	BRIHTvah
Razor blades	Леза	LEHzah
Rouge	Рум'яна	rooMYAHnah
Safety pins	Англійські шпильки	ahngLEEYS'kee SHPIHL'kih
Sanitary napkins	Гігієнічні пакети	geegeeyehNEECHnee pahKEHtih
Shampoo	Шампунь	shahmPOON'
Shaving cream	Крем для гоління	krehm dlyah gohLEEN'nyah
Sleeping pills	Снотворне	snohTVOHRneh
Soap	Мило	MIHloh
Sponge	Губка	GOOBkah
Sun-tan lotion	Масло для загару	MAHSloh dlyah zahGAHroo
Thermometer	Термометер	tehrMOHmehtehr
Throat lozenges	Таблетки для горла	tahbLEHTkih dlyah GOHRlah
Toilet paper	Туалетний папір	tooahLEHTnihy pahPEER
Tooth brush	Зубна щітка	zoobNAH SHCHEETkah
Tooth paste	Зубна паста	zoobNAH PAHStah
Tranquillizer	Заспокоююче	zahspohKOHyooyoocheh
Tweezers	Пинцет	pihnTSEHT
Vitamins	Вітаміни	veetahMEEnih

XIII. ACCIDENTS AND EMERGENCIES

Help

English	Ukrainian	Pronunciation
I need help	Мені потрібна допомога	mehNEE pohtREEBnah dohpohMOHgah
There's been an accident	Стався нещасний випадок	STAHVsyah nehSHCHAHSnihy VIHpahdohk
Please call the...	Подзвоніть, будь ласка до...	pohDZVOHneet' bood' LAHSkah doh
American/	американського/	ahmehrihKAHNS'kohgoh/
British/	англійського/	ahngLEEYS'kohgoh/
Canadian	канадського	kahNAHDS'kohgoh
embassy	посольства.	pohSOHL'stvah
consulate	консульство	KOHNsool'stvoh
ambulance	швидка допомога	shvihdKAH dohpohMOHgah
Please get...	Викличте, будь ласка...	VIHKlihchteh bood' LAHSkah
a doctor	лікаря	LEEkahryah
the police	міліцію	meeLEEtseeyoo
Please notify...	Сповістіть, будь ласка...	spohveesTEET' bood' LAHSkah
my husband	мого чоловіка	mohGOH chohlohVEEkah
my wife	мою жінку	mohYOO ZHEENkoo
my family	мою сім'ю	mohYOO seemYOO
my hotel	мій готель	meey gohTEHL'
I've had my ...stolen	У мене вкрали...	oo MEHneh VKRAHlih
I've lost my...	Я загубив/ла...	yah zahgooBIHV/lah
passport	паспорт	PAHSpohrt
wallet	гаманець	gahmahNEHTS'
purse	сумку	SOOMkoo
keys	ключі	klyooCHEE
money	гроші	GROHshee

Illness and Injury

English	Ukrainian	Pronunciation
He/She is hurt	Він хворий/ Вона хвора	veen KHVOHrihy/ vohNAH KHVOHrah
He/She is bleeding badly	У нього/неї сильна кровотеча	oo NYOHgoh/NEHyee SIHL'nah krohvohTEHchah

English	Ukrainian	Pronunciation
He/She is unconscious	Він/Вона втратив/ла свідомість	veen/vohNAH VTRAHtihv/lah sveeDOHmeest'
He/She is seriously injured	У нього/неї серйозне пошкодження	oo NYOHgoh/NEHyee sehrYOHZneh pohSHKOHDzhehnnyah
I'm in pain	Мені боляче	mehNEE BOHlyahcheh
My ... hurts	У мене болить...	oo MEHneh bohLIHT'
I can't move my...	Я не можу рухати...	yah neh MOHzhoo ROOkhahtih
I'm ill (f)	Я хворий/хвора	yah KHVOHrihy/KHVOHrah
I'm dizzy	У мене голова паморочиться	oo MEHneh gohlohVAH PAHmohrohchiht'syah
I'm nauseous	Мене нудить	mehNEH NOOdiht'
I feel feverish	Мене лихоманить	mehNEH lihkhohMAHniht'
I've vomited	Я виблював/ла	yah VIHblyoovahv/lah
I've got food poisoning	У мене отруєння їжею	oo MEHneh ohTROOyehnnyah YEEzhehyoo
I've got diarrhea	У мене розслаблення шлунку	oo MEHneh rohzSLAHBlehnnyah SHLOONkoo
I'm constipated	У мене запор	oo MEHneh zahPOHR
It hurts to swallow	Мені боляче ковтати	mehNEE BOHlyahcheh kohvTAHtih
I'm having trouble breathing	Мені важко дихати	mehNEE VAHZHkoh DIHkhahtih
I have chest pain	У мене біль в грудях	oo MEHneh beel' v GROOdyahkh
I've got indigestion	У мене розлад шлунку	oo MEHneh ROHZlahd SHLOONkoo
I've got a bloody nose	У мене кровотеча з носа	oo MEHneh krohvohTEHchah z NOHsah
I've got sun stroke	У мене сонячний удар	oo MEHneh SOHnyahchnihy ooDAHR
I'm sun-burned	Я обгорів/ла	yah ohbgohREEV/lah
I've got a cramp/cramps	У мене судорога/ схватки	oo MEHneh SOOdohrohgah/SKHVAHTkih
I've got a bladder/ vaginal infection	У мене запалення міхура/ влагалища	oo MEHneh zahPAHlehnnyah meekhooRAH/ vlahGAHlihshchah
I've broken my arm	Я зломав/ла собі руку	yah zlohMAHV/lah sohBEE ROOkoo

English	Ukrainian	Pronunciation
I've sprained my ankle	Я підвернув/ла собі ногу	yah peedvehrNOOV/lah sohBEE NOHgoo
I've dislocated my shoulder	Я вивихнув/ла собі ключицю	yah VIHvihkhnoolah sohBEE klyooCHIHtsyoo
I've been stung by a wasp/bee	Мене вкусила оса/бджола	mehNEH vkooSIHlah ohSAH/bdzhohLAH
I've got...	У мене...	oo MEHneh
arthritis	артрит	ahrtRIHT
asthma	астма	AHSTmah
diabetis	діабет	deeahBEHT
high blood pressure	високий тиск	vihSOHkihy tihsk
an ulcer	виразка	VIHrahzkah

Parts of the Body

English	Ukrainian	Pronunciation
Ankle	Щиколотка	SHCHIHkohlohtkah
Appendix	Апендикс	ahPEHNdihks
Arm	Рука	rooKAH
Back	Спина	spihNAH
Bladder	Сечовий міхур	sehchohVIHY meeKHOOR
Blood	Кров	krohv
Body	Тіло	TEEloh
Bone	Кість	keest'
Breasts	Груди	GROOdih
Calf	Литка	LIHTkah
Cheek	Щока	shchohKAH
Chest cavity	Грудинна порожнина	grooDIHNnah pohrohzhNIHnah
Ear/Ears	Вухо/Вуха	VOOkhoh/VOOkhah
Elbow	Лікоть	LEEkoht'
Eye	Око	OHkoh
Face	Обличчя	ohbLIHCHchyah
Finger	Палець	PAHlehts'
Foot	Нога	nohGAH
Gall bladder	Жовчний міхур	ZHOHVCHnihy meeKHOOR
Genitalis	Статеві органи	stahTEHvee OHRgahnih
Glands	Залози	ZAHlohzih
Hand	Рука	rooKAH
Heart	Серце	SEHRtseh
Heel	П'ятка	PYAHTkah
Hip	Бедро	behdROH
Intestines	Кишки	kihshKIH

Jaw	Щелепа	shchehLEHpah
Joint	Суглоб	sooGLOHB
Kidney	Нирка	NIHRkah
Knee	Коліно	kohLEEnoh
Leg	Нога	nohGAH
Lip	Губа	gooBAH
Liver	Печінка	pehCHEENkah
Lungs	Легені	lehGEHnee
Mouth	Рот	roht
Muscle	М'яз	myahz
Neck	Шия	SHIHyah
Nerve	Нерв	nehrv
Nose	Ніс	nees
Rib	Ребро	rehbROH
Shoulder	Плече	plehCHEH
Skin	Шкіра	SHKEErah
Spine	Хребет	khrehBEHT
Stomach	Живіт/Шлунок	zhihVEET/SHLOOnohk
Teeth	Зуби	ZOObih
Tendon	Сухожилля	sookhohZHIHL'lyah
Throat	Горло	GOHRloh
Thumb	Великий палець	vehLIHkihy PAHlehts'
Toe	Палець ноги	PAHlehts' nohGIH
Tongue	Язик	yahZIHK
Tonsils	Гланди	GLAHNdih
Vein	Вена	VEIInah
Wrist	Зап'ястя	zahPYAHStyah

Seeing a Doctor

Except for the cost of the medicine, health care in Ukraine is free.

I'd like an appointment...	Я хочу записатися на прийом...	yah KHOHchoo zahpihSAHtihsyah nah prihYOHM
for tomorrow	на завтра	nah ZAHVTrah
as soon as possible	як можна скоріше	yahk MOHZHnah skohREEsheh
Where does it hurt?	Що у вас болить?	shchoh oo vahs bohLIHT'
Is the pain sharp/ dull/constant?	Чи біль гострий/ тупий/ постійний?	chih beel' GOHSTrihy/ tooPIHY/ pohsTEEYnihy

How long have you felt this way?	Чи давно́ ви себе́ так почува́єте?	chih davNOH vih sehBEH tahk pohchooVAHyehteh
I'll take your temperature.	Я змі́ряю ва́шу температу́ру	yah ZMEEryahyoo VAHshoo tehmpehpahTOOroo
I'll measure your blood pressure.	Я змі́ряю ваш тиск	yah ZMEEryahyoo vash tihsk
I'll take your pulse	Я пощу́паю ваш пульс	yah pohSHCHOOpahyoo vahsh pool's
Roll up your sleeve	Засучі́ть рука́в	zahsooCHEET' rooKAHV
Undress to the waist	Роздягні́ться до по́яса	rohzdyahgNEET'syah doh POHyahsah
Breeth deeply	Глибо́ко вдихні́ть	glihBOHkoh vdihkhNEET'
Open your mouth	Відкри́йте рот	veedKRIHYteh roht
Cough	Пока́шляйте	pohKAHSHlyayteh
I'll need an X-ray	Потрі́бно зроби́ти рентге́н	pohTREEBnoh zroh-BIHtih rehntGEHN
Is it serious?	Це серйо́зно?	tseh sehrYOHZnoh
Do I need surgery?	Необхі́дна опера́ція?	nehohbKHEEDnah ohpehRAHtseeyah
It's broken/ sprained	Вона́ зло́мана/ підве́рнута	vohNAH ZLOHmahnah/ peedVEHRnootah
You need a cast	Вам потрі́бен гіпс	vahm pohTREEbehn geeps
You've pulled a muscle	Ви розтягну́ли м'яз	vih rohztyahgNOOlih myahz
It's infected	У вас зара́ження	oo vahs zahRAHzhehnnyah
It's not contagious	Це не зара́зне	tseh neh zahRAHZneh
Get well	Поправля́йтесь!	pohprahvLYAYtehs'

Seeing a Dentist

Dentist	Зубни́й лі́кар	zoobNIHY LEEkahr
I need a dentist	Мені́ потрі́бен зубни́й лі́кар	mehNEE pohTREEbehn zoobNIHY LEEkahr
What are the clinic's hours?	Коли́ годи́ни прийо́му в поліклі́ніці?	kohLIH gohDIHnih prihYOHmoo v pohleekLEEneetsee
I want to make an appointment	Я хо́чу записа́ти-ся на прийо́м	yah KHOHchoo zahpihSAH-tihsyah nah prihYOHM

Will I have to wait long?	Чи довго треба чекати?	chih DOHVgoh TREHbah chehKAHtih
I have... an	У мене...	oo MEHneh
abscess	нарив	nahRIHV
a broken tooth	зломався зуб	zlohMAHVsyah zoob
a broken denture	зломався протез	zlohMAHVsyah prohTEHZ
lost a filling	випала пломба	VIHpahlah PLOHMbah
a toothache	болить зуб	bohLIHT' zoob
a cavity	діра	deeRAH
sore and bleeding gums	ясна дуже запалені і кровоточать	YAHSnah DOOzheh zahPAHlehnee ee krohvohTOHchaht'
Don't pull it out	Не виривайте його	neh vihrihVAYteh yohGOH
Can you fix it temporarily?	Можна поставити тимчасову пломбу?	MOHZHnah pohsTAHvih-tih tihmchahSOHvoo PLOHMboo
When will my denture be ready?	Коли протез буде готовий?	kohLIH prohTEHZ BOOdeh gohTOHvihy
May I have an anesthetic?	Можна зробити обезболювання?	MOHZHnah zrohBIHtih ohbehzBOHlyoovahnnyah

Treatment

I'm taking medication	Я приймаю ліки	yah prihyMAHyoo LEEkih
What medicine are you taking?	Які ліки ви приймаєте?	yahKEE LEEkih vih prihyMAHyehteh
I'm taking antibiotics	Я приймаю антибіотики	yah prihyMAHyoo ahntihbeeOHtihkih
I'm on the Pill	Я приймаю про-тизачаточні таблетки	yah prihyMAHyoo prohtih-zahCHAHtohchnee tahbLEHTkih
I'm allergic to penicillin	У мене алергія на пеніцилін	oo MEHneh ahlehrGEEyah nah pehneetsihLEEN
I'll prescribe an antibiotic/a painkiller	Я пропишу вам антибіотик/ болезаспокій-ливий засіб	yah prohpihSHOO vahm ahntihbeeOHtihk/ bohlehzahspohKEEY-lihvihy ZAHseeb
Where can I have this prescrip-tion filled?	Де можна дістати ліки по цьому рецепту?	deh MOHZHnah deesTAHtih LEEkih poh TSYOHmoo rehTSEHPtoo

94

When should I take the medicine?	Коли мені приймати ці ліки?	kohLIH mehNEE prihyMAHtih tsee LEEkih
Take...	Приймайте...	prihyMAYteh
2 pills	по дві таблетки	poh dvee tahbLEHTkih
3 teaspoons	по три чайні ложки	poh trih CHAYnee LOHZHkih
every 2/6 hours	кожні дві години/шість годин	KOHZHnee dvee gohDIHnih/sheest' gohDIHN
twice a day	два рази на день	dvah RAHzih nah dehn'
before meals	перед їжею	PEHrehd YEEzhehyoo
after meals	після їжі	PEESlyah YEEzhee
as needed	коли буде потреба	kohLIH BOOdeh pohTREHbah
for 5/10 days	п'ять/десять днів	pyaht'/DEHsyaht' dneev
I feel better/ worse/ the same	Я почуваю себе краще/гірше/ так само	yah pohchooVAHyoo sehBEH KRAHshcheh/ GEERsheh/ tahk SAHmoh
Can I travel on Friday?	Можу я відправи- тися у поїздку в п'ятницю?	MOHzhoo yah veedPRAHvih- tihsyah oo pohYEEZDkoo v PYAHTnihtsyoo

At the Hospital

Hospital	Лікарня	leeKAHRnyah
Clinic	Клініка	KLEEneekah
Doctor	Лікар	LEEkahr
Surgeon	Хірург	kheeROORG
Gynecologist	Гінеколог	geenehKOHlohg
Ophthamologist	Офтальмолог	ohftahl'MOHlohg
Pediatrician	Педіатр	pehdeeAHTR
Nurse	Медсестра	mehdsehstRAH
Patient (f)	Пацієнт/ка	pahtseeEHNT/kah
Anesthesia	Анестезія	ahnehstehZEEyah
Bedpan	Судно	SOODnoh
Injection	Укол	ooKOHL
Operation	Операція	ohpehRAHtseeyah
Transfusion	Переливання крові	pehrehlihVAHNnyah KROHvee
Thermometer	Термометер	tehrMOHmehtehr

I can't sleep/eat	Я не можу спати/їсти	yah neh MOHzhoo SPAHtih/YEEStih
When will the doctor come?	Коли прийде лікар?	kohLIH PRIHYdeh LEEkahr
When can I get out of bed?	Коли я зможу вставати?	kohLIH yah ZMOHzhoo vstahVAHtih
When are visiting hours?	Коли година відвідування?	kohLIH gohDIHnih veedVEEdoovahnnyah

XIV. NUMBERS AND TIME EXPRESSIONS

Cardinal Numbers

Ukrainian numbers are highly irregular. The number "one" agrees in gender with the noun it modifies, so that it can be either masculine, feminine or neuter. The number "two" has two forms: one serves as both masculine and neuter, while the other form is reserved for feminine subjects. All the remaining numbers have only one form.

0	Нуль	nool'
I (m/f/n)	Один/Одна/Одно	ohDIHN/ohdNAH/ohdNOH
2 (m/f/n)	Два/Дві/Двоє	dvah/ dvee/ DVOHyeh
3	Три	trih
4	Чотири	chohTIHrih
5	П'ять	pyaht'
6	Шість	sheest'
7	Сім	seem
8	Вісім	VEEseem
9	Дев'ять	DEHvyaht'
10	Десять	DEHsyaht'
11	Одинадцять	ohdihNAHDtsyaht'
12	Дванадцять	dvahNAHDtsyaht'
13	Тринадцять	trihNAHDtsyaht'
14	Чотирнадцять	chohtihrNAHDtsyaht'
15	П'ятнадцять	pyahtNAHDtsyaht'
16	Шістнадцять	sheestNAHDtsyaht'
17	Сімнадцять	seemNAHDtsyaht'
18	Вісімнадцять	veeseemNAHDtsyaht'
19	Дев'ятнадцять	dehvyahtNAHDtsyaht'
20	Двадцять	DVAHDtsyaht'
21	Двадцять один	DVAHDtsyaht' ohDIHN
22	Двадцять два	DVAHDtsyaht' dvah
23	Двадцять три	DVAHDtsyaht' trih
24	Двадцять чотири	DVAHDtsyaht' chohTIHrih
25	Двадцять п'ять	DVAHDtsyaht' pyaht'
26	Двадцять шість	DVAHDtsyaht' sheest'
27	Двадцять сім	DVAHDtsyaht' seem
28	Двадцять вісім	DVAHDtsyaht' VEEseem
29	Двадцять дев'ять	DVAHDtsyaht' DEHvyaht'
30	Тридцять	TRIHDtsyaht'
31	Тридцять один	TRIHDtsyaht' ohDIHN
40	Сорок	SOHrohk

41	Сорок одйн	SOHrohk ohDIHN
50	П'ятдесят	pyahtdehSYAHT
60	Шістдесят	sheestdehSYAHT
70	Сімдесят	seemdehSYAHT
80	Вісімдесят	veeseemdehSYAHT
90	Дев'яносто	dehvyahNOHStoh
100	Сто	stoh
200	Двісті	DVEEStee
300	Триста	TRIHStah
400	Чотириста	chohTIHrihstah
500	П'ятсот	pyahtSOHT
600	Шістсот	sheestSOHT
700	Сімсот	seemSOHT
800	Вісімсот	veeseemSOHT
900	Дев'ятсот	devyahtSOHT
1.000	Тисяча	TIHsyahchah
2.000	Дві тисячі	dvee TIHsyahchee
5.000	П'ять тисяч	pyaht' TIHsyahch
100.000	Сто тисяч	stoh TIHsyahch
1.000.000	Мільйон	meel'YOHN

Ordinal Numbers

Since they act as adjectives grammatically, all ordinal numbers have masculine (-ий), feminine (-a) and neuter form (-e), which can be identified by their endings. The number "three" has irregular ("soft") endings.

First	Перший/-a, -e/	PEHRshihy/-ah, -eh/
Second	Другий /-a, -e/	DROOgihy/-ah, -eh/
Third	Третій /-я, -є/	TREHteey/-yah, -yeh/
Fourth	Четвертий	chehtVEHRtihy
Fifth	П'ятий	PYAHtihy
Sixth	Шостий	SHOHStihy
Seventh	Сьомий	S'OHmihy
Eighth	Восьмий	VOHS'mihy
Ninth	Дев'ятий	dehVYAHtihy
Tenth	Десятий	dehSYAHtihy
Eleventh	Одинадцятий	ohdihNAHDtsyahtihy
Twelfth	Дванадцятий	dvahNAHDtsyahtihy
Thirteenth	Тринадцятий	trihNAHDtsyahtihy
Fourteenth	Чотирнадцятий	chohtihrNAHDtsyahtihy
Fifteenth	П'ятнадцятий	pyahtNAHDtsyahtihy

Sixteenth	Шістнадцятий	sheestNAHDtsyahtihy
Seventeenth	Сімнадцятий	seemNAHDtsyahtihy
Eighteenth	Вісімнадцятий	veeseemNAHDtsyahtihy
Nineteenth	Дев'ятнадцятий	dehvyahtNAHDtsyahtihy
Twentieth	Двадцятий	dvahdTSYAHtihy
Thirtieth	Тридцятий	trihdTSYAHtihy
Fourtieth	Сороковий	sohrohKOHvihy
Hundredth	Сотий	SOHtihy
Thousandth	Тисячний	TIHsyahchnihy

Quantities and Measurements

Quantity	Кількість	KEEL'keest'
A lot/Much	Багато	bahGAHtoh
A little/ Few	Мало/ Декілька	MAHloh/ DEHkeel'kah
More/ Less	Більше/Менше	BEEL'sheh/ MEHNsheh
Most/ least/ best/ worst of all	Більше/менше/ найкраще/ гірше всього	BEEL'sheh/MEHNsheh/ nayKRAHshcheh/ GEERsheh VSYOHgoh
Majority/ Minority	Більшість/ Меншість	BEEL'sheest'/ MEHNsheest'
Enough/ Too much	Досить/ Занадто багато	DOHsiht'/ zahNAHDtoh bahGAHtoh
A third	Треть	treht'
A quarter	Чверть	chvehrt'
A half	Половина	pohlohVIHnah
Three quarters	Три чверті	trih CHVEHRtee
The whole	Ціле	TSEEleh
Once	Раз	rahz
Twice	Два рази	dvah RAHzih
Three times	Три рази	trih RAHzih
Five times	П'ять разів	pyaht' rahZEEV
Early/Late	Рано/Пізно	RAHnoh/PEEZnoh
Now	Зараз	ZAHrahz
Still	Ще	shcheh
Never	Ніколи	neeKOHlih
Seldom	Рідко	REEDkoh
Sometimes	Іноді	EEnohdee
Usually	Звичайно	zvihCHAYnoh
Often	Часто	CHAHStoh
Always	Завжди	zahvzgDIH
In the past	В минулому	v mihNOOlohmoo

99

In the future	В майбутньому	v mayBOOTnyohmoo
A long time ago	Давно	dahvNOH
A short while ago	Не так давно	neh tahk dahvNOH

Days and Weeks

Sunday	Неділя	nehDEElyah
Monday	Понеділок	pohnehDEElohk
Tuesday	Вівторок	veevTOHrohk
Wednesday	Середа	sehrehDAH
Thursday	Четвер	chehtVEHR
Friday	П'ятниця	PYAHTnihtsyah
Saturday	Субота	sooBOHtah
On Wednesday	У середу	oo SEHrehdoo
On Monday	В понеділок	v pohnehDEElohk
Last Saturday	Минулої суботи	mihNOOlohyee sooBOHtih
Next Thursday	Наступного четверга	nahsTOOPnohgoh chehtvehrGAH
From Monday to Friday	Від понеділка до п'ятниці	veed pohnehDEELkah doh PYAHTnihtsee
What day is it today?	Який сьогодні день тижня?	yahKIHY s'ohGOHDnee dehn' TIHZHnyah
It's Tuesday	Сьогодні вівторок	s'ohGOHDnee veevTOHrohk
Week	Тиждень	TIHZHdehn'
Last week	Минулого тижня	mihNOOlohgoh TIHZHnyah
This week	Цього тижня	tsyohGOH TIHZHnyah
Next week	Наступного тижня	nahsTOOPnohgoh TIHZHnyah
In two weeks	Через два тижні	CHEHrehz dvah TIHZHnee
In five weeks	Через п'ять тижнів	CHEHrehz pyaht' TIHZHneev
Every week	Кожного тижня	KOHZHnohgoh TIHZHnyah
For 3 weeks	На три тижні	nah trih TIHZHnee
Two weeks ago	Два тижні тому	dvah TIHZHnee TOHmoo

Months

Month	Місяць	MEEsyahts'
This month	Цього місяця	tsyohGOH MEEsyahtsyah
Last/Next month	Минулого/Наступного місяця	mihNOOlohgoh/nahsTOOPnohgoh MEEsyahtsyah

100

English	Ukrainian	Pronunciation
Every month	Кожного місяця	KOHZHnohgoh MEEsyahtsyah
In a month	Через місяць	CHEHrehz MEEsyahts'
January	Січень	SEEchehn'
February	Лютий	LYOOtihy
March	Березень	BEHrehzehn'
April	Квітень	KVEEtehn'
May	Травень	TRAHvehn'
June	Червень	CHEHRvehn'
July	Липень	LIHpehn'
August	Серпень	SEHRpehn'
September	Вересень	VEHrehsehn'
October	Жовтень	ZHOHVtehn
November	Листопад	lihsTOHpahd
December	Грудень	GROOdehn'
In July...	В липні...	v LIHPnee
Since January...	З січня...	z SEECHnyah
In the beginning of October...	На початку жовтня...	nah pohCHAHTkoo ZHOHVTnyah
In the middle of December...	В середині грудня...	v sehREHdihnee GROODnyah
In the end of April...	Наприкінці квітня	nahprihkeenTSEE KVEETnyah
We'll be here from June to August	Ми будемо тут від червня до серпня	mih BOOdehmoh toot veed CHEHRVnyah doh SEHRPnyah
We'll be here from the 3rd of May through the 19th of July	Ми будемо тут з третього травня по дев'ятнадцяте липня	mih BOOdehmoh toot z TREHtyohgoh TRAHVnyah poh dehvyahtNAHDtsyahteh LIHPnyah
I've been here since October 14th	Я тут з чотирнадцятого жовтня	yah toot z chohtihrNAHDtsyahtohgoh ZHOHVTnyah
What's the date?	Яке сьогодні число?	yahKEH s'ohGOHDnee chihsLOH
It's January 22nd	Сьогодні двадцять друге січня	s'ohGOHDnee DVAHDtsyaht' DROOgeh SEECHnyah
When did he come?	Коли він приїхав?	kohLIH veen prihYEEkhahv
He arrived on May 20th	Він приїхав двадцятого травня	veen prihYEEkhahv dvahdTSAHtohgoh TRAHVnyah

101

Year	Рік	reek
Decade	Декада	dehKAHdah
Century	Вік/ століття	veek/ stohLEETtyah
This year	Цього року	tsyohGOH ROHkoo
Next year	Наступного року	nahsTOOPnohgoh ROHkoo
Last year	Минулого року	mihNOOlohgoh ROHkoo
In a year	Через рік	CHEHrehz reek
For a year	На рік	nah reek
Three years ago	Три роки тому	trih ROHkih TOHmoo
Year round	Цілий рік	TSEElihy reek
In the 19th century	У дев'ятнадця-тому столітті	oo dehvyahtNAHDtsyah-tohmoo stohLEETtee
In the 20th century	У двадцятому столітті	oo dvahdTSYAHtohmoo stohLEETtee
In the 21st century	У двадцять пер-шому столітті	oo DVAHDtsyaht' PEHR-shohmoo stohLEETtee
In 2010	У дві тисячі де-сятому році	oo dvee TIHsyahchee deh-SYAHtohmoo ROHtsee
In 1991	У тисяча дев'ят-сот дев'я-носто першо-му році	oo TIHsyahchah dehvyaht-SOHT dehvyah-NOHStoh PEHRshoh-moo ROHtsee
In 1985	У тисяча дев'ятсот, вісімдесят п'ятому році	oo TIHsyahchah dehvyahtSOHT veeseemdehSYAHT PYAHtohmoo ROHtsee
How old are you?	Скільки вам років?	SKEEL'kih vahm ROHkeev
I'm 28/51 years old.	Мені двадцять вісім років/ п'ятдесят один рік.*	mehNEE DVAHDtsyaht' VEEseem ROHkeev/ pyahtdehSYAHT ohDIHN reek
When was he/she born?	Коли він наро-дився?/ Коли вона народилася?	kohLIH veen nahroh-DIHVsyah/ kohLIH vohNAH nahrohDIHlahsyah

* The word for year changes depending on the number that precedes it. For one year, or numbers that end in a one (41,621, etc.) the word for year is pік (reek). For two, three, four and numbers that end in any of those numbers, the word is роки (ROHkih) and for five and above, as well as numbers that end in five or higher, the word for year is років (ROHkeev).

102

He was born in...	Він народився	veen nahrohDIHVsyah
1936/1960	у... тисяча	oo... TIHsyahchah
	дев'ятсот	dehvyahtSOHT
	тридцять	TRIHDtsyaht'
	шостому	SHOHStohmoo
	роцi/ тисяча	ROHtsee/ TIHsyahchah
	дев'ятсот	dehvyahtSOHT
	шестидеся-	shehstihdehSYAH-
	тому роцi.	tohmoo ROHtsee

Other Time Expressions

Today	Сьогодні	syohGOHDnee
Tomorrow	Завтра	ZAHVTrah
Yesterday	Вчора	VCHOHrah
Day after tomorrow	Післязавтра	peeslyahZAHVTrah
Day before yesterday	Позавчора	pohzahVCHOHrah
The next day	На другий день	nah DROOgihy dehn'
Three/Five days ago	Три дні/П'ять днів тому	trih dnee/pyaht' dneev TOHmoo
Morning	Ранок	RAHnohk
In the morning	Вранці	VRAHNtsee
This morning	Сьогодні вранці	syohGOHDnee VRAHNtsee
Yesterday morning	Вчора вранці	VCHOHrah VRAHNtsee
Tomorrow morning	Завтра вранці	ZAHVTrah VRAHNtsee
All morning	Весь ранок	vehs' RAHnohk
Every morning	Кожного ранку	KOHZHnohgoh RAHNkoo
Day	День	dehn'
In the afternoon	Вдень/Після обіду	vdehn'/PEESlyah ohBEEdoo
This afternoon	Сьогодні вдень	syohGOHDnee vdehn'
Yesterday afternoon	Вчора вдень	VCHOHrah vdehn'
Tomorrow afternoon	Завтра вдень	ZAHVTrah vdehn'
All day	Цілий день	TSEElihy dehn'
Every day	Кожний день	KOHZHnihy dehn'
Evening	Вечір	VEHcheer
In the evening	Увечері	ooVEHchehree
This evening	Сьогодні ввечері	syohGOHDnee vVEHchehree
Yesterday evening	Вчора ввечері	VCHOHrah vVEHchehree
Tomorrow evening	Завтра ввечері	ZAHVTrah vVEHchehree
All evening	Весь вечір	vehs' VEHcheer

Every evening	Кожний вечір/ Щовечора	KOHZHnihy VEHcheer shchohVEHchohrah
Night	Ніч	neech
At night	Вночі	vnohCHEE
Tonight	Сьогодні вночі	syohGOHDnee vnohCHEE
All night	Всю ніч	vsyoo neech
Every night	Щоночі	shchohNOHchee
Weekend	Кінець тижня	keeNEHTS' TIHZHnyah
Holiday	Свято	SVYAHtoh
Vacation	Відпустка	veedPOOSTkah
School holiday	Канікули	kahNEEkoolih
Birthday	День народження	dehn' nahROHDzhehnnyah

Telling Time

Kyyiv is seven hours ahead of Eastern Standard Time and has no Daylight Savings Time.

Time	Час	chahs
Half hour	Півгодини	peevgohDIHnih
Hour	Година	gohDIHnah
Minute	Хвилина	khvihLIHnah
Second	Секунда	sehKOONdah
Early/Late	Рано/Пізно	RAHnoh/PEEZnoh
I'm sorry, I'm late	Вибачте, що спізнився	VIHbahchteh shchoh speezNIHVsyah
On time	Вчасно	VCHAHSnoh
What time is it?	Котра година?	kohtRAH gohDIHnah
It's...	Зараз...	ZAHrahz
one o'clock	перша година	PEHRshah gohDIHnah
five past three	п'ять хвилин четвертої	pyaht' khvihLIHN chehtVEHRtohyee
ten past six	десять хвилин сьомої	DEHsyaht' khvihLIHN SYOHmohyee
quarter after four	п'ятнадцять хвилин п'ятої	pyahtNAHDtsyaht' khvih-LIHN PYAHtohyee
twenty past twelve	двадцять хвилин першої	DVAHDtsyaht' khvihLIHN PEHRshohyee
twenty-five after two	двадцять п'ять хвилин третьої	DVAHDtsyaht' pyaht' khvihLIHN TREHtyohyee
seven thirty	половина восьмої	pohlohVIHnah VOHS'mohyee

104

twenty-five to nine	за двадцять п'ять дев'ята	zah DVAHDtsyaht' pyaht' dehVYAHtah
twenty to eleven	за двадцять одинадцята	zah DVAHDtsyaht' ohdihNAHDtsyatah
quarter to one	за чверть перша	zah chvehrt' PEHRshah
ten of eight	за десять восьма	zah DEHsyaht' VOHS'mah
five of two	за п'ять друга	zah pyaht' DROOgah
twelve o'clock	дванадцята година	dvahNAHDtsyahtah gohDIHnah
midnight	північ	PEEVneech
noon	південь	PEEVdehn'
A.M.	Зранку	ZRAHNkoo
P.M.	Увечері	ooVEHchehree
At what time?	О котрій годині?	oh kohtREEY gohDIHnee
At one	О першій	oh PEHRsheey
At 3:05	В п'ять хвилин четвертої	v pyaht' khvihLIHN chehtVEHRtohyee
At 2:10	В десять хви-лин третьої	v DEHsyaht' khvihlihn TREHtyohyee
At 5:30	В половині шостої	v pohlohVIHnee SHOHStohyee
At 7:40	О сьомій сорок	oh SYOHmeey SOHrohk
At 12:50	О дванадцятій п'ятдесят	oh dvahNAHDtsyahteey pyahtdehSYAHT

Seasons

Seasons	Пори року	POHrih ROHkoo
Spring/	Весна/	vehsNAH/
In the spring	Весною	vehsNOHyoo
Summer/	Літо/	LEEtoh/
In the summer	Влітку	VLEETkoo
Fall/	Осінь/	OHseen'/
In the fall	Восени	vohsehNIH
Winter/	Зима/	zihMAH/
In the winter	Взимку	VZIHMkoo

XV. REFERENCE

Ukrainian National Holidays

Jan. 1	New Year's Day	Новий рік
Mar. 8	International Women`s Day	Міжнародний день жінок
May 1-2	May Day	Перше Травня
May 9	V-E Day	День Перемоги
August 24	Independence Day	День Незалежності

Weather

The weather	Погода	pohGOHdah
What is it like outside?	Яка сьогодні погода?	yahKAH syohGOHDnee pohGOHdah
What's the forecast (for tomorrow)?	Який прогноз погоди на завтра?	yahKIHY prohgNOHZ pohGOHdih nah ZAHVTrah
Tomorrow it will rain	Завтра буде дощ	ZAHVTrah BOOdeh dohshch
Today it's...	Сьогодні...	syohGOHDnee
sunny	світить сонце	SVEEtiht' SOHNtseh
overcast	похмуро	pohkhMOOroh
cool	прохолодно	prohkhohLOHDnoh
warm	тепло	TEHPloh
hot	гаряче	GAHryahcheh
cold	холодно	KHOHlohdnoh
humid	вологo	vohLOHgoh
foggy	туман	tooMAHN
windy	вітер	VEEter
What's it usually like here?	Яка погода звичайно буває тут?	yahKAH pohGOHdah zvihCHAYnoh booVAHyeh toot
It's raining/snowing	іде дощ/ сніг	eeDEH dohshch/ sneeg
What a beautiful day!	Який чудовий день!	yahKIHY chooDOHvihy dehn'
What awful weather!	Яка жахлива погода!	yahKAH zhahkhLIHvah pohGOHdah

Directions

North	Північ	PEEVneech
In the north	На півночі	nah PEEVnohchee

To the north	На пі́вніч	nah PEEVneech
Northward	До пі́вночі	doh PEEVnohchee
South	Пі́вдень	PEEVdehn'
In the south	На пі́вдні	nah PEEVDnee
To the south	На пі́вдень	nah PEEVdehn'
Southward	До пі́вдня	doh PEEVDnyah
East	Схід	skheed
In the east	На схо́ді	nah SKHOHdee
To the east	На схід	nah skheed
Eastward	До схо́ду	doh SKHOHdoo
West	Захід	ZAHkheed
In the west	На за́ході	nah ZAHkhohdee
To the west	На за́хід	nah ZAHkheed
Westward	До за́ходу	doh ZAHkhohdoo

Family

Family	Сім'я́	seemYAH
Relatives	Ро́дичі	ROHdihchee
Children	Діти	DEEtih
Adults	Доро́слі	dohROHSlee
Wife/	Жі́нка/	ZHEENkah/
Spouse (f)	Дружи́на	drooZHIHnah
Husband/Spouse (m)	Чолові́к	chohlohVEEK
Mother	Ма́ти	MAHtih
Father	Ба́тько	BAHT'koh
Baby	Дити́на	dihTIHnah
Daughter	До́чка	DOHCHkah
Son	Син	sihn
Sister	Сестра́	sehstRAH
Brother	Брат	braht
Grandmother	Бабу́ся	bahBOOsyah
Grandfather	Діду́сь	deeDOOS'
Granddaughter	Вну́чка	VNOOCHkah
Grandson	Внук	vnook
Aunt	Ті́тка	TEETkah
Uncle	Дя́дько	DYAD'koh
Niece	Племі́нниця	plehMEENnihtsyah
Nephew	Племі́нник	plehMEENnihk
Cousin (m/f)	Двою́рідний брат/	dvohYOOreednihy braht/
	двою́рідна	dvohYOOreednah
	се́стра	sehstRAH

Husband's mother	Свекруха	svehkROOkhah
Husband's father	Свекор	SVEHkohr
Wife's mother	Теща	TEHSHchah
Wife's father	Тесть	tehst'

Signs

Information	Довідки/ Довід-	DOHveedkih/ dohveed-
	кове бюро	KOHveh byooROH
Bathroom (M/W)	Туалет Ч/Ж	tooahLEHT ch/zh
Don't touch	Не чіпати	neh cheePAHtih
Push/ Pull	Від себе/ До себе	veed SEHbeh/ doh SEHbeh
No admittance	Не входити	neh VKHOHdihtih
Entrance	Вхід	vkheed
Exit	Вихід	VIHkheed
No entry	Нема входу	nehMAH VKHOHdoo
No exit	Нема виходу	nehMAH VIHkhohdoo
Emergency exit	Запасний вихід	zahpahsNIHY VIHkheed
Employees' entrance	Службовий вхід	sloozhBOHvihy vkheed
Elevator	Ліфт	leeft
Stairs	Сходи	SKHOHdih
Up/Down	Вгору/Вниз	VGOHroo/vnihz
Keep to the left/	Тримайтеся	trihMAYtehsyah LEE-
right	лівої/правої	vohyee/PRAHvohyee
	сторони	stohrohNIH
Don't lean	Не притуляйтеся	neh prihtooLYAYtehsyah
Stop	Стоп	stohp
Wait	Стійте	STEEYteh
Go	Ідіть	eeDEET'
Careful!	Обережно!	ohbehREHZHnoh
Attention!	Увага!	ooVAHgah
Prohibited	Забороняється	zahbohrohNYAHyeht'syah
Danger	Небезпечно!	nehbehzPEHCHnoh
Police	Міліція	meeLEEtseeyah
Quiet!	Тихо!	TIHkhoh
Self-serve	Самообслуго-	sahmohohbslooGOH-
	вування	voovahnnyah
Occupied	Зайнято	ZAYnyahtoh
No smoking	Не курити	neh kooRIHtih
Closed for lunch/	Зачинено на обід/	zahCHIHnehnoh nah
repairs/	ремонт/сані-	ohBEED/rehMOHNT/
cleaning	тарний день	sahneeTAHRnihy dehn'

108

Closed for a break from 1 to 2	Перерва з 1 до 2	pehREHRvah z PEHRshohyee doh DROOgohyee
Office hours	Години прийому	gohDIHnih prihYOHmoo
Men working	Ремонт	rehMOHNT
Watch out for cars	Обережно, автомобіль!	ohbehREHZHnoh ahvtohmohBEEL'

Abbreviations and Acronyms

АЗС	автозаправочна станція	gas station
б.	будинок	house
бульв.	бульвар	boulevard
в.	вік	century
вул.	вулиця	street
г.	гора/година	mountain/hour
гр.	громадянин	citizen
до н.е.	до нашої ери	B.C.
ж.	жіночий	women
з.-д.	залізниця	railway
і т.д.	і так далі	etc.
і т.п.	і тому подібне	and so on
ім.	імені	named after...
к., коп.	копійка	kopeck
к., корп.	корпус	corpus
карб.	карбованець	karbovanets
кв.	квартира	apartment
КДУ	Київський державний університет	Kyyiv State University
ЛДУ	Львівський державний університет	Lviv State University
М.	метро	Metro
м.	метр/місто	meter/city
мед.	медичний	medical
наб.	набережна	embankment
напр.	наприклад	for example
н.е.	нашої ери	A.D.
обл.	область	oblast
оз.	озеро	lake

п.	пан/пані	Mr./Mrs.
пл.	площа	square
пр., просп.	проспект	prospect
р.	рік/ріка	year/river
р-н	район	region
с., стр.	сторінка	page
с.-г.	сільськогоспо-дарський	rural
СНД	Співдружність незалежних держав	Collaboration of Independent States
США	Сполучені Штати Америки	USA - United States of America
т.б.	тобто	that is, i.e.
тов.	товариш	comrade
ЦУМ	Центральний універсальний магазин	Central Department store
ч.	чоловічий	men

Metric Conversions

Temperature:

To convert Celsius into Fahrenheit, multiply degree Celsius by 1.8 and add 32. To convert Fahrenheit into Celsius, subtract 32 from degree Fahrenheit and divide by 1.8.

Distance:

To convert miles into kilometers, divide miles by 5 and multiply by 8. To convert kilometers into miles, divide kilometers by 8 and multiply by 5.

1 km = 5/8 mile	1 inch = 2.54 centimeters
1 centimeter = 0.39 inches	1 foot = 30.5 centimeters
1 meter = 3.28 foot	1 mile = 1609 meters
1 kilometer = 0.675 mile	

Weight:

1 kilogram = 2.2 pounds	
1 gram = 0.0352 ounces	
1 ounce = 28.35 grams	
1 pound = 453.60 grams	

Volume:

1 liter = 0.264 gallons	
1 liter = 1.06 quarts	
1 quart = 0.95 liter	
1 gallon = 3.8 liter	

As in all standard dictionaries, verbs are listed in the infinitive form. Adjectives are given in the masculine form and are marked by the abbreviation (adj.). Nouns are given without articles. When both masculine and feminine forms exist, the masculine form is given first, followed by the feminine (f) version.

Ukrainian-English Dictionary

A

a ah - but, and

або ahBOH - or

аварія ahVAHreeyah - breakdown; accident

авеню ahvehNYOO - avenue

авіапошта ahveeahPOHSHtah - airmail

автобус ahvTOHboos - bus

автозаправочна станція ahvtohzahPRAHvohchnah STAHNtseeyah - service station

автомат ahvtohMAHT - vending machine

автомобіліст ahvtohmohbee-LEEST - motorist

автомобіль ahvtohmohBEEL` - car

автор AHVtohr - author

адвокат ahdvohKAHT - lawyer

адміністратор ahdmeenees-TRAHtohr - manager

адреса ahdREHsah - address

аеропорт ahehrohPOHRT - airport

азбука AHZbookah - alphabet

акт ahkt - act

актор ahkTOHR - actor

актриса ahkTRIHsah - actress

актуальний ahktooAHL`nihy - current (adj.)

акуратний ahkooRAHTnihy - punctual (adj.)

акушер ahkooSHEHR - obstetrician

акцент ahkTSEHNT - accent

але ahLEH - but

алергія ahlehrGEEyah - allergy

алкоголь ahlkohGOHL` - alcohol

алло ahlLOH - hello (on the telephone)

амбулаторія ahmboolahTOHreeyah - outpatient clinic

американець/ (канка) ahmeh-rihKAHnehts`/ (-KAHNkah) - American/(f)

ананас ahnahNAHS - pineapple

англійська шпилька ahngLEEYS`kah SHPIHL`kah - safety pin

англійський ahngLEEYS`kihy - English, British (adj.)

англічанин/ (чанка) ahngleeCHAHnihn/

111

(-CHAHNkah) - Englishman/ (f)

анкета ahnKEHtah - form, blank, survey

антибіотик ahntihbeeOHtihk - antibiotic

антракт ahnTRAHKT - intermission

апельсин ahpehl`SIHN - orange

апендикс ahPEHNdihks - appendix

апендицит ahpehndihTSIHT - appendicitis

апетит (смачного! приємного апетиту!) ahpehTIHT (smahchNOHgoh! prihYEHMnohgoh ahpehTIHtoo!) - appetite (Hearty appetite!)

аптека ahpTEHkah - drugstore

аптечка ahpTEHCHkah - first-aid kit

ароматний ahrohMAHTnihy - fragrant (adj.)

артерія ahrTEHreeyah - artery

артист ahrTIHST - performer

артіль ahrTEEL` - workers cooperative

артрит ahrtRIHT - arthritis

архітектор ahrkheeTEHKtohr - architecht

архітектура ahrkheetehkTOOrah - architecture

аспірант/(-ка) ahspeeRAHNT/(-kah) - graduate student/(f)

аспірин ahspeeRIHN - aspirin

астма AHSTmah - asthma

атеїзм ahtehYEEZM - atheism

атлетика ahtLEHtihkah - athletics

атлетичний ahtlehTIHCHnihy - athletic (adj.)

афіша ahFEEshah - poster; play bill

Б

бабуся bahBOOsyah - grandmother

бавовняний bahvohvNYAHnihy - cotton

багаж bahGAHZH - baggage

багатий bahGAHtihy - rich (adj.)

багато bahGAHtoh - a lot

багатокольоровий bahgahtohkohlyohROHvihy - multicolored (adj.)

бадьорий bahDYOHrihy - cheerful (adj.)

бажання bahZHAHNnyah - wish

бажати bahZHAHtih - to wish

базар bahZAHR - market, bazaar

байдужий bayDOOzhihy - indifferent (adj.)

баклажан bahklahZHAHN

- eggplant
балаку́чий bahlahKOOchihy - talkative (adj.)
балала́йка bahlahLAYkah - balalaika
бале́т bahLEHT - ballet
балко́н bahlKOHN - balcony
бана́н bahNAHN - banana
бандеро́ль bahndehROHL` - wrapping for mailing printed matter
банк bahnk - banquette
ба́нка BAHNkah - jar; can
банке́т bahnKEHT - banket
ба́ня BAHnyah - public bath
бара́нина bahRAHnihnah - mutton; lamb
басе́йн bahSEYN - pool
батаре́я bahtahREHyah - battery
батьки́ baht`KIH - parents
батькі́вщи́на baht`keevshchihnah fatherland
ба́тько BAHT`koh - father
ба́чення BAHchehnnyah - vision
ба́чити BAHchihtih - to see
ба́шта BAHSHtah - tower
бедро́ behdROH - hip, thigh
без behz - without
безалкого́льний behzahlkohGOHL`nihy- nonalcoholic (adj.)
безбо́жник behzBOHZHnihk - atheist
безбо́жність behzBOHZNneest` -

atheism
безви́нний behzVIHNnihy - innocent (adj.)
безкольоро́вий behzkohlyohROHvihy- colorless, dull (adj.)
безкошто́вний behzkohshTOHVnihy - free of charge (adj.)
безми́тний behzMIHTnihy - duty-free
безпереса́дочний behzpehrehSAHdohchnihy - without transfer (adj.)
безпоса́дочний behzpohSAHdohchnihy nonstop (of a flight) (adj.)
без смаку́ behz smahKOO - tasteless (adj.)
безсо́ння behzSOHNnyah - insomnia
беко́н behKOHN - bacon
бензи́н behnZIHN - gas
бензоба́к behnzohBAHK - gas tank
бензозапра́вочна ста́нція behnzohzahPRAHvohchnah STAHNtseeyah - gas station
бе́рег BEHrehg - coast, bank, shore
берегти́ behrehgTIH - to save, keep; to guard
бережи́сь behrehZHIS` - caution
бере́за behREHzah - birch
бе́сіда BEHseedah - conversation
бинт bihnt - bandage
би́ти BIHtih - to beat, strike
би́тися BIHtihsyah - to fight
бібліоте́ка

113

beebleeohTEHkah - library
Біблія BEEBleeyah - Bible
біг beeg - run, race
бігати BEEgahtih - to run
біда beeDAH - misfortune
бідний BEEDnihy - poor (adj.)
бізнесмен/(-ка) beeznehsMEHN/(-kah) - businessman/(f)
бік beek - side
білий BEELihy - white (adj.)
білизна beeLIHZnah - laundry; linen
біля BEELyah - at, near
біль beel` - pain
більше BEEL`sheh - more (than), larger; bigger; greater
більшість BEEL`sheest` - majority
бінокль beeNOHKL` - binoculars; opera glasses
біфштекс beefSHTEHKS - steak
благословення blahgohslohVEHNnyah - blessing
блакитний blahKIHTnihy - light blue (adj.)
бланк blahnk - form; blank
близько BLIHZ`koh - near; close; nearby
блискавка BLIHSkahvkah - lightning
блідий bleeDIHY - pale (adj.)
блондин/(-ка) blohnDIHN/(-kah) - blonde/(f)
блузка BLOOZkah - blouse
блюдо BLYOOdoh - dish
бог bohg - God

богослужіння bohgohslooZHEENnyah - worship service
божевільний bohzhehVEEL`nihy - crazy; mad; insane (adj.)
боком BOHkohm - sideways
болевгамовуючий засіб boh-lehvgahMOOHvooyoochihy ZAHseeb - painkiller
болільник bohLEEL`nihk - sports fan
борода bohrohDAH - beard
борошно BOHrohshnoh - flour
боротьба bohroht`VAH - fight, struggle
борщ bohrshch - borscht beet soup
ботанічний сад bohtahNEECHnihy sahd - botanical garden
боятися bohYAHtihsyah - to fear; be afraid
брат braht - brother
брати BRAHtih - to take; seize
брехати brehKHAHtih - to lie
бритва BRIHTvah - razor
бритися BRIHtihsyah - to shave; get a shave
брова brohVAH - eyebrow
брошка BROHSHkah - brooch
бруд brood - dirt, filth
брудний broodNIHY - dirty; filthy (adj.)
брюки BRYOOkih - pants
брюнет/(-ка) bryooNEHT/(-kah) - brunette/(f)

114

будильник booDIHL`nihk - alarm clock

будинок booDIHnohk - building; house

будній день BOODneey dehn` - weekday

будь ласка bood' LAHSkah - please

буженина boozhehNIHnah - ham

бузок booZOHK - lilac

буква BOOKvah - letter of the alphabet

букініст bookeeNEEST` - secondhand book dealer

булка BOOLkah - roll; bun

булочна BOOlohchnah - bakery

бульвар bool`VAHR - boulevard

бульйон bool`YOHN - bouillon

бурхливий boorkhLIHvihy - stormy; violent (adj.)

буря BOORyah - storm

буряк booRYAHK - beet

бутерброд bootehrBROHD - sandwich

бюро byooROH - office

бюро Інтуриста byooROH eentooRIHstah - Intourist office

бюстгальтер byoostGAHL`ter - bra

В

в v - in, at, for, to

в один кінець v ohDIHN keeNEHTS` - one-way (ticket)

вага vahGAH - weight

вагітна vahGEETnah - pregnant (adj.)

вагон vahGOHN - railroad car

важливість vahzhLIHveest - importance

важливий vahzhLIHvihy - important (adj.)

вазалін vahzehLEEN - vaseline

валюта vahLYOOtah - hard-currency

валютний курс vahLYOOTnihy koors-rate of exchange

вальдшнеп VAHLDshnehp - woodcock

ваніль vahNEEL` - vanilla

ванна VAHNnah - bathtub

ванна кімната VAHNnah keemNAHtah - bathroom

варений vahREHnihy - boiled (adj.)

вареник vahREHnihk - filled dumpling

варення vahREHNnyah - jam

варити vahRIHtih - to cook, boil

вата VAHtah - absorbent cotton

вбивство VBIHVstvoh - murder

вбивця VBIHVtsyah - murderer

ввічливий VVEECHLihvihy - polite, courteous (adj.)

вголос VGOHlohs - aloud

вгорі vgohREE - above; overhead (location)

вгору VGOHroo - up, upwards (destination)

вдалині vdahlihNEE - in the distance

вдова vdohVAH - widow

вдовець vdohVEHTS` - widower

вдячний VDYAHCHnihy - thankful; grateful

вегетаріанець vehgehtahreeAHnehts` - vegetarian

велике спасибі vehLIHkeh spahSIHbee - thanks a lot!

великий vehLIHkihy - big; large; great

великий палець vehLIHkihy PAHLehts' - thumb

велосипед vehlohsihPEHD - bicycle

вена VEHnah - vein

верблюд vehrBLYOOD - camel

верх vehrkh - top

верхній VEHRKHneey - upper; top (adj.)

вершки vehrshKIH - cream

веселитися vehsehLIHtihsyah - to enjoy oneself; have fun

весілля vehSEEL'lyah - wedding

весна vehsNAH - spring

весняний vehsNYAHnihy - spring (adj.)

весь vehs' - all; the whole

вечеря vehCHEHryah - supper

вечір VEHcheer - evening

вечірній vehCHEERneey - evening (adj.)

вже vzheh - already

взагалі vzahgahLEE - in general

взаєморозуміння vzahyehmohroh-zooMEENnyah - mutual understanding

взліт vzleet - take off (in a plane)

взуття vzootTYAH - shoes

взяти напрокат VZYAHtih nahprohKAHT - to rent

вибір VIHbeer - choice

вибори VIHbohrih - elections

вигідний VIHgeednihy - profitable; favorable (adj.)

вигляд VIHGlyahd - appearance

виделка vihDEHLkah - fork

видно VIHDnoh - visible; clear; obvious

викладач vihklahDAHCH - professor

виключати vihklyooCHAHtih - to turn out, switch off

вимова VIHmohvah - pronunciation

вина vihNAH - guilt

винний VIHNnihy - guilty (adj.)

вино vihNOH - wine

виноград vihnohGRAHD - grapes

випадково vihpahdKOHvoh - accidentally

випадок VIHpahdohk - incident

випуск VIHpoosk - issue;

edition; output

висновок VIHSnohvohk - conclusion

високий vihSOHkihy - high; tall; lofty (adj.)

висота vihsohTAH - height; altitude

вистава vihSTAHvah - performance; play

виставка VIHStahvkah - exhibition; display

витрати VIHTrahtih - expenses

вихід VIHkheed - exit

виходити vihKHOHdihtih - to leave, go out, exit

вихідний день vihkheedNIHY dehn'- day off

вишитий VIHshihtihy - embroidered (adj.)

вівсянка veevSYAHNkah - oatmeal

від veed - from

віддаль veedDAHL' - distance

відділ VEEDdeel - section; department

від'їзд veedYEEZD - detour

відліт veedLEET - departure (airplane)

відмінок veedMEEnohk - grammatical case

відношення veedNOHshehnnyah - attitude; relationship; connection

відповідь VEEDpohveed' - answer

відпустка veedPOOSTkah - vacation from work

відрядження veedRYAHDzhehnnyah - business trip; assignment

відсутність veedSOOTneest' - absence

відхід veedKHEED - departure (train)

відчуття veedchootTYAH - feeling, sensation

віза VEEzah - visa

війна veeyNAH - war

військовий veeys'KOHvihy - military (adj.)

вік veek - century; age

вікно veekNOH - window

вільний VEEL'nihy - free; vacant (adj.)

вільно VEEL'noh - freely; voluntarily

він veen - he

вінігрет veeneeGREHT - vegetable salad

віра VEErah - belief; faith

вірити VEErihtih - to believe, have faith

вірний VEERnihy - true; faithful (adj.)

вірус VEEroos - virus

вірьовка veeRYOHVkah - rope; string; cord

вітаміни veetahMEEnih - vitamins

вітер VEEtehr - wind

вітрове скло veetrohVEH skloh - windshield

вітряний VEETryahnihy - windy

вітчизна veetCHIHZnah - homeland

вітчим VEETchihm -

stepfather

ві́чно VEECHnoh - eternally

ві́шалка VEEshahlkah - hanger

ві́я VEEyah - eyelash

ві́яло VEEyahloh - fan

включа́ти vklyooCHAHtih - to turn, switch on

влага́лище vlahGAHlihshcheh - vagina

вниз vnihz - down

внизу́ vnihZOO - down below (location)

внук vnook - grandson

вну́тршіній VNOOtreeshneey - internal (adj.)

вну́чка VNOOCHkah - granddaughter

во́вна VOHVnah - wool

вовня́ний vohvNYAHnihy - woolen (adj.)

во́гнище VOHGnihshcheh - campfire

вода́ vohDAH - water

воді́й vohDEEY - driver

водопа́д vohdohPAHD - waterfall

водопрово́дчик vohdohprohVOHDchihk - plumber

вокза́л vohkZAHL - station

воло́гий vohLOHgihy - humid (adj.)

воло́гість vohLOHgeest' - humidity

воло́сся vohLOHSsyah - hair

вольта́ж vohl'TAHZH - voltage

во́ля VOHLyah - freedom

вона́ vohNAH - she

вони́ vohNIH - they

во́рог VOHrohg - enemy

воро́та vohROHtah - gate

впе́ртий VPEHRtihy - stubborn (adj.)

впе́рше VPEHRsheh - for the first time; first

вплив vplihv - influence

впра́ва VPRAHvah - exercise

впуск vpoosk - admission; admittance

впуска́ти vpoosKAHtih - to admit, let in

вра́жения VRAHzhehnnyah - impression

все ж таки́ vseh zh tahKIH - still; all the same

всере́дині vsehREHdihnee - inside

встава́ти vstahVAHtih - to get, stand up

вступ vstoop - introduction

всю́ди VSYOOdih - every-where

вто́ма VTOHmah - exhaus-tion

втоми́тися vtohMIHtihsyah - to be tired

вузьки́й vooz'KIHY - narrow (adj.)

ву́лиця VOOlihtsyah - street

ву́са VOOsah - mustache

ву́хо VOOkhoh - ear

вхід vkheed - entrance

вхо́дити VKHOHdihtih - to enter

вча́сно VCHAHSnoh - on time

вче́ний VCHEHnihy - scholar; scientist

118

вчитель/ (-ка) VCHIHtehl'/ (-kah) - teacher/ (f)

вчитися VCHIHtihsyah - to study

вчора VCHOHrah - yesterday

вчорашній vchohRAHSHneey - yesterday's (adj.)

Г

газета gahZEHtah - newspaper

газомір gahzohMEER - gas meter

галстук GAHLStook - tie

гаманець gahmahNEHTS' - wallet; billfold

гараж gahRAHZH - garage

гаразд gahRAHZD - ok.

гардероб gahrdehROHB - cloakroom

гардеробник gahrdehROHBnihk - cloakroom attendant

гарячий gahRYAHchihy - hot (of food and drink) (adj.)

гастрит gahsTRIHT - gastritis

гастроном gahstrohNOHM - grocery store

гвоздика gvohzDIHkah - carnation

геморой gehmohROY - hemorrhoids

гемофілія gehmohfeeLEEyah - hemophilia

гепатит gehpahTIHT - hepatitis

геріатричний gehreeahTRIHCHnihy - geriatric

герой gehROY - hero

гід geed - guide

гідність GEEDneest' - value; worth

гінеколог geenehKOHlohg - gynecologist

гіпертонія geepehrtohNEEyah - high blood pressure

гіпс geeps - cast

гіркий geerKIHY - bitter (adj.)

гірчиця geerCHIHtsyah - mustard

гірше GEERsheh - worse

гість geest' - guest

гітара geeTAHrah - guitar

гладкий GLAHDkihy - smooth (adj.)

гланди GLAHNdih - tonsils

глина GLIHnah - clay

глибокий glihBOHkihy - deep; in depth (adj.)

глухий glooKHIHY - deaf (adj.)

глядач glyahDAHCH - spectator

гнів gneev - anger

гнівний GNEEVnihy - angry (adj.)

гнучкий gnoochKIHY - flexible (adj.)

говірливий gohveerLIHvihy - talkative (adj.)

говорити gohvohRIHtih - to speak, talk (about)

годи́нник gohDIHNnihk - watch

го́лий GOHLihy - naked (adj.)

голи́тися gohLIHtihsyah - to shave

го́лка GOHLkah - needle

голова́ gohlohVAH - head

головни́й gohlohvNIHY - main; principle (adj.)

головни́й біль gohlohvNIHY beel' - headache

го́лод GOHlohd - hunger

голо́дний gohLOHDnihy - hungry (adj.)

го́лос GOHlohs - voice

голосува́ти gohlohsooVAHtih - to voice

го́луб GOHloob - pigeon; dove

голубці́ gohloobTSEE - stuffed cabbage

гомосексуалі́зм gohmohsehksooahLEEZm homosexuality

гора́ gohRAH - mountain

го́рдий GOHRdihy - proud (adj.)

го́ре GOHreh - grief

горі́лка gohREELkah - vodka

горі́х gohREEKH - nut

го́рло GOHRloh - throat

горо́х gohROHKH - peas

госпо́дар gohsPOHdahr - master; boss

господи́ня gohspohDIHnyah - housewife

го́стрий GOHSTrihy - sharp; pungent; keen (adj.)

готе́ль gohTEHL' - hotel

гото́вий gohTOHvihy - ready (adj.)

готува́ти gohtooVAHtih - to prepare

гра grah - game

гра́дус GRAHdoos - temperature

гра́дусник GRAHdoosnihk - thermometer

грам grahm - gram

грама́тика grahMAHtihkah - grammar

грамплати́нка grahmplahsTIHNkah - record

грана́т grahNAHT - garnet

гра́ти GRAHtih - to play

гре́бінь GREHbeen - comb

грейпфру́т greypFROOT - grapefruit

гриби́ grihBIH - mushrooms

гри́жа GRIHzhah - hernia

грип grihp - flu

грі́зний GREEZnihy - threatening (adj.)

грім greem - thunder

гріх greekh - sin

гроза́ grohZAH - thunderstorm

громадяни́н grohmahdyahNIHN - citizen

громадя́нка grohmahDYAHNkah - a female citizen

громадя́нський grohmahDYAHNs'kihy - civil; civilian (adj.)

гро́ші GROHshee - money

грошовий переказ grohshohVIHY pehREHkahz - money order

грубий GROObihy - rude; course (adj.)

груди GROOdih - chest; breast

грузовик groozohVIHK - truck

група GROOpah - group

група крові GROOpah KROHvee - blood type

груша GROOshah - pear

губа gooBAH - lip

гудзик GOODzihk - button

гудок gooDOHK - horn; whistle

гуляти gooLYAHtih - to stroll, walk

гуляш gooLYAHSH - goulash

гума GOOmah - rubber

гумовий GOOmohvihy - rubber (adj.)

гуртожиток goorTOHzhihtohk - dormitory

гуска GOOSkah - goose (adj.)

густий goosTIHY - thick, dense (adj.)

гучний goochNIHY - loud (adj.)

Д

давай dahVAHY - let's; go ahead!

давати dahVAHtih - to give

давно dahvNOH - long ago

далі DAHlee - further; farther

далеко dahLEHkoh - far away

дамський DAHMs'kihy - ladies (adj.)

дари моря dahRIH MOHryah - sea food

дарувати dahrooVAHtih - to give (as a gift)

дача DAHchah - cottage

дах dahkh - roof

двері DVEHree - door

двоспальний dvohSPAHL'nihy - double occupancy (adj.)

двоюрідний брат dvohYOOreednihy braht - cousin (m)

двоюрідна сестра dvohYOOreednah sehsTRAH - cousin (f)

де deh - where

де-небудь deh NEHbood' - somewhere

дезінфікувати dehzeenfeekooVAHtih - to disinfect

дезодорант dehzohdohRAHNT - deoderant

денний DEHNnihy - daytime (adj.)

день dehn' - day

день народження dehn' nahROHDzhehnnyah - birthday

дерево DEHrehvoh - tree

дерев'яний dehrehvYAHnihy - wooden (adj.)

держава dehrZHAHvah - the State

державний dehrZHAHVnihy - state; government (adj.)

десерт dehSEHRT - dessert

детектив dehtehkTIHV - mystery (store/ movie)

дефицит dehfihTSIHT - deficit

дешевий dehSHEHvihy - inexpensive; cheap (adj.)

джінси DZHEENsih - jeans

дзвін dzveen - bell

дзеркало DZEHRkahloh - mirror

диван dihVAHN - sofa

дивний DIHVnihy - strange; weird; odd (adj.)

дикий DIHkihy - wild (adj.)

дим dihm - smoke

димний DIHMnihy - smokey (adj.)

диня DIHnyah - melon

директор dihREHKtohr - director; manager

диригент dihrihGEHNT - conductor (music)

дитина dihTIHnah - child, baby

дихання DIHkhahnnyah - breathing; respiration

дихати DIHkhahtih - to breath

дичина dihchihNAH - wild game

діабет deeahBEHT - diabetes

діагноз deeAHGnohz - diagnosis

діамант deeahMAHNT - diamond

дівчина DEEVchihnah - young lady; waitress

дівчинка DEEVchihnkah - little girl

дідусь deeDOOS' - grandfather

дієслово deeyehSLOHvoh - verb

дієта deeYEHtah - diet

дійсний DEEYSnihy - real; actual; effective (adj.)

дійсно DEEYSnoh - really; truly

ділити deeLIHtih - to share; divide

діловий deelohVIHY - business (adj.)

дім deem - house; home

діра deeRAH - hole

діти DEEtih - children

дія DEEyah - action

діяти DEEyahtih - to act, take action

для dlyah - for

до doh - to; toward

до побачення doh pohBAHchehnnyah - goodbye

до речі doh REHchee - incidentally; by the way

доба dohBAH - 24 hour period; day

доброта dohbrohTAH - kindness

добрий DOHBrihy - good; kind (adj.)

довгий DOHVgihy - long (physically)

довго DOHVgoh -
for a long time
довжина dohvzhihNAH -
length
довідка DOHveedkah -
reference; information
довкола dohvKOHlah -
around (location)
договір DOHgohveer -
contract; agreement
дозвіл DOHZveel -
permission
дозування
dohzooVAHNnyah -
dosage
докір DOHkeer -
rebuke
долар DOHlahr - dollar
долина dohLIHnah -
valley
долоня dohLOHnyah -
palm
доля DOHLyah -
share; lot
доля DOHLyah - fate
допитливий
dohPIHTlihvihy -
curious (adj.)
допомога dohpohMOHgah -
help
дорога dohROHgah - road
дорогий dohrohGIHY -
dear; expensive;
valuable (adj.)
дорогоцінність
dohrohgohTSEENneest'-
jewel
дорослий dohROHSlihy -
adult
досвід DOHSveed -
experience
досить DOHsiht' - enough

дослідження
dohSLEEDzhehnnyah -
research
доступ DOHStoop - access
дохід dohKHEED - income
дочка dohchKAH -
daughter
дощ dohshch - rain
драматург drahmah-
TOORG - playwright
друг droog - friend
другий DROOgihy - other;
another; the other
дружба DROOZHbah -
friendship
дружина drooZHIHnah -
wife
дружний DROOZHnihy -
friendly; amicable (adj.)
друкарська машинка
drooKAHRs'kah
mahSHINkah - typewriter
дуже DOOZHeh - very
думка DOOMkah -
opinion/thought, idea
дупло doopLOH - cavity
дура DOOrah - fool (f)
дурень DOOrehn' -
fool (m)
дурний doorNIHY - stupid;
silly (adj.)
дурниця doorNIHtsyah -
nonsense
душ doosh - shower
душа dooSHAH - soul
душевний dooSHEHV-
nihy - mental;
emotional (adj.)
душно DOOSHnoh -
stuffy
дюжина DYOOzhihnah -
dozen

123

дюйм dyooym - inch
дядько DYAHD'koh - uncle
дякувати DYAHkoovahtih
- to thank
дякую DYAHkooyoo -
thank you

Е

екземпляр
ehkzehmPLYAHR - copy;
edition
екран ehkRAHN - screen
екскурсія ehksKOORseeyah
- tour; excursion
екскурсовод
ehkskoorsohVOHD - tour
guide
експрес ehksPREHS -
express
електрика ehLEHK-
trihkah - electricity
електричний
ehlehkTRIHCHnihy -
electrical (adj.)
енергія ehNEHRgeeyah -
energy
ескалатор ehskahLAHtohr -
escalator

Є

є yeh - is, are
єврей/ (-ка) yeevREY/
(-kah) - Jew/(f)
єврейський
yehvREYS'kihy - Jewish;
Hebrew (adj.)
європеэць/ (-пейка)
yeevrohPEHyehts'/
(-PEYkah) -
European/ (f)

європейський
yehvrohPEYs'kihy -
European (adj.)
єдиний yehDIHnihy - only;
sole
єрмолка yehrMOHLkah -
skullcap

Ж

жадібний ZHAHdeebnihy -
greedy (adj.)
жаліти zhahLEEtih - to feel
sorry for; pity
жаль zhahl' - pity
жар zhahr - fever
жаркий zhahrKIHY - hot
(of the weather) (adj.)
жарт zhahrt - joke
жахливий zhahkhLIH-
vihy - horrible (adj.)
ждати ZHDAHtih - to wait
живіт zhihVEET - stomach
живий zhihVIHY - alive
живопис zhihVOHpihs -
painting
жила ZHIHlah - vein
жилет ZHIHleht - vest
жир zhihr - fat; grease
жирний ZHIHRnihy -
fatty; greasy; oily (adj.)
житель ZHIHtehl' -
resident
жити ZHIHtih - to live
жито ZHIHtoh - rye
життя zhihtTYAH - life
жінка ZHEENkah -
woman; wife
жіночий zheeNOHchihy -
feminine; woman's (f.)
жовтий ZHOHVtihy -
yellow (adj.)

124

жонáтий zhohNAHtihy -
married (men) (adj.)
жорстóкий zhohrsTOH-
kihy - cruel; brutal (adj.)
журнáл zhoorNAHL -
magazine
журналíст zhoornah-
LEEST - journalist

З

з z - with; off; since
за zah - behind; beyond
забáрвлення
zahBAHRVlehnnyah -
coloration
забороняти
zahbohrohNYAHtih - to
forbid
забувáти zahbooVAHtih -
to forget
забýтий zahBOOtihy -
forgotten
зáвжди ZAHVZHdih -
always
завíдуючий
zahVEEdooyoochihy -
manager
завíса zahVEEsah - curtain
завóд zahVOHD - factory
зáвтра ZAHVtrah - tomor-
row
зáвтрашній
ZAHVtrahshneey -
tomorrow's (adj.)
загáльний
zahGAHL'nihy - general;
common (adj.)
загáр zahGAHR - sunburn;
sun tan
загрóза zahGROHzah -
threat

загубúти zahgooBIHtih - to
lose (smth.)
зáдній ZAHDneey -
rear; back;
hind (adj.)
задовóлення
zahdohVOHLehnnyah -
satisfaction; pleasure
зáєць ZAHyehts' - hare
заздалегíдь
zahzdahlehGEED' -
in advance
зáйвий ZAYvihy -
spare; extra (adj.)
зáйнятий ZAYnyahtihy -
busy; occupied (adj.)
закíнчення
zahKEENchehnnyah -
end; completion
зáклад ZAHKLahd - institution
закóн zahKOHN - law
закóнний
zahKOHNnihy - legal;
legitimate (adj.)
закрúтий zahKRIHtihy -
closed (adj.)
закýска zahKOOSkah -
appetizer; snack
закýсочна
zahKOOsohchnah -
snackbar
зал/зáла zahl/ZAHLah - hall
замíна zahMEEnah - substitution
зáмість ZAHmeest' -
instead of
замíтка zahMEETkah -
note; mark; notice
замовляти
zahmohvLYAHtih -
to order

125

замо́к zahMOHK - lock
за́мужем ZAHmoozhehm - married (women)
заня́ття zahNYAHTtyah - occupation; work; studies
запа́лення zahPAHLehnnyah - inflammation
запа́лення леге́нь zahPAHLehnnyah lehGEHN' - pneumonia
запальни́чка zahpahl'NIHCHkah - cigarette lighter
за́пах ZAHpahkh - smell
запе́внити zahPEHV-nihtih - to assure
запере́чувати zahpehREHchoovahtih - to deny
за́пис ZAHpihs - recording
записа́тися zahpihSAHtihsyah - to sign up (for)
запізни́тися zahpeezNIHtihsyah - to be late
запі́знення zahPEEZnehnnyah - delay, tardiness
запо́р zahPOHR - constipation
запро́шення zahPROHshehnnyah - invitation
зара́ження zahRAHzhehnnyah - infection
за́раз ZAHrahz - now
за́сіб від комарів ZAHseeb ved kohmahREEV - insect repellent

зато́ка zahTOHkah - bay; gulf
захворі́ти zahkhvoh-REEtih - to fall ill
за́хід ZAHkheed - west
за́хідний ZAHkheednihy - western (adj.)
захо́плення zahKHOHPlehnnyah - enthusiasm
за́чіска ZAHcheeskah - hair-do
зберегти́ zbehrehgTIH - to save
збіг zbeeg - coincidence
збір zbeer - collection; gathering
збі́льшення ZBEEL'shehnnyah - increase
збенте́ження zbehnTEHzhehnnyah - embarrassment
збо́ри ZBOHrih - meeting
збу́джений ZBOODzhehnihy - excited (adj.)
зверх zvehrkh - over and above; in access of
звича́йно zvihCHAYnoh - of course
зви́чка ZVIHCHkah - habit
зворо́тний zvohROHTnihy - return; opposite (adj.)
звук zvook - sound; noise
згі́дний ZGEEDnihy - in agreement
зда́ча ZDAHchah - change

здоро́в'я zdohROHVyah - health
зеле́ний zehLEHnihy - green (adj.)
земля́ zehmLYAH - ground; dirt; earth
зерно́ zehrNOH - grain
зима́ zihMAH - winter
зимо́вий zihMOHvihy - winter (adj.)
зіпсо́ваний zeepSOHvahnihy - spoiled, rotten, tainted (adj.)
зір zeer - eyesight
зі́рка ZEERkah - star
з'їзд zyeezd - convention; congress
злама́ти zlahMAHtih - to break
злий zlihy - evil; wicked; mean; malicious (adj.)
зло́бний ZLOHBnihy - malicious; spiteful (adj.)
зло́дій ZLOHdeey - thief
зло́чин ZLOHchihn - crime
змага́ння zmahGAHNnyah - competition; sports match
зме́ншення ZMEHNshehnnyah - decrease
знайо́мий znahYOHmihy - acquainted; familiar (adj.)
знайо́мство znahYOHMstvoh - acquaintance
знак znahk - sign; signal
знамени́тий znahmehNIHtihy - famous (adj.)
знання́ znahnNYAH - knowledge
зна́ти ZNAHtih - to know
знахо́дити znahKHOHdihtih - to find
знахо́дитися znahKHOHdihtihsyah - to be found, located
зна́чення ZNAHchehnnyah - meaning; sense
зна́чити ZNAHchihtih - to mean
значни́й znahchNIHy - considerable; significant
значо́к znahCHOHK - badge
зно́ву ZNOHvoo - again
зо́внішній ZOHVneeshneey - outward, external (adj.)
золоти́й zohlohTIHY - gold (adj.)
зо́лото ZOHlohtoh - gold
зоопа́рк zohohPAHRK - zoo
зо́шит ZOHshiht - notebook
зразо́к zrahZOHK - sample; model; pattern
зрі́лий ZREELihy - ripe; mature (adj.)
зру́чний ZROOCHnihy - comfortable (adj.)
зру́чність ZROOCHneest' - convenience
зуб zoob - tooth
зубна́ па́ста zoobNAH PAHStah - toothpaste
зубна́ щі́тка zoobNAH SHCHEETkah - toothbrush
зубни́й біль zoobNIHY

127

beel' - toothache

зубний лікар zoobNIHY LEEkahr - dentist

зупинка zooPIHNkah - bus stop

зустріч ZOOstreech - meeting

зустрічати zoostreeCHAHtih - to meet

зять zyaht' - son-in-law; brother-in-law

I

і ee - and; also

іграшка EEGrahshka - toy

ідея eeDEHyah - idea

ікона eeKOHnah - icon

іконостас eekohnohSTAHS - iconostasis

ікра eekRAH - caviar

ім'я eemYAH - first name

інакше eeNAHKsheh - differently; otherwise

інвалід eenvahLEED - disabled person

інвалідність eenvahLEEDneest' - disability

індик eenDIHK - turkey

інженер eenzhehNEHR - engineer

іноді EEnohdee - sometimes

іноземець eenohZEHmehts' - foreigner

іноземний eenohZEHMnihy - foreign (adj.)

інструкція eensTROOKtseeyah - instructions

інсульт eenSOOLT - stroke

історія eesTOHreeyah - history; story

Ї

їда yeeDAH - food

їдальня yeeDAHL'nyah - dining hall

їжа YEEzhah - food

їжак yeeZHAHK - hedgehog

їзда yeezDAH - ride; drive

їздити YEEZdihtih - to drive

її yeeYEE - her; its

їсти YEEstih - to eat

їхати YEEkhahtih - to drive

Й

його yohGOH - his; its

йод yohd - iodine

йти ytih - to go

К

кабіна kahBEEnah - booth; cubicle

каблук kahbLOOK - heel

кава KAHvah - coffee

кавун kahVOON - water-melon

казка KAHZkah - tale

какао kahKAHoh - cocoa

календар kahlehnDAHR - calendar

калорія kahLOHreeyah - calorie

калоші kahLOHshee - rubbers; galoshes

калюжа kahLYOOzhah - puddle

кальсóни kahl'SOHnih - long underwear
кáмбала KAHMbahlah - flounder; sole
кáмінь KAHmeen' - rock
кáмера зберігáння KAHmehrah zbehreeGAHNnyah - baggage room
канáдець/ (-ка) kahNAHdehts'/ (-kah) - Canadian/ (f)
канáдський kahNAHDs'kihy - Canadian (adj.)
канáл kahNAHL - canal
канíкули kahNEEkoolih - school vacation
кáпля KAHPlyah - drop
капýста kahPOOStah - cabbage
кáра KAHrah - punishment
карáт kahRAHT - carat
караýл kahrahOOL - guard; sentry
карбóванець kahrBOHvahnehts' - karbovanets
карнавáл kahrnahVAHL - carnival
кáрта KAHRtah - map
картúна kahrTIHnah - picture; drawing
картóпля kahrTOHPLyah - potato
кáса KAHsah - ticket office; cashier's booth
касéта kahSEHtah - cassette
касúр kahSIHR - cashier
кастрýля kahsTROOlyah - pot; saucepan

катóк kahTOHK - skating rink
кафé kahFEH - cafe
кáфедра KAHfehdrah - department
кáшель KAHshehl' - cough
каштáн kahshTAHN - hard-currency store
квадратóвий kvahdrahTOHvihy - square (adj.)
квартáл kvahrTAHL - block (in a city)
квартúра kvahrTIHrah - apartment
квас kvahs - kvass
квíтка KVEETkah - flower
кéди KEHdih - sneakers
кéмпінг KEHMpeeng - camping
керівнúцтво kehreevNIHTStvoh - leadership
кефíр kehFEER - a yogurt-like drink
килíм KIHleem - rug
кúсень KIHsehn' - oxygen
кúслий KIHSlihy - sour (adj.)
кишéня kihSHEHnyah - pocket
кишенькóвий ліхтáр kihshehn'KOHvihy leekhTAHR - flash light
кишкá kihshKAH - intestine
кілогрáм keelohGRAHM - kilogram
кіломéтр keelohMEHTR - kilometer
кíлькість KEEL'keest' - quantity

кімна́та keemNAHtah - room

кіне́ць keeNEHTS' - end

кіно́ keeNOH - movie; the cinema

кінотеа́тр keenohtehAHTR - movie theater

кінь keen' - horse

кіо́ск keeOHSK - kiosk

кі́сть keest' - bone

кі́шка KEESHkah - cat

кла́довище KLAHdohvihshcheh - cemetary

класи́чний klahSIHCHnihy - classical (adj.)

клей kley - glue

клі́мат KLEEmaht - climate

клі́пс kleeps - clip-on earrings

клоп klohp - bedbug

клуб kloob - club

клю́ква KLYOOKvah - cranberries

ключ klyooch - key

кни́га KNIHgah - book

книжко́вий магази́н knihzhKOHvihy mahgahZIHN - book store

кно́пка KNOHPkah - push button; snap

ковбаса́ kohvbahSAH - sausage

ко́вдра KOHVDrah - blanket

ковзани́ kohvzahNIH - skates

ковта́ти kohvTAHtih - to swallow

ко́жен KOHzhehn - every (adj.)

колго́сп kohlGOHSP - collective farm

ко́лесо KOHlehsoh - wheel

коли́ kohLIH - when

коли́шній kohLISHneey - former; previous (adj.)

колі́но kohLEEnoh - knee

ко́ло KOHloh - circle

кома́нда kohMAHNdah - sports team

кома́р kohMAHR - mosquito

кома́ха kohMAHkhah - insect

комбіна́ція kohmbeeNAHtseeyah - slip

коме́дія kohMEHdeeyah - comedy

комуна́льний kohmooNAHL'nihy - communal (adj.)

компле́кт kohmpLEHKT - complete set

компози́тор kohmpohZIHtohr - composer

компю́тер kohmpYOOtehr - computer

конве́рт kohnVEHRT - envelope

конди́терська kohnDIHtehrs'kah - confectionery shop

кондиціоне́р kohndihtseeohNEHR - air conditioner

ко́нкурс KOHNkoors - competition; contest

консе́рви kohnSEHRvih - canned goods

консе́рвний ніж kohnSEHRVnih neezh - can opener

130

консульство
KOHNsool'stvoh - consulate

контактна лінза
kohnTAHKTnah LEENzah - contact lens

контора kohnTOHrah - office

концерт kohnTSEHRT - concert

коньяк kohn'YAHK - cognac; brandy

кооператив
kohohpehrahTIHV - cooperative store

копійка kohPEEYkah - kopeck

корабель kohrahBEHL' - ship

кордон kohrDOHN - border

корисний kohRIHSnihy - useful, helpful (adj.)

користь KOHrihst' - use; benefit

кориця kohRIHtsya - cinnamon

коричневий
kohRIHCHnehvihy - brown (adj.)

коробка kohROHBkah - box

короткий kohROHTkihy - short (adj.)

косметика kohsMEHtihkah - make up

костюм kohsTYOOM - suit

котлета kohtLEHtah - cutlet

кохання kohKHAHNnyah - love

кохати kohKHAHtih - to love

кошерний kohSHEHRnihy - kosher (adj.)

кошик KOHshihk - basket

краватка krahVAHTkah - tie

країна krahYEEnah - country

край kray - edge; rim

красивий krahSIHvihy - beautiful; pretty (adj.)

красота krahsohTAH - beauty

красти KRAHStih - to steal

краще KRAHshcheh - better

кращий KRASHchihy - better, the best (adj.)

кредитна картка
krehDIHTnah KAHRTkah - credit card

крем krehm - cream; lotion

кривда KRIHVdah - offense; insult

кривий krihVIHY - crooked (adj.)

криза KRIHzah - crisis

крик krihk - shout; cry

кришка KRIHSHkah - lid; cover

крізь kreez' - through

крілик KREElihk - rabbit

крім kreem - except for; but; besides

кріпкий KREEPkihy - strong durable (adj.)

крісло KREESloh - arm chair

кров krohv - blood

крововилив
krohvohVIHlihv - hemorrhage

кровоточити krohvohTOHchihtih - to bleed

крохмаль krohkhMAHL' - starch

крок krohk - step

куди kooDIH - where to

культура kool'TOOrah - culture

купальна шапочка kooPAHL'nah SHAHpohchkah - bathing cap

купальник kooPAHL'nihk - bathing suit

купе kooPEH - train compartment

купити kooPIHtih - to buy

курка KOORkah - hen; chicken

курити kooRIHtih - to smoke

курорт kooROHRT - resort

кусень KOOsehn' - piece

кут koot - corner

кухар KOOkhahr - cook

кухня KOOKHnyah - kitchen

Л

лавка LAHVkah - bench

лавра LAHVrah - monastery

лак lahk - polish; lacquer

лампа LAHMpah - lamp

лампочка LAHMpohchkah - light lamp

ланцюг lahnTSYOOG - chain

легальний lehGAHL'nihy - legal (adj.)

легкий LEHGkihy - easy (adj.)

легко LEHGkoh - easily

легені lehGEHNee - lungs

ледве LEHDveh - hardly; scarcely

леза LEHzah - razor blades

лекція LEHKtseeyah - lecture

лижі LIHzhee - skis

лимон lihMOHN - lemon

лимонад lihmohNAHD - lemonade

липкий lihpKIHY - sticky (adj.)

лист lihst - letter

листівка lihsTEEVkah - post card

листок lihsTOHK - leaf; sheet (of paper)

лівий LEEvihy - left (direction)

лід leed - ice

ліжко LEEZHkoh - bed

лікар LEEkahr - doctor

лікарня leeKAHRnya - hospital

ліки LEEkih - medicine

лікоть LEEkoht' - elbow

лікування leekooVAHNnyah - medical treatment

ліс lees - forest

літак leeTAHK - airplane

література leetehrahTOOrah - literature

літній LEETneey - summer (adj.)

літо LEEtoh - summer

літр leetr - liter

ліфт leeft - elevator

лоб lohb - forehead

ложа LOHzhah - theater

box
ло́жка LOHZHkah - spoon
ло́кшина LOHKshihnah - soup noodle
лососи́на lohsohSIHnah - salmon
лю́бий LYOObihy - dear; beloved (adj.)
люби́ти lyooBIHtih - to love
любо́в lyooBOHV - love
лю́ди LYOOdih - people
люди́на lyooDIHnah - man; person
ля́лька LYAHL'kah - doll

М

ма́буть MAHboot' - probably
мавзоле́й mahvzohLEY - mausoleum
магази́н mahgahZIHN - store
магніто́фон mahgneetohFOHN - tape recorder
майбу́тній mayBOOTneey - future (adj.)
ма́йже MAYzheh - almost
ма́йка MAYkah - shirt
ма́йно mayNOH - property
мак mahk - poppy
малахі́т mahlahKHEET - malachite
мале́нький mahLEHN'kihy - small (adj.)
мали́на mahLIHnah - raspberries
ма́ло MAHloh - a little; not enough
малюва́ння mahlyooVAHNnyah - drawing
маля́тко mahLYAHTkoh - baby; infant
мандари́н mahndahRIHN - tangerine
мари́нований mahrihNOHvahnihy - marinated (adj.)
ма́рка MAHRkah - stamp
ма́рний MAHRnihy - useless (adj.)
масли́ни mahsLIHnah - olives
ма́сло MAHSloh - butter
мат maht - checkmate
ма́ти MAHtih - mother
матрьо́шка mahtRYOHSHkah - wooden, nested doll
ма́чуха MAHchookhah - step-mother
маши́на mahSHIHnah - car; machine
ме́блі MEHBlee - furniture
мед mehd - honey
медсестра́ mehdsehstRAH - nurse
менструа́ція mehnstrooAHtseeyah - menstruation
ме́нше MEHNsheh - less
меню́ mehNYOO - menu
ме́ртвий MEHRTvihy - dead (adj.)
метр mehtr - meter
метро́ mehTROH - subway
механі́зм mehkhahNEEZM - mechanism
ми mih - we
ми́лий MIHlihy - dear; sweet (adj.)
ми́ло MIHloh - soap

миндалина mihnDAHlihnah - tonsil

минулий mihNOOlihy - past (adj.)

мир mihr - world; peace

миска MIHSkah - bowl

мистецтво mihsTEHTStvoh - art; skill

мито MIHtoh - duty (customs)

миша MIHshah - mouse

між meezh - between

міжнародний meezhnahROHDnihy - international

міліціонер meeleetseeohNEHR - policeman

міліція meeLEEtseeyah - the police

мільйон meel'YOHN - million

міра MEErah - measure; extent; degree

міст meest - bridge

місце MEEStseh - place; seat; site

місцевий meesTSEHvihy - local (adj.)

місяць MEEsyahts' - month

місяць MEEsyahts' - moon

міхур meeKHOOR - bladder

міцний meetsNIHY - strong, durable (adj.)

млинець mlihNEHTS' - pancake

мовчання mohvCHAHNnyah - silence

могила mohGIHlah - grave

могутній mohGOOTneey - powerful (adj.)

мода MOHdah - fashion; style

модний MOHDnihy - fashionable; stylish (adj.)

можливість mohzhLIHveest' - opportunity

можливо mohzhLIHvoh - maybe; perhaps

можна MOHZHnah - may; can

мозг mohzg - brain

мокрий MOHKrihy - wet (adj.)

молитва mohLIHTvah - prayer

молодий mohlohDIHY - young (adj.)

молодший mohLOHDshihy - younger (adj.)

молодь MOHlohd' - young people

молоко mohlohKOH - milk

молочарня mohlohCHAHRnyah - dairy

монастир mohnahsTIHR - monastary

монета mohNEHtah - coin

море MOHreh - sea

морква MOHRKvah - carrot

морожений mohROHzhehnihy - frozen (adj.)

мороз mohROHZ - frost

морозиво mohROHzihvoh - ice cream

мотор mohTOHR - motor

134

мотоцикл mohtohTSIHKL - motor-cycle

мужність MOOZHneest' - courage

музей mooZEY - museum

музика MOOzihkah - music

мультфільм mool'tFEEL'm - cartoon

муха MOOkhah - fly

м'який myahKIHY - soft (adj.)

м'яз myahz - muscle

м'ясо MYAHsoh - meat

м'яч myahch - ball

Н

на nah - on; in

набагато nahbahGAHtoh - much, far

набитий nahBIHtihy - tightly packed (adj.)

навмисно nahvMIHSnoh - deliberately; on purpose

наволочка NAHvohlohchkah - pillowcase

навпаки nahvpahKIH - on the contrary

навушники nahVOOSHnihkih earphones

нагорода nahgohROHdah reward; gratuity

наголос NAHgohlohs - grammatical stress

над nahd - over; above

надгробний камінь nahdGROHBnihy KAHmeen' - tombstone

надія nahDEEyah - hope

надпис NAHDpihs - inscription

надто NAHDtoh - too

назавжди nahZAHVZHdih - forever

назад nahZAHD - back-wards

назва NAHZvah - name; title

називати nahzihVAHtih - to be called, named

найбільший nayBEEL'shihy - the largest, greatest

найближчий nayBLIHZHchiy - nearest; next (adj.)

наліво nahLEEvoh - on the left

намисто nahMIHStoh - necklace

намір NAHmeer - intention

напам'ять nahPAHMyaht' - by heart

напевне nahPEHVneh - probably

напій nahPEEY - drink

направо nahPRAHvoh - on the right

наприклад nahPRIHKlahd - for example; for instance

напроти nahPROHtih - opposite; facing

напруга nahPROOgah - tension; stress; strain

наречена nahrehCHEHnah - bride

нарешті nahREHSHtee - at last; finally

нарив nahRIHV - abscess

наріст NAHreest - growth; tumor

135

наркоз nahrKOHZ - anesthesia

народ nahROHD - people

народження nahROHDzhehnnyah - birth

народний nahROHDnihy - national; folk (adj.)

населення nahSEHlehnnyah - population

насильство nahSIHL'stvoh - violence

наслідок NAHSleedohk - result; consequence

насморк NAHSmohrk - head cold

насолода nahsohLOHdah - enjoyment; pleasure; delight

настрій NAHSTreey - mood

наступний nahsTOOPnihy - next

натиск NAHtihsk - onset

натовп NAHtohvp - crowd

національність nahtseeohNAHL'neest'- nationality

нація NAHtseeyah - nation

начальник nahCHAHLnihk - chief; head; boss

не neh - not

небагато nehbahGAHtoh - a little; not much

небезпечний nehbehzPEHCIInihy - dangerous (adj.)

неблагополучний nehblahgohpoh-LOOCHnihy - unfortunate; unhappy (adj.)

небо NEHboh - sky; heaven

неважний nehVAHZHnihy - unimportant (adj.)

невигідний nehVIHgeednihy - unprofitable; unfavorable (adj.)

невизначений nehVIHZnahchehnihy - vague; indefinite (adj.)

невідомий nehveeDOHmihy - unknown (adj.)

невільний nehVEEL'nihy - unintentional; involuntary (adj.)

невістка nehVEESTkah - daughter-in-law; sister-in-law

негативний nehgahTIHVnihy - negative (adj.)

недавно nehDAHVnoh - not long ago; recently

недалекий nehdahLEHkihy - nearby (adj.)

недалеко nehdahLEHkoh - not far; close by

недбалий nehdBAHlihy - careless

неділя nehDEElyah - Sunday

недоброякісний nehdohbrohYAHkeesnihy - poor-quality (adj.)

недосвідчений nehdohSVEEDchehnihy - inexperienced (adj.)

недостатньо nehdohSTAHTnyoh - insufficient

недостача
nehdohSTAHchah -
shortage; scarcity;
defeat; deficiency

недосяжний
nehdohSYAHZHnihy -
unattainable (adj.)

незаконний
nehzahKOHNnihy -
illegal (adj.)

незалежний
nehzahLEHTHnihy -
independent (adj.)

незвичайний
nehzvihCHAYnihy -
unusual;
uncommon (adj.)

незвичний
nehZVIHCHnihy -
unwanted

незграбний
nehZGRAHBnihy -
awkward; clumsy (adj.)

незнайомий
nehznahYOHmihy -
unfamiliar (adj.)

незрілий
nehZREElihy - unripe; not
mature (adj)

незручний
nehZROOCHnihy -
uncomfortable (adj.)

неймовірний
neymohVEERnihy -
incredible;
unbelievable (adj.)

нейтральний
neyTRAHL'nihy -
neutral (adj.)

некрасивий
nehkrahSIHvihy -
ugly (adj.)

неможливо
nehmohzhLIHvoh -
impossible

немовля nehmohvLYAH -
baby; infant

необхідний
nehohbKHEEDnihy -
necessary;
essential (adj.)

неохайний
nehohKHAYnihy -
untidy (adj.)

неохоче nehohKHOHcheh
- reluctantly

непомітний
nehpohMEETnihy -
unnoticable (adj.)

непорозуміння
nehpohrohzooMEENnyah -
misunderstanding

неправда nehPRAHVdah -
untruth; falsehood; lie

неправильний
nehPRAHvihl'nihy - wrong;
incorrect (adj.)

неприємний
nehprihYEHMnihy -
unpleasant (adj.)

неприродний
nehprihROHDnihy -
unnatural (adj.)

непристойний
nehprihSTOYnihy - im-
proper; indecent (adj.)

непритомний
nehprihTOHMnihy -
unconscious (adj.)

нерв nehrv - nerve

нервовий nehrVOHvihy -
nervous; irritable (adj.)

несвідомий
nehsveeDOHmihy -

unreasonable (adj.)

неспокійний nehspohKEEYnihy - worried; troubled (adj.)

нижній NIHZHneey - lower (adj.)

нижня білизна NIHZHnyah beeLIHZnah - underwear

нирка NIHRkah - kidney

нитка NIHTkah - thread

ні nee - no

ніж neezh - than

ніж neezh - knife

ніколи neeKOHlih - never

німець/(-ка) NEEmehts'/ (-kah) - German/ (f)

ніс nees - nose

нісенітниця neesehNEETnihtsyah - nonsense

ніхто neekhTOH - no one

ніч neech - night

нічого neeCHOHgoh - nothing

новий nohVIHY - new (adj.)

Новий рік nohVIHY reek - New Year

новина nohvihNAH - news; information

нога nohGAH - leg; foot

ножиці NOHzhihtsee - scissors

номер NOHmehr - hotel room; number; issue

номерок nohmehROHK - (coat check) ticket

нормальний nohrMAHL'nihy - normal (adj.)

носилки nohSIHLkih - stretcher

носильник nohSIHL'nihk - porter

ну noo - well; well then

нудний noodNIHY - boring (adj.)

нужда noozhDAH - poverty

нуль nool' - zero

О

обезболювання ohbehzBOHLyoovahnnyah - anesthetization

обережно ohbehREHZHnoh - beware; careful

обидва ohBIHDvah - both

обід ohBEED - lunch; dinner

обідати ohBEEdahtih - to have lunch, dinner

обіцянка ohBEEtsyahnkah - promise

область OHBlahst' - region; area; field; domain

обличчя ohbLIHCHchyah - face

обман ohbMAHN - fraud; deception; deceit

обмін OHBmeen - exchange

обміняти ohbmeeNYAHtih - to exchange

обов'язковий ohbohvyahzKOHvihy - obligatory; mandatory (adj.)

образ OHBrahz - image; way; mode; manner

обстановка ohbstahNOHVkah - situation; setting

обурений ohBOOrehnihy - out-raged (adj.)

обхід ohbKHEED - round-about way

об'ява ohbYAHvah - announcement

овес ohVEHS - oats

овочі OHvohchee - vegetables

огірки ohgeerKIH - cucumbers

огляд OHGlyahd - examination; checkup

однак ohdNAHK - however; but

однаковий ohdNAHkohvihy - identical (adj.)

одночасний ohdnohCHAHSnihy - simultaneous (adj.)

одружений ohDROOzhehnihy - married

ожина ohZHIHnah - black-berries

озеро OHzehro - lake

означений ohZNAHchehnihy - definite; set; certain (adj.)

океан ohkehAHN - ocean

око ОНkoh - eye

окремо ohkREHmoh - separately; individually

окуляри ohkooLYAHrih - glasses

оленина ohlehNIHnah - venison

олівець ohleeVEHTS' - pencil

опера OHpehrah - opera

опис OHpihs - description

оптик OHPtihk - optician

оранжевий ohRAHNzhehvihy - orange (adj.)

оркестр ohrKEHSTR - orchestra

оса ohSAH - wasp

освіта ohSVEEtah - education

оселедець ohsehLEHdehts' - herring

осінь OHseen' - fall

основа ohsNOHvah - basis

особистий ohsohBIHStihy - personal; private (adj.)

особливо ohsohbLIHvoh - especially

останній ohsTAHNneey - last; latest (adj.)

острів OHStreev - island

ось ohs' - here (is)

офіціант ohfeetseeAHNT - waiter

офіціантка ohfeetseeAHNTkah - waitress

оформлення ohFOHRMlehnnyah - processing (of documents)

охайний ohKHAYnihy - neat, tidy (adj.)

очевидний ohchehVIHDnihy - obvious (adj.)

П

павук pahVOOK - spider

пакет pahKEHT - packet; package

палатка pahLAHTkah - tent

палац pahLAHTS - palace

палець PAHlehts' - finger
палити pahLIHtih - to burn
пальто́ pahl'TOH - coat
па́м'ятник PAHMyahtnihk
- monument
па́м'ять PAHMyaht' -
memory
пан pahn - Mr.
па́ні PAHnee - Mrs.
панчо́хи pahnCHOHkhih -
stockings
папі́р pahPEER - paper
па́ра PAHrah - pair
парасо́ля pahrahSOHlya -
umbrella
па́рений PAHrehnihy -
steamed (adj.)
парк pahrk - park
паро́м pahROHM - ferry
паропла́в pahrohPLAHV -
ship; steamship
парфу́ма pahrFOOmah -
perfume
пасажи́р pahsahZHIHR -
passenger
па́спорт PAHSpohrt -
passport
Па́сха PAHSkhah - Easter;
Passover
па́хнути PAHKHnootih -
to smell
паціє́нт pahtseeYEHNT -
patient
па́чка PAHCHkah - pack;
bundle
педіа́тр pehdeeAHTR -
pediatrician
пеніцилі́н
pehneetsihLEEN -
penicillin
пе́рвісний PEHRveesnihy -
original (adj.)

перебі́льшення
pehrehBEEL'shehnnyah -
exaggeration
перебува́ння
pehrehbooVAHNnyah -
stay
перев'я́зка
pehrehvYAHZkah - ban-
dage; dressing
переговори
pehrehgohVOHrih - nego-
tiations
пе́ред PEHrehd - before; in
front of
переда́ча
pehrehDAHchah -
broadcast; transmission
передмі́стя
pehrehdMEETyah -
suburb
пере́дній pehREHDneey -
front (adj.)
перека́з pehREHkahz -
(money) order
пере́клад pehREHKlahd -
translation
переклада́ч
pehrehklahDAHCH -
translator; interpreter
перекла́сти
pehrehkLAHStih -
to translate
перемо́га pehrehMOHgah -
victory
переносний
pehrehnohsNIHY - portable
(adj.)
пере́пустка
pehREHpoostkah - admis-
sion; admittance
пере́рва pehREHRvah -
break; recess

140

пересадка pehrehSAHDkah - change; transfer (on planes, trains, buses, etc.)

перехід pehrehKHEED - place to cross; crosswalk

перешкода pehrehSHKOHdah - hinderance

перець PEHrehts' - pepper

перлина pehrLIHnah - pearl

перманент pehrmahNEHNT - permanent wave

персик PEHRsihk - peach

перукар pehrooKAHR - hairdresser; barber

перцовка pehrTSOHVkah - pepper vodka

петрушка pehtROOSHkah - parsley

печиво PEHchihvoh - cookie; pastry

печінка pehCHEENkah - liver

пиво PIHvoh - beer

пилюля pihLYOOlyah - pill

пинцет pihnTSEHT - tweezers

пиріг pihREEG - pie

писати pihSAHtih - to write

письменник pihs'MEHNnihk - writer

письмово pihs'MOHvoh - in writing

питання pihTAHNnyah - question

пити PIHtih - to drink

півгодини peevgohDIHnih - half hour

південний peevDEHNnihy - southern (adj.)

південь PEEVdehn' - south

північ PEEVneech - north

північний peevNEECHnihy - northern (adj.)

півтора peevtohRAH - one and a half

під peed - under; beneath

підгрузник peedGROOZnihk - diaper

піджак peedZHAHK - man's suit jacket

підметка peedMEHTkah - sole (of a shoe)

підпис PEEDpihs - signature

підписати peedpihSAHtih - to sign

підручник peedROOCHnihk - textbook

підтвердження peedTVEHRDzhehnnyah - confirmation

піжама peeZHAHmah - pajamas

пізній PEEZneey - late (adj.)

пізніше peezNEEsheh - later

після PEESlyah - after

після обіду PEESlyah ohBEEdoo - afternoon

післязавтра peeslyahZAHVTrah - day after tomorrow

пісня PEESnyah - song

піт peet - sweat

піч peech - stove

пішки PEESHkih - on, by foot

плавати PLAHvahtih - to swim

плакат plahKAHT - poster

план plahn - city map

пластир PLAHStihr - band-aide

платити plahTIHtih - to pay

плаття PLAHTtyah - dress

плацкартний plahtsKAHRtnihy - reserved (on a train) (adj.)

плащ plahshch - raincoat

племінник plehMEENnick - nephew

племінниця plehMEENnihtsyah - niece

плече plehCHEH - shoulder

плитка PLIHTkah - (chocolate) bar

плівка PLEEVkah - film

плов plohv - pilaf

пломба PLOHMbah - (tooth) filling

площа PLOHSHchah - area; square

пляж plyahzh - beach

пляма PLYAHmah - spot; stain

побачення pohBAHchehnnyah - appointment; meeting

повар POHvahr - cook

повертати pohvehrTAHtih - to return

повз pohvz - by; past

повинен pohVIHnehn - must; should; ought to

повільний pohVEEL'nihy - slow

повітря pohVEETryah - air

повний POHVnihy - full; complete (adj.)

повністю POHVneestyoo - fully; quite

повстання pohvSTAHNnyah - uprising; revolt

повторити pohvtohRIHtih - to repeat

поганий pohGAHnihy - bad; poor (adj.)

погано pohGAHnoh - badly

погляд POHGlyahd - look; glance

погода pohGOHdah - weather

подарунок pohdahROOnohk - present; gift

подзвонити pohdzvohNIHtih - to call (on the phone)

подібний pohDEEBnihy - similar; like (adj.)

подія pohDEEyah - event

подобатися pohDOHbahtihsyah - to enjoy

подробиця pohDROHbihtsyah - detail

подушка pohDOOSHkah - pillow

поезія pohEHzeeyah - poetry

поет pohEHT - poet

пожежа pohZHEHzhah - fire

поза POHzah - outside; out of

позавчора pohzahVCHOHrah - day before yesterday

поздоровити pohzdohROHvihtih - to congratulate

142

позити́вний
pohzihTIHVnihy - positive;
affirmative (adj.)

познайо́мити
pohznahYOHmihtih - to
introduce

позоло́чений
pohzohLOHchehnihy -
gilded (adj.)

поїзд POHyeezd - train

показа́ти pohkahZAHtih -
to show

по́ки POHkih - meanwhile

по́ки що POHkih shchoh -
in the meanwhile

поко́ївка pohkohYEEVkah
- maid

покупе́ць pohkooPEHTS' -
customer

поку́пка pohKOOPkah -
purchase

по́ле POHleh - field; area

полікліні́ка
pohleeKLEEneekah - clinic

полі́т pohLEET - flight

полі́тика pohLEEtihkah -
politics

полови́на pohlohVIHnah -
half

поло́ження
pohLOHzhehnnyah -
situation; condition

поми́лка pohMIHLkah -
mistake

помідо́р pohmeeDOHR -
tomato

поно́с pohNOHS - diarrhea

по́нчик POHNchihk -
doughnut

попере́дження
pohpehREHDzhehnnyah -
warning

попере́дній
pohpehREHDneey -
former; previous (adj.)

попе́реду pohPEHrehdoo -
in front; ahead

попі́льниця
pohpeel'NIHtsyah - ashtray

попра́вка pohPRAHVkah -
correction; adjustment

пора́ pohRAH - it's time

пора́да pohRAHdah -
advice

пора́дити pohRAHdihtih -
to recommend

пора́нений
pohRAHnehnihy - wounded
(adj.)

поро́жній pohROHZHneey
- empty; vacant (adj.)

по́рох POHrohkh - powder

порт pohrt - port

портре́т pohrtREHT -
portrait

портсига́р pohrtsihGAHR -
cigarette case

портфе́ль pohrtFEHL' -
briefcase

по́ряд POHryahd - alongside; beside; next to

поря́док pohRYAHdohk -
order; sequence

поса́дка pohSAHDkah -
landing

посила́ти pohsihLAHtih -
to send

поси́лка pohSIHLkah -
package

по́смішка POHSmeeshkah
- smile

посо́льство
pohSOHL'stvoh -
embassy

постійний pohsTEEYnihy
- constant;
continuous (adj.)
постіль POHSteel' - bed
поступово pohstooPOHvoh
- gradually
посуд POHsood - dishes
потиск POHtihsk - hand-
shake
потім POHteem - then; next;
afterwards
похмурий pohkhMOOrihy
- overcast (adj.)
походження
pohKHOHDzhehnnyah -
origin
поцілунок
pohtseeLOOnohk - kiss
початок pohCHAHtohk -
beginning
починання
pohchihNAHNnyah -
undertaking; venture
почувати pohCHOOvahtih
- to feel
почуття pohchootTYAH -
feeling
пошта POHSHtah - mail;
post office
поштамт pohshTAHMT -
main post office
поштова скринька
pohshTOHvah SKRIHN'kah
- mailbox
пояс POHyahs - belt; waist
пояснення
pohYAHSnehnnyah -
explanation
правда PRAHVdah - truth
правий PRAHvihy - right
(direction)
правило PRAHvihloh - rule

правильний
PRAHvihl'nihy - correct;
right (adj.)
православний
prahvohSLAHVnihy -
orthodox
прання prahnNYAH -
laundry
працювати
prahtsyooVAHtih - to work
праця PRAHtsyah - work
предмет prehdMEHT -
subject
презерватив
prehzehrvahTIHV - contra-
ceptive
прекрасний
prehKRAHSnihy - beautiful
(adj.)
при prih - attached to; in the
presence of; in the time of
привіт prihVEET - hi
приємний prihYEHMnihy
- pleasant (adj.)
приїзд prihYEEZD - arrival
приймати prihyMAHtih -
to accept
прийом prihYOHM -
reception
приклад PRIHKlahd -
example
прикраса prihKRAHsah -
decoration
приліт prihLEET - arrival
(on a plane)
принаймні prihNAYMnee
- at least
природа prihROHdah -
nature
природно prihROHDnoh -
naturally
прислів'я prihsLEEVyah -

proverb

приста́нь PRIHStahn' -
dock; pier; wharf

присті́йний
prihsTEEYnihy - proper;
civilized (adj.)

пристрастний
PRIHSTrahstnihy - passionate (adj.)

причи́на prihCHIHnah -
reason

прі́звище PREEZvihshcheh
- last name; sur name

про proh - about

проба́чати prohBAHchahtih
- to excuse, pardon

проба́чте prohBAHCHteh -
sorry, excuse me

пробле́ма probLEHmah -
problem

прову́лок prohVOOlohk -
side street

прогно́з prohgNOHZ -
prognosis; forecast

продава́ти prohdahVAHtih
- to sell

продаве́ць prohdahVEHTS'
- salesman

про́даж PROHdahzh - sale

продо́вження
prohDOHVzhehnnyah -
continuation

продо́вжитися
prohDOHVzhihtihsyah -
to last

промо́ва prohMOHvah -
speech

проносне́ prohnohsNEH -
laxative

пропи́ска prohPIHSkah -
registration

прости́й prohsTIHY -

simple; easy (adj.)

простира́дло
prohstihRAHDloh - sheet

про́сто PROHStoh - simply

просту́да prohsTOOdah -
head cold

проте́з prohTEHZ - denture

проти PROHtih - against

прото́ка prohTOHkah -
strait; channel

профе́сія prohFEHseeyah -
profession

профе́сор prohFEHsohr -
professor

проха́ння prohKHAHNnyah
- request

прохоло́дний
prohkhohLOHDnihy - cool
(adj.)

проща́вай
prohshchahVAHY -
farewell

проя́влення
prohYAHVlehnnyah -
(film) development

прями́й pryahMIHY -
straight (adj.)

птах ptahkh - bird

пуло́вер pooLOHvehr -
sweater

пульс pool's - pulse

пункт poonkt - point;
station; center

путівни́к pooteevNIHK -
guidebook

пшени́ця pshehNIHtsyah -
wheat

п'є́са PYEHsah - play; drama

п'я́ний PYAHnihy - drunk;
intoxicated (adj.)

п'яни́ця pyahNIHtsyah -
drunkard

145

Р

равін rahVEEN - rabbi

рагу́ rahGOO - stew

ра́дий RAHdihy - glad; pleased

ра́діо RAHdeeoh - radio

радіоста́нція rahdeeohSTAHNtseeyah radio station

ра́дісний RAHdeesnihy - joyful; joyous (adj.)

ра́зом RAHzohm - together

рак rahk - crayfish

ра́ковина RAHkohvihnah - (bathroom) sink

ра́на RAHnah - wound

рані́ше rahNEEsheh - earlier; sooner

ра́нній RAHNneey - early (adj.)

ра́нок RAHnohk - morning

ра́птом RAHPtohm - suddenly

рва́ний RVAHnihy - torn; ripped (adj.)

ребро́ rehbROH - rib

ревмати́зм rehvmahTIHZM - rheumatism

реди́ска rehDIHSkah - radish

режисе́р rehzhihSEHR - (theater) director

ре́йка REYkah - rail; track

рейс reys - trip; flight

рекла́ма rehkLAHmah - advertising; sign

ремо́нт rehMOHNT - repair

ремо́нт взуття́ rehMOHNT vzootTYAH - shoemaker

рентге́н rehntGEHN - x-ray

респу́бліка rehsPOBleekah - republic

рестора́н rehstohRAHN - restaurant

реце́пт rehTSEHPT - prescription

ри́ба RIHbah - fish

ри́ма RIHmah - rhyme

рис rihs - rice

ри́са RIHsah - feature

рі́вень REEvehn' - level

рі́вний REEVnihy - equal (adj.)

рідки́й reedKIHY - rare; infrequent (adj.)

рі́дко REEDkoh - rarely

рі́дний REEDnihy - native (adj.)

рі́заний REEzahnihy - cut; sliced (adj.)

Різдво́ reezdVOH - Christmas

рі́зний REEZnihy - different

різномані́тний reeznohmahNEETnihy - various

рік reek - year

ріка́ reeKAH - river

рі́па REEpah - turnip

ріст reest - growth; height

рі́шення REEshehnnyah - decision

роби́ти rohBIHtih - to do

робі́тник rohbeetNIHK - worker

родзи́нки rohdZIHNkih - raisin

роди́на rohDIHnah - relatives

ро́дич ROHdihch - relative

розва́га rohzVAHgah - amusement; entertainment

розвиток ROHZvihtohk - development

роздратування rohzdrahtooVAHNnyah - irritation

роздутий rohzDOOtihy - swollen; puffed up (adj.)

роздягальня rohzdyahGAHL'nyah - cloakroom

розетка rohZEHTkah - electrical socket

розкішний rohzKEESHnihy - luxurious (adj.)

розклад ROHZKlahd - schedule; timetable

розлад шлунку ROHZlahd SHLOONkoo - indigestion

розмір ROHZmeer - size

розмова rohzMOHvah - conversation

розмовний rohzMOHVnihy - conversational; colloquial (adj.)

розмовник rohzMOHVnihk - phrasebook

розповідь ROHZpohveed' - story; tale; account

розпродано rohzPROHdahnoh - sold out

розсольник rohzSOHL'nihk - cucumber soup

розтягнення rohzTYAHGnehnnyah - strain; sprain

розумний rohZOOMnihy - sensible; rational (adj.)

роль rohl' - role; part

роман rohMAHN - novel

рослина rohsLIHnah - plant

ростбиф ROHSTbihf - roast beef

рот roht - mouth

рубин rooBIHN - ruby

рука rooKAH - hand; arm

рукав rooKAHV - sleeve

рукавиця rookahVIHtsyah - mitten

рукопис rooKOHpihs - manuscript

рукоплескання rookohplehsKAHNnyah - applause

рулет rooLEHT - meat loaf

рух rookh - movement; traffic

ручка ROOCHkah - pen

рюкзак ryookZAHK - backpack

рябчик RYAHBchihk - hazel grouse

ряд ryahd - row; file

С

сад sahd - garden

салат sahLAHT - salad

саме SAHmeh - exactly; precisely

самовар sahmohVAHR - samovar

самовпевнений sahmohVPEHVnehnihy - self confident (adj.)

самогубство sahmohGOOBstvoh - suicide

самообслуговування sahmohohbslooGOHvoovahnnyah - self-service (adj.)

самостійний

самohSTEEYnihy - independent (adj.)

санітарний день sahneeTAHRnihy dehn' - one day a month for cleaning

санки SAHNkih - sleigh; sled

сапфір sahpFEER - sapphire

сарказм sahrKAHZM - sarcasm

сатира sahTIHrah - satire

сахарин sahkhahRIHN - saccharin

светер SVEHtehr - sweater

свинина svihNIHnah - pork

свиня svihNYAH - pig

свіжий SVEEzhihy - fresh (adj.)

світанок sveeTAHnohk - dawn; daybreak

світлий SVEETlihy - light; bright (adj.)

світло SVEET'loh - light

світло-... SVEETloh-... - light-(color)

світлофор sveetlohFOHR - traffic light

свічка SVEECHkah - candle

свобода svohBOHdah - freedom

святий svyahTIHY - holy; sacred (adj.)

священик svyahSHCHEHnihk - priest; clergyman

село sehLOH - village

секретар sehkrehTAHR - secretary

секунда sehKOONdah - second (time measure)

секція SEHKtseeyah - section

серветка sehrVEHTkah - napkin

сервіз sehrVEEZ - set (of dishes or silverware)

серги SEHRgih - earrings

сердечний приступ sehrDEHCHnihy PRIHStoop - heart attack

сердитий sehrDIHtihy - angry

середина sehREHdihnah - middle

середній sehREHDneey - middle; average (adj.)

серйозний sehrYOHZnihy - serious (adj.)

серце SEHRtseh - heart

сестра sehsTRAH - sister

сигара sihGAHrah - cigar

сигарета sihgahREHtah - cigarette

сила SIHlah - strength

сильний SIHL'nihy - strong (adj.)

син sihn - son

синагога sihnahGOHgah - synagogue

синій SIHneey - dark blue (adj.)

синяк sihNYAHK - bruise

сир sihr - cheese

сирий sihRIHY - raw (adj.)

система sihsTEHmah - system

ситечко SIHtehchkoh - strainer

ситий SIHtihy - full (of food)

сік seek - juice

сіль seel' - salt

148

сім'я́ seemYAH - family

сі́рий SEErihy - grey (adj.)

сірни́к seerNIHK - match

ска́рга SKAHRgah - complaint

ски́дка SKIHDkah - sale

скі́льки SKEEL'kih - how much

складни́й sklahdNIHY - complex; difficult (adj.)

скло́ skloh - glass

скля́нка SKLYAHNkah - (drinking) glass

сковорода́ skohvohrohDAH - frying pan

скоро́чення skohROHchehnnyah - abbreviation

скрізь skreez' - everywhere

скро́мний SKROHMnihy - modest (adj.)

скульпту́ра skool'pTOOrah - sculpture

слабки́й slahbKIHY - weak (adj.)

сла́ва SLAHvah - glory

сли́ва SLIHvah - plum

слизьки́й slihz'KIHY - slippery (adj.)

слі́дство SLEEDstvoh - result; consequence

словни́к slohvNIHK - dictionary

сло́во SLOHvoh - word

слу́жба SLOOZHbah - church service

сльо́зи SLYOHzih - tears

сма́жити SMAHzhihtih - to fry, roast, broil

смара́гд smahRAHGD - emerald

смачни́й smahchNIHY - tasty (adj.)

смілй́вий smeeLIHvihy - brave; courageous (adj.)

сміття́ smeetTYAH - trash; rubbish

сміх smeekh - laughter

смішни́й smeeshNIHY - funny (adj.)

смерть smehrt' - death

смета́на smehTAHnah - sour cream

сморо́дина smohROHdihnah - currants

сніг sneeg - snow

сніда́нок sneeDAHnohk - breakfast

соба́ка sohBAHkah - dog

собо́р sohBOHR - cathedral

солда́т sohlDAHT - soldier

соло́дке (на) sohLOHDkeh (nah) - (for) dessert

соло́дкий sohLOHDkihy - sweet (adj.)

соло́ний sohLOHnihy - salted (adj.)

сон sohn - sleep; dream

со́нце SOHNtseh - sun

со́нячний SOHnyahchnihy - sunny (adj.)

со́ром SOHrohm - shame

соромли́вість sohrohmLIHveest' - embarrassment

соро́чка sohROHCHkah - shirt

сорт sohrt - kind; sort

со́ска SOHSkah - pacifier

со́тня SOHTnyah - hundred

со́ус SOHoos - sauce; gravy

сою́з sohYOOZ - union

спа́льня SPAHL'nyah - bedroom

149

спаси́бі spahSIHbee - thank you

спа́ти SPAHtih - to sleep

спиціа́льність spehtseeAHL'neest' - speciality

спина́ spihNAH - back; spine

спи́сок SPIHsohk - list

співа́к speeVAHK - singer

співа́чка speeVAHCHkah - singer (f)

співчуття́ speevchootTYAH - sympathy

спідни́ця speedNIHtsyah - skirt

спір speer - argument

спі́рний SPEERnihy - controversial (adj.)

спі́шний SPEESHnihy - hurried; rushed (adj.)

сповіща́ти spohveeSHCHAHtih - to notify, inform

спо́вна SPOHVnah - fully; completely; quite

споко́йний spohKEEYnihy - calm; tranquil (adj.)

сполу́чення spohLOOchehnnyah - combination

спо́мин SPOHmihn - memory; recollection

споча́тку spohCHAHTkoo - at first; in the beginning

спра́ва SPRAHvah - matter; affair; business

спра́вжній SPRAHVZHneey - real; true (adj.)

спра́га SPRAHgah - thirst

срібло́ SREEBloh - silver

срі́бний SREEBnihy - silver (adj.)

стадіо́н stahdeeOHN - stadium

стан stahn - condition

ста́нція STAHNtseeyah - station

стари́й stahRIHY - old (adj.)

старода́вній stahrohDAHVneey - ancient (adj.)

ста́рший STAHRshihy - older; elder (adj.)

стіл steel - table

стіна́ steeNAH - wall

столи́ця stohLIHtsyah - capital (of a state)

столі́ття stohLEETtyah - century

стоп stop - stop

сторі́нка stohREENkah - page

сторона́ stohrohNAH - side

стоя́нка stohYAHNkah - (bus) stop

стоя́нка для маши́н stohYAHNkah dlyah mahSHIN - parking lot

стра́ва STRAHvah - dish; food; course

страх strahkh - fear

стра́шний strahshNIHY - horrible; terrifying (adj.)

стри́жка STRIHZHkah - haircut; trim

строк strohk - (period of) time; date; deadline

студе́нт stooDEHNT - student

стук stook - knock

сту́пінь STOOpeen' - degree; extent

стюардеса styooahrDEHsah - stewardess

сувенір soovehNEER - souvenir

суворий sooVOHrihy - strict; harsh; severe (adj.)

суд sood - court

сумний soomNIHY - sad; melancholy (adj.)

сумнів SOOMneev - doubt

суниці sooNIHtsee - strawberries

суп soop - soup

сусід sooSEED - neighbor

сухий sooKHIHY - dry (adj.)

сучасний sooCHAHSnihy - contemporary (adj.)

схвильований skhvihLYOHvahnihy - worried, troubled (adj.)

схід skheed - east/sunrise

східний SKHEEDnihy - eastern (adj.)

сходи SKHOHdih - stairs

сцена STSEHnah - stage

сьогодні syohGOHDnee - today

сьогоднішній syohGOHDneeshneey - today's (adj.)

сьомга SYOHMgah - lox

Т

табір TAHbeer - camp

таблетка tahbLEHTkah - pill; tablet

так tahk - so; true, yes

також TAHkohzh - as well

таксі tahkSEE - taxi

талія TAHleeyah - waist

талон tahLOHN - coupon

тальк tahl'k - talcum powder

там tahm - there

таможеник tahMOHzhehnihk - customs official

таможня tahMOHZHnyah - customs

тампон tahmPOHN - tampon

танець TAHnehts' - dance

тапочки TAHpohchkih - slippers

таракан tahrahKAHN - cockroach

тарілка tahREELkah - plate

тварина tvahRIHnah - animal

твердий tvehrDIHY - hard (adj.)

творчість TVOHRcheest' - creative work

театр tehAHTR - theater

телебачення tehlehBAHchehnnyah - television

телевізор tehlehVEEzohr - TV set

телеграма tehlehGRAHmah - telegram

телеграф tehlehGRAHF - telegraph office

телефон tehlehFOHN - telephone

телефон-автомат tehlehFOHN-ahvtohMAHT - pay phone; phone booth

телефоністка tehlehfohNEESTkah - operator

теля́тина tehLYAHtihnah - veal

те́мні окуля́ри TEHMnee ohkooLYAHrih - sunglasses

те́мний TEHMnihy - dark (adj.)

те́мно- TEHMnoh - dark (color)

температу́ра tehmpehrahTOOrah - temperature

те́ніс TEHnees - tennis

тепе́р tehPEHR - now

те́плий TEHPlihy - warm (adj.)

терміно́вий tehrmeeNOHvihy - urgent; emergency (adj.)

те́рмос TEHRmohs - thermos

терпели́вий tehrpehLIHvihy - patient (adj.)

ти́ждень TIHZHdehn' - week

тимчасо́во tihmchahSOHvoh - temporarily

тиск tihsk - (blood) pressure

ти́сяча TIHsyahchah - thousand

ти́хий TIHkhihy - quite (adj.)

ті́ло TEEloh - body

ті́льки TEEL'kih - only

тінь teen' - shadow

тісни́й teesNIHY - crowded

ті́стечко TEEStehchkoh - pastry

ті́тка TEETkah - aunt

ткани́на tkahNIHnah - fabric

това́р tohVAHR - merchandise

товари́ство tohvahRIHSTvoh - company

това́риш tohVAHrihsh - comrade

товсти́й tohvsTIHY - fat (adj.)

тоді́ tohDEE - then

тому́ tohMOO - therefore

тому́ що tohMOOshchoh - because

тонки́й tohnKIHY - thin (adj.)

топа́з tohPAHZ - topaz

торка́тися tohrKAHtihsyah - to touch

торт tohrt - cake

той toy - that (one)

то́чно TOHCHnoh - exactly

трава́ trahVAH - grass

траге́дія trahGEHdeeyah - tragedy

трамва́й trahmVAY - street car

тра́са TRAHsah - highway

тре́ба TREHbah - must

трима́ти trihMAHtih - to hold, keep, support

тріска́ treesKAH - cod

троле́йбус trohLEYboos - trolley bus

тротуа́р trohtooAHR - side walk

троя́нда trohYAHNdah - rose

тру́бка TROOBkah - pipe

труси́ trooSIH - underpants

туале́т tooahLEHT - toilet

туале́ний папір tooahLEHTnihy pahPEER -

toilet paper
туди́ tooDIH - that way
туди́ й наза́д tooDIH y nahZAHD - roundtrip (ticket)
тума́н tooMAHN - fog
туне́ць tooNEHTS' - tuna
турбо́та toorBOHtah - care; concern
турбува́ти toorbooVAHtih - to worry, trouble
тури́ст tooRIHST - tourist
тут toot - here
ту́флі TOOFlee - shoes
тютю́н tyooTYOON - tobacco
тюфте́лі tyoofTEHlee - meatballs
тяжки́й tyahzhKIHY - difficult (adj.)

У

у оо - at
уби́вство ooBIHVstvoh - murder
уби́вця ooBIHVtsyah - murderer
убира́льня oobihRAHL'nyah - bathroom, toilet
ува́га ooVAHgah - attention
уго́да ooGOHdah - agreement
укли́н ookLEEN - bias; incline
уко́л ooKOHL - injection
украї́нець/ (-ка) ookrahYEENehts'/ (-kah) - Ukrainian/ (f)
украї́нський ookrahYEENs'kihy -

Ukrainian (adj.)
умо́ва ooMOHvah - condition
універма́г ooneevehrMAHG - department store
університе́т ooneevehrsihTEHT - university
ури́вок ooRIHvohk - passage; excerpt
уро́к ooROHK - lesson
у́ряд OOryahd - government
ускла́днення oosKLAHDnehnnyah - complication
у́смішка OOSmeeshkah - smile
у́сний OOSnihy - oral; verbal (adj.)
у́спіх OOSpeekh - success
устано́ва oostahNOHvah - institution
уся́кий ooSYAHkihy - any
утю́г ooTYOOG - iron
у́часть OOchahst' - participation
уче́ний ooCHEHnihy - scholar; scientist
учи́тель ooCHIHtehl' - teacher
учи́телька ooCHIHtehl'kah - teacher (f)
учи́тися ooCHIHtihsyah - to study
уя́ва ooYAHvah - imagination

Ф

фальши́вий fahl'SHIHvihy - fake; falsified (adj.)
фарбува́ння

153

fahrbooVAHNnyah - dye; hair coloring

фарбува́ти fahrbooVAHtih - to color

фари FAHrih - headlights

фарфор fahrFOHR - china

фарцо́вщик fahrTSOHVshchihk - blackmarketeer

фарширо́ваний fahrshihROHvahnnihy - stuffed (food) (adj.)

фен fehn - hairdryer

фе́рма FEHRmah - farm

фільм feel'm - movie

флот floht - navy

фойе́ foyEH - lobby

фонта́н fohnTAHN - fountain

форе́ль fohREHL' - trout

фотоапара́т fohtohahpahRAHT - camera

фотогра́фія fohtohGRAHfeeyah - photograph

фра́за FRAHzah - phrase; sentence

фрукт frookt - fruit

фунт foont - pound

фут foot - foot (measure)

футбо́л footBOHL - soccer

Х

хаба́р khahBAHR - bribe

хала́т khahLAHT - robe

харчо́ khahrCHOH - mutton soup

ха́та KHAHtah - peasant's nut; cabin

хвилюва́тися

khvihlyooVAHtihsyah - to be worried, agitated

хви́ля KHVIHlyah - wave

хво́рий KHVOHrihy - sick (adj.)

хворі́ти khvohREEtih - to be ill

хворо́ба khvohROHbah - illness; disease

хи́бний KHIHBnihy - false (adj.)

хіба́? kheeBAH - really? is that so?

хімчи́стка kheemCHIHSTkah - dry cleaning

хіру́рг kheeROORG - surgeon

хліб khleeb - bread

хлібосо́льний khleebohSOHL'nihy - hospitable (adj.)

хло́пчик KHLOHPchihk - boy

хмарочо́с khmahrohCHOHS - skyscraper

хокей khohKEY - hockey

холоде́ць khohlohDEHTS' - aspic

холоди́льник khohlohDIHL'nihk - refrigerator

холо́дний khohLOHDnihy - cold (adj.)

хор khohr - choir

хоро́ший khohROHshihy - good (adj.)

хоті́ти khohTEEtih - to want

хоча́ khohCHAH - although

храм khrahm - cathedral; temple

хрест khrehst - cross

хрін khreen - horse-radish
хто khtoh - who
хто-небудь khtoh-
NEHbood' - anyone,
someone
художник
khooDOHZHnihk - artist
худий khooDIHY - thin
(adj.)
хуліган khooleeGAHN -
hooligan
хустка KHOOSTkah -
kerchief
хутро KHOOTroh - fur

Ц

цар tsahr - tsar
цвях tsvyahkh - nail, tack
це tseh - it; this (one) (n.)
цей tsehy - this (one) (m.)
центр tsehntr - center
церква TSEHRKvah -
church
цибуля tsihBOOlyah -
onion
циган TSIHgahn - gypsy
цигарка tsihGAHRkah -
cigarette
цирк tsihrk - circus
цитата tsihTAHtah - quote
цифра TSIHFrah - number;
numeral
цікавий tseeKAHvihy -
interesting (adj.)
цілий TSEElihy - whole;
entire (adj.)
цілком tseelKOHM - fully;
quite
ціль tseel' - goal; aim
цінний TSEENnihy -
valuable

цукерки tsooKEHRkih -
candy
цукор TSOOkohr - sugar
ця tsyah - this (one) (f)

Ч

чай chay - tea
чайник CHAYnihk - tea
kettle
чайниця CHAYnihtsyah -
tea caddy
чайові chahyohVEE - tip
чарівний chahREEVnihy -
charming (adj.)
час chahs - time
часник chahsNIHK - garlic
часто CHAHStoh - often
частота chahstohTAH -
frequency
чашка CHAHSHkah - cup
чверть chvehrt' - quarter
чек chehk - check
чекати chehKAHtih - to
wait
чемодан chehmohDAHN -
suitcase
червоний chehrVOHnihy -
red
черга CHEHRgah - line
чергова chehrGOHvah - hall
monitor
через CHEHrehz - through;
within
черешня chehREHSHnyah
- sweet cherries
чесний CHEHSnihy -
honest (adj.)
чи chih - if, whether
чиновник chihNOHVnihk
- clerk
число chihsLOH - number

155

чистий CHIHStihy - clean (adj.)

читати chihTAHtih - to read

читач chihTAHCH - reader

чіткий cheetKIHY - clear; distinct (adj.)

член chlehn - member

чоботи CHOHbohtih - boots

човен CHOHvehn - boat

чоловік chohlohVEEK - man; husband; person

чоловічий chohlohVEE-chihy - men's (adj.)

чому chohMOO - why

чомусь chohMOOS' - for some reason

чорний CHOHRnihy - black; dark (adj.)

чорний ринок CHOHRnihy RIHnohk - black market

чорнило chohrNIHloh - ink

чорниця chohrNIHtsyah - blueberries

чорно-білий CHOHRnoh BEElihy - black-and-white (adj.)

чорт chohrt - devil

чудесний chooDEHSnihy - wonderful; miraculous (adj.)

чужак chooZHAHK - stranger

чужий chooZHIHY - not one's own; foreign (adj.)

чучело CHOOchehloh - stuffed animal

Ш

шампанське shahmPAHNs'keh - champagne

шампунь shahmPOON' - shampoo

шановний shahNOHVnihy - respected

шапка SHAHPkah - hat

шарф shahrf - scarf

шафа SHAHfah - closet; cabinet

шах shahkh - check

шахи SHAHkhih - chess

шашки SHAHSHkih - draughts; checkers

шашлик shahshLIHK - shish kebob

швейцар shveyTSAHR - doorman

швидкість SHVIHDkeest' - speed

швидко SHVIHDkoh - quickly

швидка допомога shvihdKAH dohpohMOHgah - ambulance

шепіт SHEHpeet - whisper

шерстяний shehrstyahNIHY - woollen (adj.)

шинка SHIHNkah - beckon

ширина shihrihNAH - width

широкий shihROHkihy - wide; broad (adj.)

шия SHIHyah - neck

шкаралупа shkahrahLOOpah - (egg) shell

шкарпетки shkahrPEHTkih - socks

шкідливий shkeedLIHvihy - harmful

шкіра SHKEErah - skin;

156

leather
шкіряний shkeeryahNIHY
- leather (adj.)
шкода SHKOHdah - harm;
hurt; injury
шкодувати
shkohdooVAHtih - to be
sorry for; pity
школа SHKOHlah - school
шкура SKKOOrah - skin;
hide
шлях shlyahkh - way; path;
trip
шнурки shnoorKIH - shoe
laces
шовк shohvk - silk
шоколад shohkohLAHD -
chocolate
шорти SHOHRtih - shorts
шосе shohSEH - highway
шофер shohFEHR - driver
штат shtaht - state
штатський SHTAHTs'kihy
- civilian (adj.)
штопор SHTOHpohr -
corkscrew
штраф shtrahf - fine
штучний SHTOOCHnihy -
artificial (adj.)
шуба SHOObah - fur coat
шум shoom - noise
шумкий shoomKIHY -
noisy (adj.)

Щ

щасливий shchahsLIHvihy
- happy; lucky (adj.)
щастя SHCHAHStyah -
happiness
ще shcheh - still, yet
щедрий SHCHEHDrihy -

generous (adj.)
ще раз shcheh rahz - once
again
щиколотка
SHCHIHkohlohtkah -
ankle
щирий SHCHIHrihy -
sincere (adj.)
щітка SHCHEETkah -
brush
що shchoh - what
щоби SHCHOHbih - in
order to
щока shchohKAH - cheek
щомісячний
shchohMEEsyahchnihy -
monthly (adj.)
що-небудь
shchohNEHbood' - any-
thing; something
щорічний
shchohREECHnihy -
yearly, annual (adj.)
щука SHCHOOkah - pike

Ю

ювелірний
yoovehLEERnihy - jewelry
(adj.)
ювілей yooveeLEY -
anniversary
юнак yooNAHK - youth
юний YOOnihy -
youthful
юність YOOneest' - youth
юридичний
yoorihDIHCHnihy -
judicial
юрист yooRIHST - lawyer
юшка YOOSHkah - potato/
fish soup

Я

я yah - I

яблоко YAHBlohkoh - apple

ягоди YAHgohdih - berries

яйце́ yayTSEH - egg

яєшня yahYEHSHnyah - fried eggs; omelet.

язик yahZIHK - tongue

як yahk - how

як давно́ yahk dahvNOH - how long

як далеко yahk dahLEHkoh - how far

який yahKIHY - what, which

якість YAHkeest' - quality

якось YAHkohs' - once; one day; somehow

як-то yahkTOH - as for instance

якщо́ yahkSHCHOH - if, whether

ялинка yahLIHNkah - fir-tree

янтар yahnTAHR - amber

ярмарок YAHRmahrohk - fair

яскравий yahskRAHvihy - bright (adj)

ясний YAHSnihy - clear (adj)

ясно YAHSnoh - clear

яшма YAHSHmah - jasper

ящик YAHSHchihk - box

ENGLISH-UKRAINIAN DICTIONARY

A

abbreviation - **скорочення**
skohROHchehn'nyah
about - **про** proh
above - **нагорі/над**
nahgohREE/nahd
abscess - **нарив** nahRIHV
absence - **відсутність**
veedSOOTneest'
absorbent cotton - **вата**
VAHtah
accent - **акцент** ahkTSEHNT
accept (to) - **приймати**
prihyMAHtih
access - **доступ** DOHStoop
accident - **нещасний**
випадок nehshCHAHS-
hihy VIHpahdok
accidentally - **випадково**
vihpahdKOHvoh
acquaintance - **знайомство**
znahYOHMstvoh
acquainted; familiar(adj) -
знайомий znahYOHmihy
act - **дія** DEEyah
act, take action(to) - **діяти**
DEEyahtih
action - **дія/подія**
pohDEEyah
actor - **актор** ahkTOHR
actress - **актриса** ahktRIHsah
address - **адреса** ahdREHsah
admission pass - **перепустка**
pehREHpoostkah
admission; admittance - **впуск**
vpoosk
admit,let in (to) - **впускати**
vpoosKAHtih
adult - **дорослий**

dohROHSlihy
advertising, sign - **реклама**
rehkLAHmah
advice - **порада** pohRAHdah
after - **після** PEESlyah
afternoon - **після обіду**
PEESlyah ohBEEdoo
afterwards - **потім** POHteem
again - **знову/ще раз**
ZNOHvoo/shcheh rahz
against - **проти** PROHtih
age - **вік** veek
agreement (in) - **згода**
ZGOHdah
agreement; contract - **договір**
DOHgohveer
air - **повітря** pohVEETryah
air conditioning -
кондиціонер
kohndihtseeohNEHR
airmail - **авіапошта**
ahveeahPOHSHtah
airplane - **літак** leeTAHK
airport - **аеропорт**
ahehrohPOHRT
alarm clock - **будильник**
booDIHL'nihk
alcohol - **алкоголь**
ahlkohGOHL'
all; the whole - **весь** vehs'
allergy - **алергія**
ahlehrGEEyah
almost - **майже** MAYzheh
along; about; according to - **по/**
згідно poh/ZGEEDnoh
alongside; beside; next to -
поряд POHryahd
aloud - **вголос** VGOHlohs
alphabet - **азбука** AHZbookah
already - **вже** vzheh

also; as well - **також** TAHkohzh

although - **хоч** khohch

always - **завжди** ZAHVZHdih

ambulance - **швидка допомога** shvihdKAH dohpohMOHgah

American (adj) - **американский** ahmehrihKAHNs'kihy

american/(f) - **американець/(-канка)** ahmehrihKAHnehts'/(-KAHNkah)

amusement; entertainment - **розвага** rohzVAHgah

ancient (adj) - **стародавній** stahrohDAHVneey

and; also - **і/та** ee/tah

anesthesia - **наркоз** nahrKOHZ

anesthetization - **обезболвання** ohbehzBOHlyoovahnnyah

anger - **гнів** gneev

angry (adj) - **гнівний** GNEEVnihy

animal - **тварина** tvahRIHnah

ankle - **щиколотка** SHCHIHkolohtkah

anniversary - **ювілей** yooveeLEY

announcement - **об'ява** ohbYAHvah

answer - **відповідь** VEEDpohveed'

anthology; collection - **збірник** ZBEERnihk

antibiotic - **антибіотик** ahntihbeeOHtihk

any - **любий** lyooBIHY

anyone - **хто-небудь** khtoh-NEHboood'

anything - **що-небудь** shchoh-NEHbood'

apartment - **квартира** kvahrTIHrah

apparently; evidently - **очевидно** ohchehVIHDnoh

appearance - **вигляд** VIHGlyahd

appendicitis - **апендицит** ahpehnditTSIHT

appendix - **апендикс** ahPEHNdihks

appetite (hearty appetite!) **апетит (смачного!)** ahpehTIHT (smahchNOHgoh)

appetizer - **закуска** zahKOOSkah

applause - **аплодисменти** ahplohdihsMEHNtih

apple - **яблуко** YAHBlookoh

appointment - **побачення** pohBAHchehnnyah

approximately; about - **біля** BEElyah

architect - **архітектор** ahrkheeTEHKtor

architecture - **архітектура** ahrkheetehkTOOrah

area; square - **площа** PLOHshchah

argument - **спір** speer

arm; hand - **рука** rooKAH

arm chair - **крісло** KREESloh

around (location) - **довкола** dohvKOHlah

arrival (on a plane) **приліт** prihLEET

arrival (on a train) **приїзд**

prihYEEZD
art - **мисте́цтво**
mihsTEHTSTvoh
artery - **арте́рія**
ahrTEHreeyah
arthritis - **артри́т** ahrtRIHT
artificial (adj) - **шту́чний**
SHTOOCHnihy
artist - **худо́жник**
khooDOHZHnihk
as well; also - **та́кож**
TAHkohzh
ashtray - **попі́льни́ця**
pohpeel/NIHtsyah
aspic - **холоде́ць**
khohlohDEHTS'
aspirin - **аспіри́н**
ahspeeRIHN
assurance - **запе́вння**
zahPEHVnehnnyah
asthma - **а́стма** AHSTmah
at - **у/бі́ля** oo/BEElyah
at first; in the beginning -
споча́тку
spohCHAHTkoo
atheism - **атеї́зм** ahtehYEEZM
athletic (adj) **атлети́чний**
ahtlehTIHCHnihy
athletics - **атле́тика**
ahtLEHtihkah
at least - **принайми́нні**
prihNAYMnee
attention - **ува́га** ooVAHgah
attitude; relationship -
відно́шення
veedNOHshehnnyah
attentively - **ува́жно**
ooVAHZHnoh
audible (adj) - **чу́тний**
CHOOTnihy
aunt - **ті́тка** TEETkah
author - **а́втор** AHVtohr

autumn - **о́сінь** OHseen'
avenue - **авеню́/проспе́кт**
ahvehNYOO/prohsPEHKT
awkward; clumsy (adj) -
незгра́бний
nehZGRAHBnihy

B

baby; infant - **дити́на**
dihTIHnah
back; backwards - **наза́д**
nahZAHD
back; spine - **спина́** spihNAH
backpack - **рюкза́к**
ryookZAHK
bacon - **ши́нка** SHINkah
bad; poor (adj) - **пога́ний**
pohGAHnihy
badge - **значо́к** znahCHOHK
badly - **пога́но** pohGAHnoh
bag; sack - **су́мка; то́рба**
SOOMkah; TOHRbah
baggage - **бага́ж** bahGAHZH
baggage room - **ка́мера**
зберіга́ння KAHmerah
zbehreeGAHNnyah
bakery - **бу́лочна**
BOOlohchnah
balalaika - **балала́йка**
bahlahLAYkah
balcony - **балко́н** bahlKOHN
ball - **м'яч** myahch
ballet - **бале́т** bahLEHT
banana - **бана́н** bahNAHN
bandage - **бинт** bihnt
bandaging; dressing -
перев'я́зка
pehrehVYAHZkah
band-aide - **пла́стир**
PLAHStihr
bank - **ба́нк** bahnk

161

banquet - **банкет** bahnKEHT

bar of chocolate - **плитка шоколаду** PLIHTkah shohkohLAHdoo

barber; hairdresser - **перукар** pehrooKAHR

basket - **кошик** KOHshihk

bath(to) - **купатися** kooPAHtihsyah

bathing cap - **купальна шапочка** kooPAHL'nah SHAHpohchkah

bathing suit - **купальник** kooPAHL'nihk

bathroom - **ванна кімната** VAHNah keemNAHtah

bathtub - **ванна** VAHNnah

battery - **батарея** bahtahREHyah

bay; gulf - **затока** zahTOHkah

bazaar - **базар** bahZAHR

beach - **пляж** plyahzh

beads - **намисто** nahMIHStoh

beans - **квасоля** kvahSOHlyah

beard - **борода** bohrohDAH

beat, strike (to) - **бити** BIHtih

beautiful (adj) - **гарний** GAHRnihy

beauty - **краса** krahSAH

because - **тому що** tohMOO shchoh

bed - **ліжко/постіль** LEEZHkoh/POHSteel'

bedbug - **клоп** klohp

bedroom - **спальня** SPAHL'nyah

bee - **бджілка** BDZHEELkah

beef - **яловичина** YAHlohvihchihnah

beer - **пиво** PIHyoh

beet soup - **холодний борщ** khohLOHDnihy bohrshch

beets - **буряки** booryahKIH

before; formerly - **раніше/до** rahNEEsheh/doh

before; in front of - **перед** PEHrehd

begin, start(to) - **починати** pohchihNAHtih

beginning - **початок** pohCAHtohk

behind; beyond; past; for; in; after - **за** zah

belief; faith - **віра** VEErah

believe, have faith(to) - **вірити** VEErihtih

bell - **дзвін** dzveen

belt; waist - **пояс** POHyahs

bench - **лавка** LAHVkah

berries - **ягоди** YAHgohdih

berth; shelf - **полиця** pohLIHtsyah

better - **краще** KRAHshcheh

better; the best - **найкращий** nayKRAHshchihy

between - **між** meezh

beware - **обережно** ohbehREHZHnoh

bias; incline; slant - **уклін** ooKLEEN

bible - **біблія** BEEBleeyah

bicycle - **велосипед** vehlohsihPEHD

big; large; great (adj) - **великий** vehLIHkihy

bill - **рахунок** rahKHOOnohk

billion - **мільярд** meel'yahrd

binoculars; opera glasses - **бінокль** beeNOHKL'

birch - **береза** behREHzah

bird - **птах** ptahkh

birth - **народження**

162

nahROHDzhehnnyah
birthday - день
  народження dehn'
  nahROHDzhehnnyah
bitter (adj) - гіркий
  geerKIHY
black-and-white (adj) -
  чорнобілий
  CHOHRnoh-BEElihy
black; dark (adj) - чорний
  CHOHRnihy
blackberries - ожина
  ohZHIHnah
black market - чорний
  ринок CHOHRnihy
  RIHnohk
blackmarketeer -
  фарцовщик
  fahrTSOHVshchihk
bladder - сечовий міхур
  sehchohVIHY meeKHOOR
blanket - ковдра KOHVDrah
bleed (to) - кровоточити
  krohvohTOHchihtih
blessing - благословення
  blahgohslohVEHNnyah
blister - міхур meeKHOOR
block (in a city) - квартал
  kvahrTAHL
blonde/(f) - блондин/(-ка)
  blohnDIHN/(-kah)
blood - кров krohv
blood pressure - тиск tihsk
blood type - група крові
  GROOpah KROHvee
blouse - блузка BLOOZkah
blue (adj) - синій SIHneey
blue (light) (adj) -
  блакитний
  blahKIHTnihy
blueberries - чорниці
  chohrNIHtsee

boat - човен CHOHvehn
body - тіло TEEloh
boiled (adj) - варений
  vahREHnihy
bone - кість keest'
book - книга KNIHgah
book store - книгарня
  knihGAHRnyah
booth; cubicle - кабіна
  kahBEEnah
boots - чоботи CHOHbohtih
border - кордон kohrDOHN
boring (adj) - нудний
  noodNIHY
borscht; beet soup - борщ
  bohrshch
botanical garden -
  ботанічний сад
  bohtahNEECHnihy sahd
both - обоє ohBOHyeh
bottle - пляшка PLYASHkah
bouillon - бульйон
  bool'YOHN
boulevard - бульвар
  bool'VAHR
bowl - миска MIHSkah
box - коробка/ящик
  kohROHBkah/YAHshchihk
boy - хлопчик
  KHLOHPchihk
bra - бюстгальтер
  byoostGAHL'tehr
brain - мозок MOHzohk
brakes (car) - гальма
  GAHL'mah
brave: courageous(adj) -
  сміливий smeeLIHvihy
bread - хліб khkeeb
break (to) - зламати
  zlahMAHtih
break; recess - перерва
  pehREHRvah

breakdown (car) - **аварія**
ahVAHreeyah

breakfast - **сніданок**
sneeDAHnohk

breakfast (to eat) - **снідати**
SNEEdahtih

breathe (to) - **дихати**
DIHkhahtih

breathing; respiration -
дихання DIHkhahnnyah

bribe - **хабар** khahBAHR

bride - **наречена**
nahrehCHEHnah

bridge - **міст** meest

brief; not long - **не довго** neh
DOHVgoh

briefcase - **портфель**
pohrtFEHL'

bright(adj) - **яскравий**
yahsKRAHvihy

British(adj) - **англійський**
ahngLEEYs'kihy

broadcast; transmission -
передача
pehrehDAHchah

brooch - **брошка**
BROHSHkah

brother - **брат** braht

brother-in-law - **зять** zyaht'

brown (adj) - **коричневий**
kohRIHCHnehvihy

bruise - **синяк** sihNYAHK

brunette/(f) - **брюнет**
bryooNEHT

brush - **щітка** SHCHEETkah

bucket - **відро** veedROH

building - **будинок**
booDIHnohk

burn - **палити** pahLIHtih

bus - **автобус** ahvTOHboos

bus stop - **зупинка**
zooPIHNkah

business (adj) - **діловий**
deelohVIHY

business trip - **відрядження**
veedRYAHDzhehnnyah

businessman/(f) - **бізнесмен**/-
ка beeznehsMEHN/-kah

busy; occupied (adj) -
зайнятий ZAYnyahtihy

but - **але** ahLEH

butter - **масло** MAHSloh

button - **гудзик** GOODzihk

buy (to) - **купити** kooPIHtih

by heart - **напам'ять**
nahPAHMyaht'

by; near - **близько**
BLIHZ'koh

C

cabbage - **капуста**
kahPOOStah

cabbage soup - **капусняк**
kahpoosNYAHK

café · **кафе** kahFEH

cake - **торт** tohrt

calendar - **календар**
kahlehnDAHR

call (to) - **подзвонити**
pohdzvohNIHtih

called, named (to be) -
називати nahzihVAHtih

calm; tranquil (adj) -
спокійний
spohKEEYnihy

calorie - **калорія**
kahLOHreeyah

camel - **верблюд**
vehrbLYOOD

camera - **фотоапарат**
fohtohahpahRAHT

camp - **табір** TAHbeer

campfire - **вогнище**

VOHGnihshcheh
camping - ке́мпінг
KEHMpeeng
Canadian (adj) - кана́дський
kahNAHDs'kihy
Canadian/(f) - кана́дець/
-на́дка kahNAHdehts'/
-NAHDkah
canal - кана́л kahNAHL
candle - сві́чка SVEECHkah
candy - цуке́рки
tsooKEHRkih
canned goods - консе́рви
kohnSEHRvih
can opener - консе́рвний
ніж kohnSEHRVnihy
neezh
capital (of a state) - столи́ця
stohLIHtsyah
car - автомаши́на /
автомобі́ль
ahvtohmahSHIHnah/
ahvtohmohBEEL'
carat - кара́т kahRAHT
care; concern - турбо́та
toorBOHtah
careful - обере́жно
ohbehREHZHnoh
careless; negligent; sloppy;
slipshod (adj) недба́лий
nehdBAHlihy
carnation - гвозди́ка
gvohzDIHkah
carnival - карнава́л
kahrnahVAHL
carrots - мо́рква MOHRKvah
cartoon (film) - мультфі́льм
mool'tFEEL'M
cashier- каси́р kahSIHR
cassette - касе́та kahSEHtah
cast - гіпс geeps
cat - кі́шка KEESHkah

cathedral - собо́р/храм
sohBOHR/khrahm
caution - бережи́сь
behrehZHIHS'
caviar- ікра́ eekRAH
cavity - дупло́ doopLOH
ceiling - стеля́ STEHlyah
cemetary - кла́довище/
цвинтар
KLAHdohvihshcheh/
TSVIHNtahr
center - центр tsehntr
century - столі́ття
stohLEETtyah
century; age - вік veek
certainly; absolutely -
безумо́вно
behzooMOHVnoh
chain - ланцю́г
lahnTSYOOG
chair - стіле́ць steeLEHTS'
champagne - шампа́нське
shahmPAHNs'keh
change (coins) - зда́ча
ZDAHchah
change; transfer (on planes,
trains, buses
etc).переса́дка
pehrehSAHDkah
check - раху́нок/чек
rahKHOOnohk/chehk
check mate - мат maht
cheek - щока́ shchohKAN
cheerful (adj) - бадьо́рий
bahDYOHrihy
cheese - сир sihr
cherries (sour) - ви́шня
VIHSHnyah
cherries (sweet) - чере́шня
chehREHSHnyah
chess - ша́хи SHAHkhih
chest; breast - груди

165

GROOdih

chicken - курча́ koorCHAH

chief; boss - керівни́к kehreevNIHK

child - дити́на dihTIHnah

children - ді́ти DEEtih

children's (adj) - дитя́чий dihTYAHchihy

china - порцеля́на pohrtsehLYAHnah

chocolate - шокола́д shohkohLAHD

choice; assortment; selection - ви́бір VIHbeer

choir - хор khohr

Christmas - різдво́ reezdVOH

church - це́рква TSEHRKvah

church service - слу́жба SLOOZHbah

cigar - сига́ра sihGAHrah

cigarette - сигаре́та sihgahREHtah

cigarette case - портсига́р pohrtsihGAHR

cigarette lighter - запа́льни́чка zahpahl'NIHCHkah

cinnamon - кори́ця kohRIHtsyah

circle - ко́ло KOHloh

circus - цирк tsihrk

circular; round (adj) - кру́глий KROOGlihy

citizen/(f) - громадя́нин/-дя́нка grohmahdyahNIHN/-DYAHNkah

citizenship - громадя́нство grohmahDYAHNstvoh

city - мі́сто MEEStoh

civil; civilian(adj) - громадя́нський

grohmahDYAHNs'kihy

classical (adj) - класи́чний

clay- гли́на GLIHnah

clean (adj) - чи́стий CHIHStihy

cleaning woman - прибира́льниця prihbihRAHL'nihtsyah

clear; distinct (adj) - чі́ткий cheetKIHY

clearly - я́сно YAHSnoh

clerk - чино́вник chihNOHVnihk

climate - клі́мат KLEEmaht

clinic - ліка́рня leeKAHRnyah

clip-on earrings - кліпс kleeps

cloakroom - гардеро́б/ роздяга́льня gahrdehROHB/ rohzdyahGAHL'nyah

cloakroom attendant/(f) - гардеро́бник/ниця gahrdehROHBnihk/nihtsyah

close by; not far - недале́ко nehdahLEHkoh

closed (adj) - зачи́нений zahCHIHnehnihy

closet; cabinet - ша́фа SHAHfah

clothes - о́дяг OHdyahg

club - клуб kloob

coast; bank; shore - бе́рег BEHrehg

coat - пальто́ pahl'TOH

coat-check ticket - номеро́к nohmehROHK

cockroach - тарака́н tahrahKAHN

cocoa - кака́о kahKAHoh

cod - тріска́ treesKAH

coffee - ка́ва KAHvah

166

cognac; brandy - коньяк kohn'YAHK

coin - монета mohNEHtah

coincidence - співпадання speevpahDAHNnyah

cold (adj) - холодний khohLOHDnihy

cold (head) - простуда prohsTOOdah

collection; gathering - збір zbeer

collective farm - колгосп kohlGOHSP

color - колір KOHleer

colorless; dull (adj) - безкольоровий kohl'ohROHvihy

comb - гребінь GREHbeen'

combination - сполучення spohLOOchehn'nyah

comedy - комедія kohMEHdeeyah

comfortable (adj) - зручний ZROOCHnihy

communal (adj) - комунальний kohmooNAHL'nihy

competition; contest; sports match конкурс/ змагання KOHNkoors/ zmahGAHNnyah

complaint - скарга SKAHRgah

completion; end - закінчення zahKEENchehnnyah

completely; absolutely - цілком/зовсім tseelKOHM/ZOHVseem

complex; difficult (adj) - складний sklahdNIHY

complication - ускладнення

ooskLAHDnehnnyah

composer - композитор kohmpohZIHtohr

computer - комп'ютер kohmPYOOtehr

comrade - товариш tohVAHrihsh

concert - концерт kohnTSEHRT

conclusion - висновок VIHSnohvohk

condition; state - стан stahn

conditions - умови ooMOHvih

conductor (musical) - диригент dihrihGEHNT

confectionery shop - кондитерська kohnDIHtehrs'kah

confirmation - підтвердження peedTVEHRdzhehnnyah

congratulate (to) - вітати veeTAHtih

consequently - таким чином /отже tahKIHM CHIHnohm/ OHTzheh

considerable; significant (adj) - значний znahchNIHY

constant; continuous (adj) - постійний pohsTEEYnihy

constipation - запор zahPOHR

consulate - консульство KOHNsool'stvoh

contact lens - контактна лінза kohnTAHKTnah LEENzah

contemporary (adj) - сучасний sooCHAHSnihy

continuation - продовження

167

prohDOHVzhehnnyah

contraceptive - **презерватив**
prehsehrvahTIHV

controversial (adj) - **спірний**
SPEERnihy

convenience - **зручність**
ZROOCHneest'

convention; congress - **з'їзд**
zyeezd

conversation - **розмова/**
бесіда rohzMOHVah/
BEHseedah

conversational; colloquial (adj)
- **розмовний**
rohzMOHVnihy

cook - **кухар** KOOkhahr

cook, boil(to) - **варити**
vahRIHtih

cookie; pastry - **печиво**
PEHchihvoh

cool (adj) - **холодний**
khohLOHDnihy

cooperative store -
кооператив
kohohpehrahTIHV

copy; edition - **примірник**
prihMEERnihk

corkscrew - **штопор**
SHTOHpohr

corner - **кут/ріг** koot/reeg

correct (adj) - **правильний**
PRAHvihl'nihy

correction; adjustment -
поправка pohPRAHVkah

correspondence -
листування
lihstooVAHNnyah

cottage - **дача** DAHchah

cotton (adj) - **бавовняний**
bahvohvNYAHnihy

cough - **кашель** KAHshehl'

country - **країна** krahYEEnah

countryside - **село** sehLOH

coupon - **талон/купон**
tahLOHN/kooPOHN

courage - **мужність**
MOOZHneest'

cousin(f) - **двоюрідна**
сестра dvohYOOreednah
sehstRAH

cousin (m) - **двоюрідний**
брат dvohYOOreednihy
braht

cranberries - **клюква**
KLYOOKvah

crayfish - **рак** rahk

crazy; mad; insane (adj) -
божевільний
bohzhehVEEL'nihy

cream (dairy) - **вершки**
vehrshKIH

cream; lotion - **крем** krehm

creative work - **творчість**
TVOHRcheest'

credit card - **кредитна**
картка krehDIHTnah
KAHRTkah

crime - **злочин** ZLOHchihn

crisis - **криза** KRIHzah

crooked (adj) - **кривий**
krihVIHY

cross - **хрест** khrehst

crosswalk - **перехід**
pehrehKHEED

crowd - **натовп** NAHtohvp

crowded (adj) - **тісний**
teesNIHY

cruel; brutal (adj) -
жорстокий
zhohrsTOHkihy

cruise - **круїз** krooEEZ

cucumber soup - **розсольник**
rohzSOHL'nihk

cucumbers - **огірки**

ohgeerKIH

culture - **культу́ра**
kool'TOOrah

cup - **ча́шка** CHAHSHkah

curious (adj) - **ціка́вий**
tseeKAHvihy

currants - **сморо́дина**
smohROHdihnah

current (adj) - **актуа́льний**
ahktooAHL'nihy

curtain - **заві́са** zahVEEsah

customer - **покупе́ць**
pohkooPEHTS'

customs; habits - **зви́чаї**
ZVIHchahyee

customs - **тамо́жня**
tahMOHZHnyah

customs official -
tahMOHzhehnihk

customs charge; duty - **ми́то**
MIHtoh

cut; sliced (adj) - **рі́заний**
REEsahnihy

cute; sweet; dear - **ми́лий**
MIHlihy

cutlet - **котле́та** kohtLEHtah

D

daily (adj) - **щоде́нний**
shchohDEHNnihy

dairy - **молоча́рня**
mohlohCHAHRnyah

dance - **та́нець** TAHnehts'

dangerous (adj) -
небезпе́чний
nehbehzPEHCHnihy

dark (adj) - **те́мний**
TEHMnihy

dark-(color) - **те́мно -**
TEHMnoh

daughter - **до́чка** dohchKAH

daughter-in-law - **неві́стка**
nehVEESTkah

dawn; daybreak - **світа́нок**
sveeTAHnohk

day - **день** dehn'

day after tomorrow -
післяза́втра
peeslyahZAHVTrah

day before yesterday -
позавчо́ра
pohzahVCHOHrah

day off - **вихідни́й день**
vihkheedNIHY dehn'

daytime (adj) - **де́нний**
DEHNnihy

dead (adj) - **ме́ртвий**
MEHRTvihy

deaf (adj) - **глухи́й**
glooKHIHY

death - **смерть** smehrt'

deception; deceit; fraud -
обма́н ohbMAHN

decision - **рі́шення**
REEshehnnyah

decoration; embellishment -
прикра́са prihKRAHsah

decrease - **зме́ншення**
ZMEHNshehnnyah

deep; in depth (adj) -
глибо́кий glihBOHkihy

deficit - **дефіци́т**
dehfihTSIHT

deficiency - **недоста́ча**
nehdohsTAHchah

definite; set; certain (adj)
ви́значений
VIHZnahchehnihy

degree; extent - **мі́ра/ступі́нь**
MEErah/STOOpeen'

delay; tardiness - **запі́знення**
zahPEEZnehnnyah

deliberately; on purpose -

навмисно nahvMIHSnoh

demon - диявол dihYAHvohl

dentist - зубний лікар
zoobNIHY LEEkahr

denture - протез prohTEHZ

deodorant - дезодорант
dehzohdohRAHNT

department - відділ/
кафедра VEEDdeel/
KAHfehdrah

department store - універмаг
ooneevehrMAHG

departure (airplane) відліт
veedLEET

departure (train) - відхід
veedKHEED

description - опис OHpihs

dessert - десерт/на солодке
dehSEHRT/nah
sohLOHDkeh

detail - деталь dehTAHL'

detour - об'їзд/
обхід ohbYEEZD/
ohbKHEED

development (film) -
проявлення
prohYAHVlehnnyah

devil - чорт chohrt

diabetes - діабет
deeahBEHT

diagnosis - діагноз
deeAHGnohz

diamond - діамант
deeahMAHNT

diaper - підгрузник
peedGROOZnihk

diarrhea - понос pohNOHS

dictionary - словник
slohvNIHK

diet - дієта deeYEHtah

difference; distinction -
різниця reezNIHtsyah

different (adj) - різний
REEZnihy

differently; otherwise -
інакше eeNAHKsheh

dining hall - їдальня
yeeDAHL'nyah

director (theater) - режисер
rehzhihSEHR

dirt; filth - бруд brood

dirty; filthy (adj) - брудний
broodNIHY

disability - інвалідність
eenvahLEEDneest'

disabled person - інвалід
eenvahLEED

dish; food; course - страва
STRAHvah

dishes - посуд POHsood

dishonest (adj) -
нечесний
nehCHEHSnihy

disinfect (to) -
дезинфікувати
dehzihnfeekooVAHtih

dissatisfied (adj) -
незадоволений
nehzahdohVOHlehnihy

distance - віддаль
VEEDdahl'

diverse (adj) різноманітний
reeznohmahNEETnihy

do (to) - робити rohBIHtih

dock; pier; wharf - пристань
PRIHStahn'

doctor - лікар LEEkahr

dog - собака sohBAHkah

doll; puppet - лялька
LYAHL'kah

dollar - долар DOHlahr

door - двері DVEHree

doorman - швейцар
shveyTSAHR

dormitory - **гуртожиток**
goortohZHIHtohk

dosage - **дозування**
dohzooVAHNnyah

double occupancy (adj) -
двоспальний
dvohSPAHL'nihy

doubt - **сумнів** SOOMneev

doughnut - **пончик**
POHNchihk

down; below (location) -
внизу vnihZOO

down; downward (destination) -
вниз vnihz

dozen - **дюжина**
DYOOzhihnah

drawing - **малювання**
mahlyooVAHNnyah

dress - **сукня** SOOKnyah

drink (to) - **пити** PIHtih

drink - **напій** nahPEEY

drive (to) - **їздити/їхати**
YEEZdihtih/VEEkhahtih

driver - **водій** vohDEEY

driver's license - **права водія**
prahVAH vohdeeYAH

drop - **капля** KAHPlyah

drugstore - **аптека**
ahpTEHkah

drunk (adj) - **п'яний**
PYAHnihy

drunkard - **п'яниця**
PYAHnihtsyah

dry (adj) - **сухий** sooKHIHY

dry cleaning - **хімчистка**
kheemCHIHSTkah

duty (customs) **мито** MIHtoh

duty-free - **безмитний**
behzMIHTnihy

dye; hair coloring -
фарбування
fahrbooVAHNnyah

E

ear - **вухо** VOOkhoh

earlier; sooner - **раніше**
rahNEEsheh

early (adj) - **ранній**
RAHNneey

earmuff; headphone -
навушник
nahVOOSHnihk

earrings - **серги** SEHRgih

easily - **легко** LEHGkoh

east - **схід** skheed

eastern (adj) - **східний**
SKHEEDnihy

Easter; Passover - **пасха**
PAHSkhah

easy (adj) - **легкий**
LEHGkihy

eat (to) - **їсти** YEEStih

edge; rim - **край** kray

education - **освіта** ohsVEEtah

egg - **яйце** yayTSEH

egg shell - **шкаралупа**
shkahrahLOOpah

eggplant - **баклажан**
bahklahZHAHN

elbow - **лікоть** LEEkoht'

elderly (adj) - **літній**
LEETneey

elections - **вибори** VIHbohrih

electrical (adj) -
електричний
ehlehkTRIHCHnihy

electrical socket - **розетка**
rohZEHTkah

electricity - **електрика**
ehLEHKtrihkah

elevator - **ліфт** leeft

embarrassment -
збентеження
zbehnTEHzhehnnyah

171

embassy - **посо́льство**
pohSOHL'stvoh

embroidered (adj) -
ви́шитий VIHshihtihy

emerald - **смара́гд**
smahRAHGD

empty; vacant (adj) -
поро́жній pohROHZneey

end - **кіне́ць** keeNEHTS'

enemy - **во́рог** VOHrohg

engineer - **інжене́р**
eenzhehNEHR

English, British (adj) -
англі́йський
ahngLEEYs'kihy

Englishman/(f) -
англіча́нин/-ча́нка
ahngleeCHAHnihn/
-CHAHNkah

enjoy (to) - **подо́батися**
pohDOHbahtihsyah

enjoy oneself (to); have fun -
весели́тися
vehsehLIHtihsyah

enough; sufficiently - **до́сить**
DOHsiht'

enter (to) - **вхо́дити**
VKHOHdihtih

enthusiastic (adj)
захо́плений
zahKHOHPlehnihy

entrance - **вхід** vkheed

envelope - **конве́рт**
kohnVEHRT

equal (and) - **рі́вний**
REEVnihy

escalator - **ескала́тор**
ehskahLAHtohr

especially - **особли́во**
ohsohbLIHvoh

eternally - **ві́чно** VEECHnoh

European (adj) -
європе́йський
yehvrohPEYS'kihy

European/(f) - **європе́єць/**
-пейка yehvrohPEHyehts/
-PEYkah

evening (adj) - **вечі́рній**
vehCHEERneey

evening - **ве́чір** VEHcheer

event - **поді́я** pohDEEyah

every (adj) - **ко́жний**
KOHZHnihy

everything - **все** vseh

everywhere - **скрізь** skreez'

evil; mean; malicious (adj) -
злий zlihy

exactly - **то́чно/са́ме**
TOHCHnoh/SAHmeh

exaggeration -
перебі́льшення
pehrehBEEL'shehnnyah

examination; checkup - **о́гляд**
OHGlyahd

example - **при́клад**
PRIHKlahd

except for; but; besides - **крім**
kreem

excessive; superfluous (adj) -
за́йвий ZAYvihy

exchange - **о́бмін** OHBmeen

exchange (to) - **обміня́ти**
ohbmeeNYAHtih

excited (adj) - **збу́джений**
ZBOODzhehnihy

excursion - **екску́рсія**
ehksKOOrseeyah

excuse, pardon (to) -
проба́чте prohBAHCHteh

exercise- **впра́ва** VPRAHvah

exhaustion - **вто́ма** VTOHmah

exhibition; display - **ви́ставка**
VIHStahvkah

exit - **ви́хід** VIHkheed

172

expenses - **ви́трати**
VIHTrahtih
expensive; valuable; dear (adj)
- **дороги́й** dohrohGIHY
experience - **до́свід**
DOHSveed
explanation - **поя́снення**
pohYAHSnehnnyah
express - **експре́с**
ehksPREHS
eye - **око** OHkoh
eyebrow - **брова́** brohVAH
eyelash - **ві́я** VEEyah
eyesight - **зір** zeer

F

fabric - **ткани́на** tkahNIHnah
face - **обли́ччя**
ohbLIHCHchyah
factory - **заво́д** zahVOHD
fair - **я́рмарок**
YAHRmahrohk
fake; falsified (adj)
фальши́вий
fahl'SHIHvihy
fall; autumn - **о́сінь** OHseen'
false (adj) - **хи́бний**
KHIHBnihy
family - **сім'я́** seemYAH
famous (adj) - **відо́мий**
veeDOHmihy
fan - **ві́яло** VEEyahloh
far away - **дале́ко**
dahLEHkoh
farewell - **прощава́й**
prohshchahVAY
farm - **фе́рма** FEHRmah
father; continue - **да́лі** DAHlee
fashion; style - **мо́да** MOHdah
fashionable; stylish (adj) -
мо́дний MOHDnihy

fast; quickly; rapidly -
шви́дко SHVIHDkoh
fat (adj) - **то́встий**
TOHVStihy
fat; grease - **жир** zhihr
fate - **до́ля** DOHlyah
father - **ба́тько** BAHT'koh
fatherland - **батьківщи́на**
baht'keevSHCHIHnah
faucet - **кран** krahn
fear, be afraid (to) - **боя́тися**
bohYAHtihsyah
fear - **страх** strahkh
feature; trait; characteristic -
ри́са RIHsah
feel (to) - **почува́ти себе́**
pohchooVAHtih sehBEH
feel sorry for, pity (to) -
шкодува́ти
shkohdooVAHtih
feeling; sensation - **відчуття́**
veedchootTYAH
feeling; sensitivity - **почуття́**
pohchootTYAH
feminine; woman's (adj)
жіно́чий zheeNOHchihy
ferry - **паро́м** pahROHM
fever - **жар** zhahr
few; some; several - **декілька́**
DEHkeel'kah
field; area - **по́ле** POHleh
fight (to) - **би́тися** BIHtihsyah
fight, struggle - **боротьба́**
bohroht'BAH
filled dumpling - **варе́ник**
vahREHnihk
filling (tooth) - **пло́мба**
PLOHMbah
film - **плі́вка** PLEEVkah
finally; at least - **наре́шті**
nahREHSHtee
find (to) - **знайти́** znayTIH

fine - **штраф** shtrahf
finger - **палець** PAHlehts'
fire - **вогонь** vohGOHN'
first-aid kit - **аптечка** ahpTEHCHkah
fish - **риба** RIHbah
fish soup - **юшка з риби** YOOSHkah z RIHbih
fishing pole - **вудка** VOODkah
flashlight - **кишеньковий ліхтар** kihshehn'KOHvihy leekhTAHR
flexible (adj) - **гнучкий** gnoochKIHY
flight - **політ** pohLEET
flood - **повінь** POHveen'
floor; story - **поверх** POHvehrkh
flounder; sole - **камбала** KAHMbahlah
flour - **борошно** BOHrohshnoh
flower - **квітка** KVEETkah
flu - **грип** grihp
fly - **муха** MOOkhah
fog - **туман** tooMAHN
food - **їжа/їда** YEEzhah/yeeDAH
fool (f) - **дура** DOOrah
fool (m) - **дурень** DOOrehn'
foot (by,on) - **пішки** PEESHkih
foot (measure) - **фут** foot
foot; leg - **нога** nohGAH
for - **для** dlyah
for example - **наприклад** nahPRIHKlahd
for some reason - **чомусь** chohMOOS'
for the first time; first - **вперше** VPEHRsheh

forbid (to) - **забороняти** zahbohrohNYAHtih
forbidden (to be) - **заборонено** zahbohROHnehnoh
forehead - **чоло** chohLOH
foreign (adj) - **іноземний** eenohZEHMnihy
foreign; not one's own (adj) **чужий** chooZHIHY
foreigner/(f) - **іноземець/-земка** eenohZEHmehts'/-ZEHMkah
forest - **ліс** lees
forever - **назавжди** nahZAHVZHdih
forget (to) - **забувати** zahbooVAHtih
forgotten (adj) - **забутий** zahBOOtihy
fork - **виделка** vihDEHLkah
form, blank, survey - **анкета** ahnKEHtah
former; previous (adj) - **колишній/минулий** kohLIHSHneey/mihNOOlihy
forward; ahead - **вперед** vpehREHD
found, located (to be) - **знаходитися** znahKHOHdihtihsyah
fountain - **фонтан** fohnTAHN
fragile (adj) - **крихкий** krihkhKIHY
fragrant (adj) - **пахучий** pahKHOOchihy
free of charge (adj) - **безкоштовний** behzkohshTOHVnihy
free; vacant (adj) - **вільний** VEEL'nihy

freedom - свобода/воля
svohBOHdah/VOHlyah

freely; voluntarily - вільно
VEEL'noh

frequency - частота
chahstohTAH

fresh (adj) свіжий
SVEEzhihy

fried eggs - яєшня
yahYEHSHnyah

friend - друг droog

friendly; amicable (adj) -
дружно DROOZHnoh

friendship - дружба
DROOZHbah

from - від veed

front (and) - передній
pehREHDneey

frost - мороз mohROHZ

frozen (adj) - заморожений
zahmohROHzhehnihy

fruit - фрукт frookt

fry, roast, broil - смажити
SMAHzhihtih

frying pan - сковорода
skohvohrohDAH

full (of food); satiated (adj) -
ситий SIHtihy

full; complete (adj) - повний
POHVnihy

fully; completely; quite -
цілком tseelKOHM

funny (adj) - смішний
smeeshNIHY

fur (adj) хутряний
khootryahNIHY

fur - хутро KHOOTroh

fur coat - шуба SHOObah

fur hat - хутряна шапка
khootryahNAH SHAHPkah

furniture - меблі MEHBlee

further; father - далі DAHlee

future - майбутній
mayBOOTneey

G

game - гра grah

garage - гараж gahRAHZH

garden - сад sahd

garlic - часник chahsNIHK

garnet - гранат grahNAHT

gas - бензин behnZIHN

gas meter - газомір
gahzohMEER

gas station -
бензозаправочна
станція
behnzohzahPRAHvohchnah
STAHN tseeyah

gas tank - бензобак
behnzohBAHK

gastritis - гастрит gahsTRIHT

gate - ворота vohROHtah

general; common; total (adj) -
загальний
zahGAHL'nihy

generous (adj) - щедрий
SHCHEHDrihy

genitals - статеві органи
stahTEHvee OHRgahnih

geriatric (adj) -
геріатричний
gehreeahTRIHCHnihy

German (adj) - німецький
neeMEHTS'kihy

German/(f) - німець/-ка
NEEmehts'/NEEMkah

get, stand up (to) - вставати
vstahVAHtih

gift; souvenir - подарунок
pohdahROOnohk

gilded (adj) - позолочений
pohzohLOHchehnihy

girl - **дівчина/-ка**
DEEVchihnah/-kah
give (to) - **давати** dahVAHtih
give as a gift (to) - **дарувати**
dahrooVAHtih
glad; pleased - **радий**
RAHdihy
gland - **залоза** ZAHlohzah
glass (drinking) - **склянка**
SKLYAHNkah
glass - **скло** skloh
glasses - **окуляри**
ohkooLYAHrih
glory - **слава** SLAHvah
gloves - **рукавички**
rookahVIHCHkih
glue - **клей** kley
go by, past - **повз** pohvz
go, walk (to) - **ходити/йти**
khohDIHtih/ytih
goal; aim - **мета** mehTAH
God - **бог** bohg
gold - **золото** ZOHlohtoh
good (adj) - **хороший**
khohROHshihy
goodbye - **до побачення**
doh pohBAHchehnnyah
goodbye (call) - **будь здоров**
bood' zdohROHV
goose - **гуска** GOOSkah
goulash - **гуляш**
gooLYAHSH
government - **уряд** OOryahd
gradually - **поступово**
pohstooPOHvoh
graduate student/(f) -
аспірант/-ка
ahspeeRAHNT/-kah
grain - **зерно** zehrNOH
gram - **грам** grahm
grammer - **граматика**
grahMAHtihkah

grammatical case - **відмінок**
veedMEEnohk
granddaughter - **внучка**
VNOOCHkah
grandfather - **дідусь**
deeDOOS'
grandmother - **бабуся**
bahBOOsyah
grandson - **внук** vnook
grapes - **виноград**
vihnohGRAHD
grapefruit - **грейпфрут**
greypFROOT
grass - **трава** trahVAH
grave - **могила** mohGIHlah
greasy; oily; fatty (adj) -
. **жирний** ZHIHRnihy
great (adj) **великий**
vehLIHkihy
greedy (adj) - **жадібний**
ZHAHdeebnihy
green (adj) - **зелений**
zehLEHnihy
greengrocer - **зеленщик**
zehLEHNshchihk
grey (adj) - **сірий** SEErihy
grief - **горе** GOHreh
grocery store - **гастроном**
gahstrohNOHM
ground; dirt; earth - **земля**
zehmLYAH
group - **група** GROOpah
growth; height - **ріст** reest
growth; tumor - **наріст**
NAHreest
guard; sentry - **караул**
kahrahOOL
guest - **гість** geest'
guide - **гід** geed
guidebook - **путівник**
pooteevNIHK
guilt - **вина** vihNAH

guilty (adj) - **винний** VIHNnihy

guitar - **гітара** geeTAHrah

gynecologist - **гінеколог** geenehKOHlohg

gypsy - **циган** TSIHgahn

Н

habit - **звичка** ZVIHCHkah

hair - **волосся** vohLOHSsyah

haircut; trim - **стрижка** STRIHZHkah

hair-do - **зачіска** ZAHcheeskah

hairdresser; barber - **перекар** pehrooKAHR

hairdryer - **фен** fehn

half - **половина** pohlohVIHnah

half hour - **півгодини** peevgohDIHnih

hall; room - **зала** ZAHlah

hall monitor - **чергова** chehrGOHvah

ham - **шинка** SHIHNkah

hand; arm - **рука** rooKAHN

handshake - **потиск** POHtihsk

hanger - **вішалка** VEEshahlkah

happy; lucky (adj) - **щасливий** shchahsLIHvihy

hard (adj) - **твердий** tvehrDIHY

hard currency - **валюта** vahLYOOtah

hard-currency store - **Каштан** kahshTAHN

hardly; scarsely; barely - **ледве** LEHDveh

hare - **заяць** ZAHyahts'

harmful (adj) - **шкідливий** shkeedLIHvihy

hat - **шапка** SHAHPkah

hazel grouse - **рябчик** RYAHBchihk

he - **він** veen

head **голова** gohlohVAH

headache - **головний біль** gohlohvNIHY beel'

head cold - **насморк** NAHSmohrk

headlights - **фари** FAHrih

headphone; earmuff - **навушник** nahVOOSHnihk

health - **здоров'я** zdohROHVyah

healthy (adj) - **здоровий** zdohROHvihy

heart - **серце** SEHRtseh

heart attack - **сердечний приступ** sehrDEHCHnihy PRIHStoop

heavy (adj) - **тяжкий** tyahzhKIHY

hedgehog - **їжак** yeeZHAHK

heel - **каблук** kahbLOOK

height; altitude - **висота** vihsohTAH

hello - **добрий день** DOHBrihy dehn'

hello (on the telephone) - **алло** ahlLOH

help - **допомога** dohpohMOHgah

hemophilia - **гемофілія** gehmohfeeLEEyah

hemorrhage - **крововилив** krohvohVIHlihv

hemorrhoids - **геморой** gehmohROHY

hepatitis - **гепатит**

gehpahTIHT

her; its - **її** yeeYEE

here (is) - **ось** ohs'

here - **тут** toot

hernia - **грижа** GRIHzhah

hero - **герой** gehROY

herring - **оселедець**
ohsehLEHdehts'

hi - **привіт** prihVEET

hidden; secret (adj) -
схований
SKHOHvahnihy

high blood pressure -
гіпертонія
geepehrtohNEEyah

high; tall; lofty (adj) -
високий vihSOHkihy

highway - **траса/шосе**
TRAHsah/shohSEH

hindrance - **перешкода**
pehrehSHKOHdah

hip; thigh - **бедро** behdROH

his; its - **його** yohGOH

history; story - **історія**
eesTOOreeyah

hockey - **хокей** khohKEY

hold, keep, support (to) -
тримати trihMAHtih

hole - **діра** deeRAH

holiday - **свято** SVYAHtoh

holy; sacred (adj) - **святий**
svyahTIHY

homeland - **вітчизна**
veetCHIHZnah

homosexuality -
гомосексуалізм
gohmohsehksooahLEEZM

honest (adj) - **чесний**
CHEHSnihy

honey - **мед** mehd

hooligan - **хуліган**
khooleeGAHN

hope - **надія** nahDEEyah

horn; whistle - **гудок**
gooDOHK

horrible (adj) - **жахливий**
zhahkhLIHvihy

horrible; terrifying (adj) -
страшний strahshNIHY

horse - **кінь** keen'

horseradish - **хрін** khreen

hospitable (adj) - **гостинний**
gohsTIHNnihy

hospital - **лікарня**
leeKAHRnyah

hot; intense (adj) - **гарячий**
gahRYAHchihy

hot (weather) (adj) - **жаркий**
zhahrKIHY

hotel - **готель** gohTEHL'

hotel room; issue - **номер**
NOHmehr

hour - **година** gohDIHnah

house; home - **дім** deem

housewife - **господиня**
gohspohDIHnyah

how - **як** yahk

how far - **як далеко** yahk
dahLEHkoh

how long - **як довго** yahk
DOHVgoh

how much - **скільки**
SKEEL'kih

however; but - **однак/але**
ohdNAHK/ahLEH

humid (adj) - **вологий**
vohLOHgihy

humidity - **вологість**
vohLOHgeest'

humor - **гумор** GOOmohr

hundred - **сто/сотня** stoh/
SOHTnyah

hunger - **голод** GOHlohd

hungry (adj) - **голодний**

gohLOHDnihy
hurried; rushed (adj)
спішний SPEESHnihy
husband - **чоловік**
chohlohVEEK

I

I - **я** yah
ice - **лід** leed
ice cream - **морозиво**
mohROHzihvoh
icon - **ікона** eeKOHnah
idea - **ідея** eeDEHyah
identical (adj) - **однаковий**
ohdNAHkohvihy
identification - **посвідчення**
pohSVEEDchehnnyah
if; when - **якщо**
yahkSHCHOH
if; whether - **чи** chih
ill (to be) - **хворіти**
khvohREEtih
ill (to fall) - **захворіти**
zahkhvohREEtih
illegal (adj) - **незаконний**
nehzahKOHNnihy
illness; disease - **хвороба**
khvohROHbah
image; way; mode; manner -
образ OHBrahz
imagination - **уява** ooYAHvah
impatience - **нетерпіння**
nehtehrPEENnyah
importance - **важливість**
vahzhLIHveest'
important (adj) - **важливий**
vahzhLIHvihy
impossible; one can not -
неможливо
nehmohzhLIHvoh
impression - **враження**

VRAHzhehnnyah
improper; indecent (adj)
непристойний
nehprihSTOYnihy
in advance - **заздалегідь**
zahzdahlehGEED'
in front; ahead - **перед/**
попереду PEHrehd/
pohPEHrehdoo
in general - **взагалі**
vzahgahLEE
in order to - **щоби**
SHCHOHbih
in the distance - **вдалині**
vdahlihNEE
in vain; for nothing - **даремно**
dahREHMnoh
in,at,for,to - **в** v
inaudible (adj) - **нечутний**
nehCHOOTnihy
inch - **дюйм** dyooym
incident - **випадок**
VIHpahdohk
incidentally; by the way - **до**
речі doh REHchee
income - **прибуток**
prihBOOtohk
incomprehensible (adj) -
незрозумілий
nehzrohzooMEElihy
increase - **збільшення**
ZBEEL'shehnnyah
incredible; unbelievable -
неймовірний
neymohVEERnihy
independence -
незалежність
nehzahLEHZHneest'
independent (adj) -
самостійний
sahmohSTEEYnihy
indifferent (adj) - **байдужий**

bayDOOzhihy

indigestion - **розлад шлунку** ROHZlahd SHLOONkoo

inexpensive; cheap - **дешевий** dehSHEHvihy

inexperienced (adj) - **недосвідчений** nehdohSVEEDchehnihy

infection - **зараження** zahRAHzhehnnyah

inflammation - **запалення** zahPAHlehnnyah

influence - **вплив** vplihv

influential (adj) - **впливовий** vplihVOHvihy

injection - **укол** ooKOHL

ink - **чорнило** chohrNIHloh

innocent (adj) - **невинний** nehVIHNnihy

inscription - **напис** NAHpihs

insect - **комаха** kohMAHkhah

insect repellent - **засіб від комарів** ZAHseeb veed kohmahREEV

inside - **усередині** oosehREHdihnee

insomnia - **безсоння** behzSOHNnyah

instead of - **замість** ZAHmeest'

institution - **заклад/ установа** ZAHKlahd/ oostahNOHvah

instructions - **інструкція** eensTROOKtseeyah

insufficient - **недостатньо** nehdohSTAHTnyoh

intention - **намір** NAHmeer

interesting (adj) - **цікавий** tseeKAHvihy

intermission - **антракт** ahnTRAKT

internal (adj); inner - **внурішній** VNOOTreeshneey

international (adj) - **міжнародний** meezhnahROHDnihy

interpreter - **перекладач** pehrehklahDAHCH

intestine - **кишка** kihshKAH

Intourist office - **бюро Інтуриста** byooROH eentooRIHStah

introduction - **вступ** vstoop

invitation - **запрошення** zahPROHshehnnyah

iodine - **йод** yohd

iron (to) - **прасувати** prahsooVAHtih

iron - **утюг** ooTYOOG

irritation - **дратування** drahtooVAHNnyah

island - **острів** OHStreev

issue; edition; output - **випуск** VIHpoosk

issue; number - **номер** NOHmehr

J

jam - **варення** vahREHNnyah

janitor; yardsman - **прибиральник** prihbihRAHL'nihk

jar; can - **банка** BAHNkah

jeans - **джінси** DZHEENsih

Jew/(f) - **єврей/-ка** yehvREY/-kah

jewel - **дорогоцінність** dohrohgohTSEENneest'

jewelry (adj) - **ювелірний** yoovehLEERnihy

180

Jewish; Hebrew (adj) -
єврейський
yehvREYS'kihy
joke - жарт zhahrt
journalist - журналіст
zhoornahLEEST
joyful; joyous (adj) -
радісний RAHdeesnhy
juice - сік seek

K

kerchief - хустка
KHOOSTkah
key - ключ klyooch
kidney - нирка NIHRkah
kilogram - кілограм
keelohGRAHM
kilometer - кілометр
keelohMEHTR
kind; good (adj) - добрий
DOHBrihy
kind; sort - сорт sohrt
kindness - доброта
dohbrohTAH
kiosk - кіоск keeOHSK
kiss - поцілунок
pohtseeLOOnohk
kitchen - кухня
KOOKHnyah
knee - коліно kohLEEnoh
knife - ніж neezh
knock - стук stook
know (to) - знати ZNAHtih
knowledge - знання
znahnNYAH
known (well) (adj) - відомий
veeDOHmihy
kopeck - копійка
kohPEEYkah
kosher (adj) - кошерний
kohSHEHRnihy

kvass (fermented drink) - квас
kvahs

L

ladies (adj) - дамський
DAHMs'kihy
lake - озеро OHzehroh
lame (adj) - кривий
krihVIHY
lamp - лампа LAHMpah
landing - посадка
pohSAHDkah
language; tongue - мова
MOHvah
larger; bigger; greater -
більше BEEL'sheh
last; latest (adj) - останній
ohsTAHNneey
last (to) - продовжитися
prohDOHVzhihtihsyah
last name; sir name -
прізвище
PREEZvihshcheh
late (adj) - пізній PEEZneey
late (to be) - спізнитися
speezNIHtihsyah
later - пізніше peezNEEsheh
laughter - сміх smeekh
laundry; linen - білизна
beeLIHZnah
law - закон zahKOHN
lawyer - адвокат
ahdvohKAHT
laxative - проносне
prohnohsNEH
leadership - керівництво
kehreevNIHTStvoh
leaf; sheet (of paper) - листок
lihsTOHK
leather (anj) - шкіряний
shkeeryahNIHY

181

leave, go out, exit (to) - **виходити** vihKHOHdihtih

lecture - **лекція** LEHKtseeyah

left (direction) - **лівий** LEEvihy

leg - **нога** nohGAH

legal; legitimate (adj) - **законний** zahKOHNnihy

lemon - **лимон** LIHmohn

lemonade - **лимонад** lihmohNAHD

length - **довжина** dohvzhihNAH

less - **менше** MEHNsheh

lesson - **урок** ooROHK

let's go ahead! - **давай** dahVAHY

letter - **лист** lihst

letter of the alphabet - **літера** LEEtehrah

level - **рівень** REEvehn'

library - **бібліотека** beebleeohTEHkah

lid; cover - **кришка** KRIHSHkah

lie, tell lies (to) - **брехати** brehKHAHtih

life - **життя** zhihtTYAH

light - **світло** SVEETloh

light bulb - **лампочка** LAHMpohchkah

light-(color) - **світло-** SVEETloh

light; bright (adj) - **світлий** SVEETlihy

lightning - **блискавка** BLIHSkahvkah

lilac - **бузок** booZOHK

line - **черга** CHEHRgah

lip - **губа** gooBAH

list - **список** SPIHsohk

liter - **літр** leetr

literature - **література** leetehrahTOOrah

little; not enough - **мало** MAHloh

little; not much - **небагато** nehbahGAHtoh

live (to) - **жити** ZHIHtih

liver (anatomy) - **печінка** pehCHEENkah

liver (the food) - **печінка** pehCHEENkah

loaf of bread - **буханець** bookhahNEHTS'

lobby - **фойе** fohYEH

local (adj) - **місцевий** meesTSEHvihy

lock - **замок** zahMOHK

long (measure) (adj) - **довгий** DOHVgihy

long (time) (adj) - **тривалий** trihVAHlihy

long ago - **давно** dahvNOH

long time (for a) - **задовго** zahDOHVgoh

long underwear - **кальсони** kahl'SOHnih

look (to) - **дивитися** dihVIHtihsyah

look; glance - **погляд** POHGlyahd

lose (to) - **загубити** zahgooBIHtih

loud (adj) - **голосний** gohlohsNIHY

love (to) - **кохати** kohKHAHtih

love - **кохання** kohKHAHNnyah

lower (adj) - **нижній** NIHZHneey

lox - сьо́мга SYOHMgah
luggage - бага́ж bahGAHZH
lunch - по́лудник POHloodnihk
lunch (to eat) - по́лудничати POHloodnihchahtih
lungs - легені lehGEHnee
luxurious (adj) розкі́шний rohzKEESHnihy

M

magazine - журна́л zhoorNAHL
maid - поко́ївка pohkohYEEVkah
mail; post office - по́шта POSHtah
mailbox - пошто́ва скри́нька pohshTOHvah SKRIHNkah
main; principal (adj) - головни́й gohlohvNIHY
majority - бі́льшість BEEL'sheest'
make-up - косме́тика kohsMEHtihkah
malachite - малахі́т mahlahKHEET
malicious; spiteful (adj) - зло́бний ZLOHBnihy
man - чолові́к chohlohVEEK
manager - адміністра́тор/ дире́ктор dihREHKtohr
manager - заві́дуючий zahVEEdooyoochihy
manuscript - руко́пис rooKOHpihs
map (of the city) - план plahn
map - ка́рта KAHRtah
marinated (adj) -
маринований mahrihNOHvahnihy
market - база́р bahZAHR
marriage - шлюб shlyoob
married (for woman) - за́мужем ZAHmoozhehm
married (for men) - одру́жений ohDROOzhehnihy
match - сірни́к seerNIHK
matroshka doll (wooden, nested doll) - матрьо́шка mahTRYOHSHkah
matter; affair; business - спра́ва SPRAHvah
mausoleum - мавзоле́й mahvzohLEY
may; can - мо́жна MOHZHnah
mean (to) - зна́чить ZNAHchiht'
meaning; sense - зна́чення ZNAHchenhhyah
meanwhile - по́ки POHkih
measure; extent; degree - мі́ра MEErah
meat - м'я́со MYAHsoh
meat loaf - руле́т rooLEHT
meatballs - тюфте́лі tyoofTEHlee
mechanism - механі́зм mehkhahNEEZM
medical treatment - лікува́ння leekooVAHNnyah
medicine - лі́ки LEEkih
meet (to) - зустріча́ти zoostreeCHAHtih
meeting - збо́ри ZBOHrih
meeting; encounter - зу́стріч ZOOStreech
melon - ди́ня DIHnyah

183

member - член chlehn
memory - пам/ять PAHMyaht'
memory; recollection - спомин SPOHmihn
men's (adj) - чоловічий chohlohVEEchihy
menstruation - менструація mehnstrooAHtseeyah
mental; emotional (adj) - душевний dooSHEHVnihy
menu - меню mehNYOO
merchandise - товар tohVAHR
meter - метр mehtr
middle - середина sehrehDIHnah
middle; average (adj) - середній sehREHDneey
midnight - північ PEEVneech
military (adj) - військовий veeys'KOHvihy
milk - молоко mohlohKOH
million- мільйон meel'YOHN
minute - хвилина khvihLIHnah
mirror - дзеркало LYOOStehrkoh
misfortune - біда beeDAH
mistake - помилка POHmihlkah
misunderstanding - непорозуміння nehpohrohzooMEEN'nyah
mitten - рукавиця rookahVIHtsyah
modest (adj) - скромний SKROHMnihy
monastery - монастир/лавра mohnahsTIHR/LAHVrah

money - гроші GROHshee
money order - грошовий переказ grohshohVIHY pehREHkahz
month - місяць MEEsyahts'
monthly (adj) - щомісячно shchohMEEsyahchnoh
monument - пам'ятник PAHMyahtnihk
mood - настрій NAHStreey
moon - місяць MEEsyahts'
more - більше BEEL'sheh
morning (adj) - ранковий rahnKOHvihy
morning - ранок RAHnohk
mosquito - комар kohMAHR
mother - мати MAHtih
motor - мотор mohTOHR
motorcycle - мотоцикл mohtohTSIHKL
motorist - автомобіліст ahvtohmohbeeLEEST
mountain - гора gohRAH
mouse - миша MIHshah
mouth - рот roht
movement; traffic - рух rookh
movie - фільм feel'm
movie theater - кінотеатр keenohtehAHTR
movie; the cinema - кіно keeNOH
Mr. (pre-revolutionary) - пан pahn
Mrs. (pre-revolutionary) - пані PAHnee
much; a lot - багато bahGAHtoh
much, far - набагато nahbahGAHtoh
multicolored (adj) - багатобарвний bahgahtohBAHRVnihy

184

murder - **убивство**
ooBIHVstvoh
murderer - **убивця**
ooBIHVtsyah
muscle - **м'яз** myahz
museum - **музей** mooZEY
mushrooms - **гриби** grihBIH
music - **музика** MOOzihkah
must - **треба/мусиш**
TREHbah/MOOsish
mustache - **вуса** VOOsah
mustard - **гірчиця**
geerCHIHtsyah
mutton; lamb - **баранина**
bahRAHnihnah
mutton soup - **харчо**
KHAHRchoh
mutual understanding -
взаєморозуміння
vzahyehmohrohzooMEENnyah
mystery (story/movie) -
детектив dehtehkTIHV

N

nail, tack - **цвях** tsvyahkh
naked (adj) - **голий** GOHlihy
name (first) - **ім'я** eemYAH
name (last); sir name -
прізвище
PREEZvihshcheh
name; title - **назва** NAHZvah
napkin - **серветка**
sehrVEHTkah
narrow (adj) - **вузький**
vooz'KIHY
nasty; foul; vile (adj) -
гидкий gihdKIHY
nation - **нація** NAHtseeyah
national; folk (adj) -
народний nahROHDnihy
nationality -

національність
nahtseeohNAHL'neest'
native (adj) - **рідний**
REEDnihy
naturally - **природно**
prihROHDnoh
nature - **природа**
prihROHdah
nausea - **нудота** nooDOHtah
navy - **флот** floht
near; nearby - **поблизу**
pohBLIHzoo
nearby; not far off (adj) -
недалекий
nehdahLEHkihy
nearest; next (adj) -
найближчий
nayBLIHZHchihy
neat, punctual (adj) -
охайний ohKHAYnihy
necessary; essential (adj) -
необхідний
nehohbKHEEDnihy
neck - **шия** SHIHyah
necklace - **намисто**
nahMIHStoh
need - **потреба** pohTREHbah
needle - **голка** GOHLkah
negative (adj) - **негативний**
nehgahTIHVnihy
negotiations - **переговори**
pehrehgohVOHrih
neighbor - **сусід** sooSEED
nephew - **племінник**
plehMEENnihk
nerve - **нерв** nehrv
nervous; irritable (adj) -
нервовий nehrVOHvihy
neutral (adj) - **нейтральний**
neyTRAHL'nihy
never - **ніколи** neeKOHlih
new (adj) - **новий** nohVIHY

New Year - **Новий рік**
   nohVIHY reek
news - **новина** nohvihNAH
newspaper - **газета**
   gahZEHtah
next (adj) - **наступний**
   nahSTOOPnihy
nice; sweet; dear; darling (adj) -
   милий MIHlihy
niece - **племінниця**
   plehMEENnihtsyah
night - **ніч** neech
no - **ні** nee
no one - **ніхто** neeKHTOH
no way - **ніяк** neeYAHK
noise - **шум** shoom
noisy (adj) - **шумний**
   SHOOMnihy
nonalcoholic -
   безалкогольний
   behzahlkohGOHL'nihy
nonsense - **нісенітниця**
   neesehNEETnihtsyah
nonstop (of a flight) -
   безпосадочний
   behzpohSAHdohchnihy
noon - **південь** PEEVdehn'
normal (adj) - **нормальний**
   nohrMAHL'nihy
north - **північ** PEEVneech
northern (adj) - **північний**
   peevNEECHnihy
nose - **ніс** nees
not - **не** neh
not long ago; recently -
   недавно nehDAHVnoh
notebook - **зошит** ZOHshiht
nothing - **нічого**
   neeCHOHgoh
noticeably; visibly - **помітно**
   pohMEETnoh
notify (to) - **сповіщати**
   spohveeSHCHAHtih
novel - **роман** rohMAHN
now - **зараз/тепер** ZAHrahz/
   tehPEHR
number - **число** chihsLOH
numeral - **цифра** TSIHFrah
nurse - **медсестра**
   mehdsehsTRAH
nut - **горіх** gohREEKH

O

oatmeal - **вівсянка**
   veevSYAHNkah
oats - **овес** ohVEHS
objection - **заперечення**
   zahpehREHchehnnyah
obligatory; mandatory (adj) -
   обов'язковий
   ohbohvyahzKOHvihy
obstetrician - **акушер**
   ahkooSHEHR
obvious (adj) - **очевидний**
   ohchehVIHDnihy
occupation; work; studies -
   заняття zahNYAHTtyah
ocean - **океан** ohkehAHN
of course - **звичайно**
   zvihCHAYnoh
offense; insult - **образа**
   ohbRAHzah
offer; proposal; suggestion -
   пропозиція
   prohpohZIHtseeyah
office - **контора** konTOHrah
office; bureau - **бюро**
   byooROO
often - **часто** CHAHStoh
ok - **гаразд** gahRAHZD
old (adj) - **старий** stahRIHY
older; elder (adj) - **старший**
   STAHRshihy

olive - **маслина** mahsLIHnah

on; in - **на** nah

on the contrary; the other way around - **навпаки** nahvpahKIH

on the left - **наліво** nahLEEvoh

on the right - **направо** nahPRAHvoh

on time - **вчасно** VCHAHSnoh

once; one day - **одного дня** ohdNOHgoh dnyah

one and a half - **півтора** peevtohRAH

one-way (ticket) - **в один кінець** v ohDIHN keeNEHTS'

onion - **цибуля** - tsihBOOlyah

only - **тільки** TEEL'kih

open (adj) - **відчинений** veedCHIHnehnihy

opera - **опера** OHpehrah

opera glasses - **бінокль** beeNOHKL'

operator - **телефоністка** tehlehfohNEESTkah

opinion - **думка** DOOMkah

opportunity - **можливість** mohzhLIHveest'

opposite; facing - **напроти** nahPROHtih

optician - **оптик** OHPtihk

or - **чи/або** chih/ahBOH

oral; verbal (adj) - **усний** OOSnihy

orange (adj) - **оранжовий** ohRAHNzhohvihy

orange (fruit) - **апельсин** ahpehl'SIHN

orchestra - **оркестр** ohrKEHSTR

order; sequence - **порядок** pohRYAHdohk

order (to) - **замовити** zahMOHvihtih

origin - **походження** pohKHOHDzhehnnyah

original (adj) - **первісний/ початковий** PEHRveesnihy/ pohchahtKOHvihy

orthodox (adj) - **православний** prahvohSLAHVnihy

other; another; the other - **другий** DROOgihy

out-raged (adj) - **обурений** ohBOOrehnihy

outpatient clinic - **амбулаторія** ahmboolahTOHreeyah

outside; out of - **поза** POHzah

outward; external (adj) - **зовнішній** ZOHVneeshneey

over and above; in access of - **понад** POHnahd

overcast (adj) - **похмурий** pohKHMOOrihy

oxygen - **кисень** KIHsehn'

P

pacifier - **соска** SOHSkah

pack; bundle - **пачка** PAHCHkah

package - **посилка** pohSIHLkah

packet; package - **пакет** pahKEHT

page - **сторінка** stohREENkah

pain - **біль** beel'
painkiller -
   болезаспокійливий
   засіб
   bohlehzahspohKEEYlihvihy
   ZAHseeb
painting - **живопис**
   zhihYOHpihs
pair - **пара** PAHrah
palace - **палац** pahLAHTS
pale (adj) - **блідий** bleeDIHY
palm (anatomy) - **долоня**
   dohLOHnyah
pancake - **млинець**
   mlihNEHTS'
pants - **брюки** BRYOOkih
paper - **папір** pahPEER
parents - **батьки** baht'KIH
park - **парк** pahrk
parking lot - **стоянка для**
   машин stohYAHNkah
   dlyah mahSHIHN
parsley - **петрушка**
   pehtROOSHkah
part - **частина** chahsTIHnah
participation - **участь**
   OOchahst'
passage; excerpt -
   уривок ooRIHvohk
passenger - **пасажир**
   pahsahZHIHR
passionate (adj) -
   пристрасний
   PRIHSTrahsnihy
passport - **паспорт**
   PAHSpohrt
past (adj) - **минулий**
   mihNOOlihy
pastry - **тістечко**
   TEEStehchkoh
patient (adj) - **терпеливий**
   tehrpehLIHvihy

patient - **пацієнт**
   pahtseeYEHNT
patronymic - **по-батькові**
   poh VAHT'kohvee
pay (to) - **платити**
   plahTIHtih
pay phone - **телефон-**
   автомат tehlehFOHN-
   ahvtohMAHT
peace - **мир** mihr
peach - **персик** PEHRsihk
pear - **груша** GROOshah
pearl - **перлина** pehrLIHnah
peas - **горох** gohROHKH
peasant's hut; cabin - **хата**
   KHAHtah
pediatrician - **педіатр**
   pehdeeAHTR
pen - **ручка** ROOCHkah
pencil - **олівець**
   ohleeVEHTS'
penicillin - **пеніцилін**
   pehneetsihLEEN
people (a) - **народ** nahROHD
people - **люди** LYOOdih
pepper - **перець** PEHrehts'
pepper vodka - **перцовка**
   pehrTSOHVkah
performance; play - **вистава**
   vihsTAHvah
performer - **актор** ahkTOHR
perfume - **парфума**
   pahrFOOmah
perhaps - **можливо**
   mohzhLIHvoh
period of twenty-four hours;
   day - **доба** dohBAH
permanent wave - **перманент**
   pehrmahNEHNT
permission; permit - **дозвіл**
   DOHZveel
person - **особа** ohSOHbah

personal; private (adj) -
особистий
ohsohBIHStihy

photograph - **фотографія**
fohtohGRAHfeeyah

phrasebook - **розмовник**
rohzMOHVnihk

phrase; sentence - **фраза**
FRAHzah

picture; drawing - **картина**
kahrTIHnah

pie - **пиріг** pihREEG

piece - **шматок** shmahTOHK

pig - **свиня** svihNYA

pigeon; dove - **голуб**
GOHloob

pike - **щука** SHCHOOkah

pilaf - **плов** plohv

pill - **пилюля** pihLYOOlyah

pill; tablet- **таблетка**
tahbLEHTkah

pillow - **подушка**
pohDOOSHkah

pillowcase - **наволочка**
NAHvohlohchkah

pin - **шпилька** SHPIHL'kah

pineapple - **ананас**
ahnahNAHS

pipe - **люлька** LYOOL'kah

pity - **жалість** ZHAHleest'

place; seat; site - **місце**
MEEStseh

plant - **рослина** rohsLIHnah

plate - **тарілка** tahREELkah

play (to) - **грати** GRAHtih

play; drama - **п'єса** PYEHsah

playwright - **драматург**
drahmahTOORG

pleasant (adj) - **приємний**
prihYEHMnihy

please - **будь ласка** bood'
LAHSkah

pleasure - **задоволення**
zahdohVOHlehnnyah

plum - **слива** SLYHvah

plumber - **водопровідник**
vohdohprohVEEDnihk

pneumonia - **запалення
легень** zahPAHlehnnyah
lehGEHN'

pocket - **кишеня**
kihSHEHnyah

poet - **поет** pohEHT

poetry - **поезія** pohEHzeeyah

point; station; center - **пункт**
poonkt

poison - **отрута** ohTROOtah

police - **міліція**
meeLEEtseeyah

policeman - **міліціонер**
meeleetseeohNEHR

polish; lacquer - **лак** lahk

polite; courteous (adj)
ввічливий
VVEECHlihvihy

politics - **політика**
pohLEEtihkah

pond - **ставок** stahVOHK

pool - **басейн** bahSEYN

poor (adj) - **бідний**
BEEDnihy

poor-quality (adj) -
недоброякісний
nehdohbrohYAHkeesnihy

poppy - **мак** mahk

population - **населення**
nahSEHlehnnyah

pork - **свинина** svihNIHnah

port - **порт** pohrt

portable (adj) - **переносний**
pehrehnohsNIHY

porter - **носильник**
nohSIHL'nihk

portrait - **портрет** pohrTREHT

positive; affirmative (adj) - **позитивний** pohzihTIHVnihy

postcard - **поштова картка** pohshTOHvah KAHRTkah

poster - **плакат** plahKAHT

poster; play bill - **афіша** ahFEEshah

post office (main branch) - **поштамт** pohshTAHMT

post office - **пошта** POHSHtah

pot; saucepan - **каструля** kahsTROOlyah

pot cheese - **сир** sihr

potato - **картопля** kahrTOHPlyah

pound - **фунт** foont

powder - **порох** POHrohkh

powerful (adj) - **могутній/ сильний** mohGOOTneey/ SIHL'nihy

prayer book - **молитвеник** mohLIHTvehnihk

pregnant (adj) **вагітна** vahGEETnah

prepare (to) - **готувати** gohtooVAHtih

prescription - **рецепт** rehTSEHPT

present - **подарунок** pohdahROOnohk

present; real; true (adj) **теперішній/ справжній** tehPEHreeshneey/ SPRAHVZHneey

pressure (physical) - **натиск** NAHtihsk

pretty (adj) - **гарний** GAHRnihy

price - **ціна** tseeNAH

priest; clergyman - **священик** svyahSHCHEHnihk

prison - **в'язниця** vyahzNIHtsyah

probably - **напевно/ можливо** nahPEHVnoh/ mohzhLIHvoh

problem - **проблема** prohbLEHmah

processing - **оформлення** ohFOHRMlehnnyah

profession - **професія** prohFEHseeyah

professor - **професор** prohFEHsohr

profitable; favorable (adj) - **вигідний** VIHgeednihy

prognosis; forecast - **прогноз** prohGNOHZ

promise - **обіцянка** ohBEEtsyahnkah

pronunciation - **вимова** VIHmohvah

proper (adj) - **правильний** PRAHvihl'nihy

property - **власність** VLAHSneest'

proud (adj) - **гордий** GOHRdihy

proverb - **прислів'я** prihSLEEVyah

public bath - **баня** BAHnyah

puddle - **калюжа** kahLYOOzhah

pulse - **пульс** pool's

punishment - **покарання** pohkahRAHNnyah

purchase - **купівля** kooPEEVlyah

push button; snap - **кнопка** KNOHPkah

190

pajamas · **пижа́ма**
pihZHAHmah

Q

quality - **я́кість** YAHkeest'
quantity - **кі́лькість**
  KEEL'keest'
quarter - **чверть** chvehrt'
question - **пита́ння**
  pihTAHNnyah
quickly! - **шви́дше!**
  SHVIHDsheh
quickly; rapidly (adj) -
  швидки́й shvihdKIHY
quiet (adj) - **ти́хий** TIHkhihy
quote - **цита́та** tsihTAHtah

R

rabbi - **раві́н** rahVEEN
rabbit - **крі́лик** KREElihk
radio - **ра́діо** RAHdeeoh
radio station - **радіоста́нція**
  rahdeeohSTAHNtseeyah
radish - **реди́ска** rehDIHSkah
rail; track - **ре́йка** REYkah
railroad car - **ваго́н** vaGOHN
rain - **дощ** dohshch
raincoat - **плащ** plahshch
raisin - **родзи́нка**
  rohDZIHNkah
rare; infrequent (adj) - **рідки́й**
  reedKIHY
rarely - **рі́дко** REEDkoh
raspberries - **мали́на**
  mahLIHnah
rate of exchange - **валю́тний**
  курс vahLYOOTnihy
  koors
rather; fairly - **до́сить**
  DOHsight'

raw (adj) - **сири́й** sihRIHY
razor - **бри́тва** BRIHTvah
razor blades - **ле́за** LEHzah
read (to) - **чита́ти**
  chihTAHtih
reader - **чита́ч** chihTAHch
ready (adj) - **гото́вий**
  hohTOHvihy
real; actual; effective (adj) -
  ді́йсний DEEYSnihy
really; truly - **ді́йсно**
  DEEYSnoh
really?; is that so? - **спра́вді?**
  SPRAHVdee
rear; back; hind (adj) - **за́дній**
  ZAHDneey
reason - **причи́на**
  prihCHIHhah
reception - **прийо́м**
  prihYOHM
recommend (to) - **ра́дити**
  RAHdihtih
record - **грампласти́нка**
  grahmplahsTIHNkah
recording (record/tape) -
  за́пис ZAHpihs
red (adj) - **черво́ний**
  chehrVOHnihy
reference; information -
  дові́дка DOHveedkah
refrigerator - **холоди́льник**
  khohlohDIHL'nihk
refusal - **відмо́ва**
  veedMOHvah
region; area; field; domain -
  о́бласть OHBlahst'
registration - **реєстра́ція**
  rehyehSTRAHtseeyah
relationship; connection -
  відно́шення
  veedNOHshehnnyah
relatives - **ро́дичі**

ROHdihchee
reluctantly - **неохо́че**
nehohKHOHcheh
remainder - **за́лишок**
ZAHlihshohk
rent (to) - **взя́ти напрока́т**
VZYAHtih nahprohKAHT
repeat (to) - **повтори́ти**
pohvtohRIHtih
republic - **респу́бліка**
rehsPOOBleekah
request - **проха́ння**
prohKHAHNnyah
research - **дослі́дження**
dohSLEEDzhehnnyah
reserved (on a train) (adj) -
плацка́ртний
plahtsKAHRTnihy
resident - **жи́тель** ZHIHtehl'
resort - **куро́рт** kooROHRT
respected (adj) - **шано́вний**
shahNOHVnihy
rest - **відпочи́нок**
veedpohCHIHnohk
restaurant - **рестора́н**
rehstohRAHN
return (to) - **поверта́ти**
pohvehrTAHtih
return; reverse; opposite (adj)
зворо́тний
zvohROHTnihy
reward - **нагоро́да**
nahgohROHdah
rheumatism - **ревмати́зм**
rehvmahTIHZM
rib - **ребро́** rehbROH
rice - **рис** rihs
rich (adj) - **бога́тий**
bohGAHtihy
ride; drive - **їзда́** yeezDAH
right; correct (adj) -
пра́вильний

PRAHvihl'nihy
right (direction) - **пра́вий**
PRAHvihy
ripe; mature (adj) - **зрі́лий**
ZREElihy
river - **піка́** reeKAN
road - **доро́га** dohROHgah
roast beef - **ро́стбиф**
ROHSTbihf
robe - **хала́т** khahLAHT
rock - **ка́мінь** KAHmeen'
role; part - **роль** rohl'
roll; bun - **бу́лка** BOOLkah
roof - **дах** dahkh
room - **кімна́та** keemNAHtah
rope; string; cord - **вірьо́вка**
veeRYOHVkah
rose - **троя́нда** trohYAHNdah
roundtrip (ticket) - **туди́ й
наза́д** tooDIH y nahZAHD
row - **ряд** ryahd
rubber (adj) - **гу́мовий**
GOOmohvihy
rubbers; galoshes - **кало́ші**
kahLOHshee
ruble - **рубль** roobl'
ruby - **рубі́н** rooBEEN
rude; course (adj) - **гру́бий**
GROObihy
rug - **ки́лим** KIHlihm
rule - **пра́вило**
PRAHvihloh
run (to) - **бі́гати**
BEEgahtih
run; race - **біг** beeg
Russian (adj) - **росі́йський**
rohSEEYS'kihy
Russian/(f) - **росія́нин/
росія́нка** rohseeYAHnihn/
rohseeYAHNkah
rye - **жи́то** ZHIHtoh
rhyme- **ри́ма** RIHmah

S

saccharin - **сахари́н**
sahkhahRIHN
sad; melancholy (adj) -
су́мний soomNIHY
safe - **сейф/вогнетривка́
ша́фа** seyf
safe (adj) - **безпе́чний**
behzPEHCHnihy
safely; without mishap -
благополу́чно
blahgohpohLOOCHnoh
safety pin - **англі́йська
шпи́лька**
ahngLEEYS'kah
SHPIHL'kah
sail boat - **вітри́льний
чо́вен** veetRIHL'nihy
CHOHvehn
salad - **сала́т** sahLAHT
sale - **про́даж/ски́дка**
PROHdahzh/SKIHDkah
salesman - **продаве́ць**
prohdahVEHTS'
salmon **лососи́на**
lohsohSIHnah
salt - **сіль** seel'
salty (adj) - **соло́ний**
sohlohNIHY
samovar - **самова́р**
sahmohVAHR
sample; model; pattern -
взіре́ць vzeeREHTS'
sand - **пісо́к** peeSOHK
sandals - **босоні́жки**
bohsohNEEZHkih
sandwich - **бутербро́д**
bootehrBROHD
sanitary day (one day a month
when stores/museums are
closed for cleaning) -

саніта́рний день
sahneeTAHRnihy dehn'
sapphire - **сапфі́р** sahpFEER
sarcasm - **сарка́зм**
sahrKAHZM
satire - **сати́ра** sahTIHrah
satisfaction - **задово́лення**
zahdohVOHlehnnyah
sauce; gravy - **со́ус** SOHoos
sausage - **ковбаса́**
kohvbahSAH
save, keep (to); to guard -
берегти́ behrehgTIH
scarf - **шарф** shahrf
schedule; timetable - **ро́зклад**
ROHZklahd
scholar; scientist - **вче́ний**
VCHEHnihy
school - **шко́ла** SHKOHlah
school vacation - **кані́кули**
kahNEEkoolih
scissors - **но́жиці**
NOHzhihtsee
screen - **екра́н** ehkRAHN
sculpture - **скульпту́ра**
skool'pTOOrah
sea - **мо́ре** MOHreh
sea food - **дари́ мо́ря** dahRIH
MOHryah
seat - **мі́сце** MEEStseh
second (time measure)
секу́нда sehKOONdah
secondhand book dealer -
букі́ніст bookeeNEEST
secretary - **секрета́р**
sehkrehTAHR
section - **се́кція** SEHKtseeyah
sedative - **заспокі́йливий
за́сіб** zahspohKEEYlihvihy
ZAHseeb
see (to) - **ба́чити** BAHchihtih
self confident (adj) -

самовпе́внений
sahmohVPEHVnehnihy
self-service -
самообслуго́вування
sahmohohbslooGOHvoovahnnyah
sell (to) - прода́ти
prohDAHtih
send (to) - наділа́ти
nahdeeSLAHtih
sensibly; rationally (adj) -
розу́мно rohZOOVnoh
sensitive (adj) - чутли́вий
chootLIHvihy
separately; individually -
окре́мо ohkREHmoh
serious (adj) - серйо́зний
sehrYOHZnihy
service station -
автозапра́вочна
ста́нція
ahvtohzahPRAHvohchnah
STAHNtseeyah
set (of dishes or silverware) -
серві́з sehrVEEZ
set - компле́кт
kohmPLEHKT
shadow - тінь teen'
shame - со́ром SOHrohm
shampoo - шампу́нь
shahmPOON'
share, divide (to) - діли́ти
deeLIHtih
share; lot - до́ля DOHlyah
sharp; pungent; keen (adj) -
го́стрий GOHSTrihy
shave (to); get a shave -
голи́тися gohLIHtihsyah
she - вона́ vohNAH
sheet - простира́дло
prohstihRAHDloh
ship - корабе́ль
kohrahBEHL'

ship; steamship - паропла́в
pahrohPLAHV
shirt - соро́чка
sohROHCHkah
shish kebob - шашли́к
shahshLIHK
shoe laces - шнурки́
shnoorKIH
shoemaker - ремо́нт взуття́
rehMOHNT vzootTYAH
shoes - взуття́ vzootTYAH
short (adj) - коро́ткий
kohROHTkihy
shortage; scarcity; defect;
deficience недоста́ча
nehdohSTAHchah
shorts - шо́рти SHOHRtih
should; must; ought to -
пови́нен pohVIHnehn
shoulder - плече́ plehCHEH
shout; cry - крик krihk
show (to) - показа́ти
pohkahZAHtih
shower - душ doosh
sick (adj) - хво́рий
KHVOHrihy
side - сторона́/бік
stohrohNAH/beek
side street - прову́лок
prohVOOlohk
side walk - тротуа́р
trohtooAHR
sideways - вбік vbeek
sight; vision - ба́чення
BAHchehnnyah
sign (to) - підписа́ти
peedpihSAHtih
sign; signal - знак znahk
sign up (to) - записа́тися
zahpihSAHtihsyah
signature - пі́дпис PEEDpihs
silence - тишина́

194

tihshihNAH

silver (adj) - **срібний**
SREEBnihy

silver - **срібло** SREEBloh

similar; like (adj) - **подібний**
pohDEEBnihy

simple; easy (adj) - **простий**
prohsTIHY

simply - **просто** PROHStoh

simultaneous (adj) -
одночасний
ohdnohCHAHSnihy

sin - **гріх** greekh

since - **з** z

sincere (adj) - **щирий**
SHCHIHrihy

singer - **співак** speeVAHK

sink (bathroom) - **раковина**
RAHkohvihnah

sister - **сестра** sehstRAH

sister-in-law - **невістка**
nehVEESTkah

situation; condition - **стан**
stahn

situation; setting -
обстановка
ohbstahNOHVkah

size - **розмір** ROHZmeer

skates - **ковзани** kohvzahNIH

skating rink - **каток**
kahTOHK

skis - **лижі** LIHzhee

skin; hide - **шкура**
SHKOOrah

skin; leather - **шкіра**
SHKEErah

skirt - **спідниця**
speedNIHtsyah

skullcap - **єрмолка**
yehrMOHLkah

sky; heaven - **небо** NEHboh

skyscraper - **хмарочос**

khmahrohCHOHS

sleep; dream - **сон** sohn

sleep (to) - **спати** SPAHtih

sleeve - **рукав** rooKAHV

sleigh; sled - **санки** SAHNkih

slip - **комбінація**
kohmbeeNAHtseeyah

slippers - **тапочки**
TAHpohchkih

slippery (adj) - **слизький**
slihz'KIHY

slow (adj) - **повільний**
pohVEEL'nihy

small (adj) - **малий** mahLIHY

small change - **копійки**
kohPEEYkih

smart; intelligent (adj)
розумний rohZOOMnihy

smell (to) - **пахнути**
PAHKHnootih

smell - **запах** ZAHpahkh

smile - **посмішка**
POHSmeeshkah

smoke (to) - **курити**
kooRIHtih

smoke - **дим** dihm

smokey (adj) - **димний**
DIHMnihy

smooth (adj) - **гладкий**
glahdKIHY

snack bar - **буфет** booFEHT

snack; appetizer - **закуска**
zahKOOSkah

snackbar - **закусочна**
zahKOOsohchnah

sneakers - **кеди** KEHdih

sneezing - **чхання**
CHKHAHNnyah

snow - **сніг** sneeg

so; true - **так** tahk

soap - **мило** MIHloh

soccer - **футбол** footBOHL

society; company -
товари́ство
tohvahRIHSTvoh

socks - **шкарпе́тки**
shkahrPEHTkih

sofa - **дива́н** dihVAHN

soft (adj) - **м'яки́й**
myahKIHY

sold out - **розпро́дано**
rohzPROHdahnoh

soldier - **солда́т** sohlDAHT

sole (of a shoe) - **підме́тка**
peedMEHTkah

somehow - **як-не́будь** yahk
NEHbood'

someone - **хто-не́будь** khtoh
NEHbood'

something - **що-не́будь**
shchoh NEHbood'

sometimes - **іноді** EEnohdee

somewhere - **де-не́будь** deh
NEHbood'

son - **син** sihn

son-in-law **зять** zyaht'

song - **пі́сня** PEESnyah

sorry - **проба́чте/виба́чте**
prohBAHCHteh/
VIHbachteh

sort; kind; type - **рід/вид** reed/
vihd

soul - **душа́** dooSHAH

sound; noise - **звук** zvook

soup - **суп** soop

soup noodle - **ло́кшина**
LOHKshihnah

sour (adj) - **ки́слий** KIHSlihy

sour cream - **смета́на**
smehTAHnah

south - **пі́вдень** PEEVdehn'

southern (adj) - **півде́нний**
peevDEHNnihy

souvenir - **сувені́р**
soovehNEER

spare; extra - **за́йвий**
ZAYvihy

speak (to); talk (about) -
говори́ти gohvohRIHtih

specialty - **спеціа́льність**
spehtseeAHL'neest'

spectator - **гляда́ч**
glyahDAHCH

speech - **промо́ва**
prohMOHvah

speed - **шви́дкість**
SHVIHDkeest'

spider - **паву́к** pahVOOK

spoiled; rotten; tainted (adj) -
зіпсо́ваний
zeePSOHvahnihy

spoon - **ло́жка** LOHZHkah

sports fan - **болі́льник**
bohLEEL'nihk

sports match - **матч** mahtch

sports team - **кома́нда**
kohMAHNdah

spot; stain - **пля́ма**
PLYAHmah

spring - **весна́** vehsNAH

spring (adj) - **весня́ний**
vehsNYAHnihy

spruce; Christmas tree -
яли́нка yahLIHNkah

square (adj) - **квадра́товий**
kvahdrahTOHvihy

stadium - **стадіо́н**
stahdeeOHN

stage - **сце́на** STSEHnah

stairs - **схо́ди** SKHOHdih

stamp - **ма́рка** MAHRkah

star - **зі́рка** ZEERkah

starch - **крохма́ль**
krohkhMAHL'

State - **держа́ва**
dehrZHAHvah

196

state - штат shtaht
state; government (adj) - державний dehrZHAHVnihy
station - станція STAHNtseeyah
station (train) - вокзал vohkZAHL
stay - перебування pehrehbooVAHNnyah
steak - біфштекс beefSHTEHKS
steal (to) - красти KRAHStih
steam room - парилка pahRIHLkah
steamed (adj) - парений PAHrehnihy
step - крок krohk
step-mother - мачуха MAHchookhah
stepfather - відчим VEEDchihm
stew - рагу rahGOO
stewardess - стюардеса styooahrDEHsah
sticky (adj) - липкий lihpKIHY
still; all the same - усе-таки ooSEH tahKIH
still; yet; else; more; another - ще shcheh
stockings - панчохи pahnCHOHkhih
stomach - живіт zhihVEET
stop - стоп stohp
store - магазин mahgahZIHN
storm - буря BOOryah
stormy; violent (adj) - бурхливий boorkhLIHvihy
story; floor - поверх POHvehrkh

story; tale; account - оповідання ohpohyeeDAHNnyah
stove - пічка PEECHkah
straight (adj) - прямий pryahMIHY
strain; sprain - розтягнення rohzTYAHGnehnnyah
strainer - ситечко SIHtehchkoh
strait; channel - протока prohTOHkah
strange; weird; odd (adj) дивний DIHVnihy
stranger - незнайомий nehznahYOHmihy
strawberries - суниці sooNIHtsee
street - вулиця VOOlihtsyah
street car - трамвай trahmVAY
strength - сила SIHlah
stress (grammatical) - наголос NAHgohlohs
stretcher - носилки nohSIHLkih
strict; harsh; severe (adj) - суворий sooVOHrihy
stroke - інсульт eenSOOLT'
stroll, walk (to) - гуляти gooLYAHtih
strong (adj) - сильний SIHL'nihy
strong; durable - міцний meetsNIHY
stubborn (adj) - наполегливий nahpohLEHGlihvihy
student/(f) - студент /-ка stooDEHNT/-kah
study (to) - вчитися VCHIHtihsyah

stuffed (food) (adj) -
  фаршированиий
  fahrshihROHvahnihy
stuffed animal - чучело
  CHOOchehloh
stuffed cabbage - голубці
  gohloobTSEE
stuffy - душно DOOSHnoh
stupid; silly (adj) - дурний
  doorNIHY
subject - предмет
  prehdMEHT
substitution - заміна
  zahNEEnah
suburb - передмістя
  pehrehdMEEStyah
subway - метро mehtROH
success - успіх OOSpeekh
suddenly - раптом
  RAHPtohm
suede - замша ZAHMshah
sugar - цукор TSOOkohr
suicide - самовбивство
  sahmohVBIHVstvoh
suit - костюм kohsTYOOM
suit jacket (man's) - піджак
  peedZHAHK
suitcase - чемодан
  chehmohDAHN
summer - літо LEEtoh
summer (adj) - літній
  LEETneey
sun - сонце SOHNtseh
sunburn; sun tan - загар
  zahGAHR
sunglasses - темні окуляри
  TEHMnee ohkooLYAHrih
sunny (adj) - сонячний
  SOHnyahchnihy
sunrise - схід skheed
supper - вечеря
  vehCHEHryah

supper (to eat) - вечеряти
  vehCHEHryahtih
surgeon - хірург
  kheeROORG
surprising (adj) - дивний
  DIHVnihy
swallow (to) - ковтати
  kohvTAHtih
sweat - піт peet
sweater - светер SVEHtehr
sweet (adj) - солодкий
  sohLOHDkihy
swim (to) - плавати
  PLAHvahtih
swollen; puffed up (adj) -
  роздутий ROHZdootihy
sympathy - співчуття
  speevchootTYAH
synagogue - синагога
  sihnahGOHgah
system - система
  sihsTEHmah

T

t-shirt - майка MAYkah
table - стіл steel
take, seize (to) - брати/взяти
  BRAHtih/VZYAHtih
takeoff (airplane) - зліт zleet
talcum powder - тальк tahl'k
tale - казка KAHZkah
talk, chat (to) - розмовляти
  rohzmohvLYAHtih
talkative (adj) - говірливий
  gohveerLIHvihy
tampon - тампон tahmPOHN
tangerine - мандарин
  mahndahRIHN
tape recorder - магнітофон
  mahgneetohFOHN
tasteless (adj) - без смаку

198

behz smahKOO

tasty - **смачний** smahchNIHY

tax - **податок** pohDAHtohk

taxi - **таксі** tahkSEE

taxi stop - **стоянка** stohYAHnkah

tea - **чай** chay

tea caddy - **чайниця** CHAYnihtsyah

tea kettle - **чайник** CHAYnihk

teacher (f) - **викладач/-ка / вчитель/-ка** vihklahDAHCH/-kah/ VCHIHtehl'/-kah

tears - **сльози** SLYOHzih

teddy bear - **ведмедик** vehdMEHdihk

telegram - **телеграма** tehlehGRAHmah

telegraph office - **телеграф** tehlehGRAHF

telephone - **телефон** tehlehFOHN

telephone booth - **телефон-автомат** tehlehFOHN ahvtohMAHT

television - **телебачення** tehlehBAHchehnnyah

television set - **телевізор** tehlehVEEzohr

temperature - **температура** tehmpehrahTOOrah

temporarily - **тимчасово** tihmchahSOHvoh

tender; gentle; delicate (adj) - **ніжний** NEEZHnihy

tennis - **теніс** TEHnees

tension; stress; strain - **напруження** nahPROOzhennyah

tent - **палатка** pahLAHTkah

textbook - **підручник** peedROOCHnihk

than - **ніж** neezh

thank (to) - **дякувати** DYAHkoovahtih

thank you - **дякую** DYAHkooyoo

thankful; grateful (adj) - **вдячний** VDYAHCHnihy

thanks a lot - **дуже дякую** DOOzheh DYAHKooyoo

that (one) - **цей** tsey

that way - **туди** tooDIH

theater - **театр** tehAHTR

theater box - **ложа** LOHzhah

then - **тоді** tohDEE

then; next; afterwards - **потім** POHteem

there - **там** tahm

therefore - **тому** tohMOO

thermometer - **термометр** tehrMOHmehtr

thermos - **термос** TEHRmohs

they - **вони** vohNIH

thick, dense (adj) - **густий** goosTIHY

thief - **злодій** ZLOHdeey

thin (adj) **тонкий/худий** tohnKIHY/khooDIHY

thirst - **спрага** SPRAHgah

though; idea - **думка** DOOMkah

thousand - **тисяча** TIHsyahchah

thread - **нитка** NIHTkah

threat - **загроза** zahGROHzah

threatening (adj) - **грізний** GREEZnihy

throat - **горло** GOHRloh

through - **крізь** kreez'

through; within - **через**

199

CHEHrehz
thumb - **великий палець**
vehLIHkihy PAHlehts'
thunder - **грім** greem
thunderstorm - **гроза**
grohZAH
ticket - **квиток** kvihTOHK
ticket office - **квиткова каса**
kvihtKOHvah KAHsah
tie - **галстук/краватка**
GAHLstook/krahVAHTkah
tie; connection - **зв'язок**
zvyahZOHK
tightly packed (adj) -
набитий nahBIHtihy
time (it's) - **пора** pohRAH
time (period of); date; dealing -
строк strohk
time - **час** chahs
time; hour - **година**
gohDIHnah
timetable - **розклад**
ROHZklahd
time; once; one - **раз** rahz
timid; shy (adj) -
соромливий
sohrohmLIHvihy
tip - **чайові** chayohVEE
tired (f) (adj) - **стомлений/-а**
STOHMlehnihy/-ah
to; toward - **до** doh
to; up to; before - **до** doh
tobacco - **тютюн**
tyooTYOON
today - **сьогодні**
syohGOHDnee
today's (adj) -
сьогоднішній
syohGOHDneeshneey
together - **разом** RAHzohm
toilet - **туалет** tooahLEHT
toilet paper - **туалетний**

папір tooahLEHTnihy
pahPEER
tomato - **помидор**
pohmeeDOHR
tombstone - **надгробний**
камінь nahdGROHBnihy
KAHmeen'
tomorrow - **завтра** ZAHVtrah
tomorrow's (adj)
завтрашній
ZAHVtrahshneey
tongue; language - **мова**
MOHvah
tonsil - **мигдалина**
mihnDAHlihnah
tonsils - **гланди** GLAHNdih
too (much) - **занадто**
zahNAHDtoh
tooth - **зуб** zoob
toothache - **зубний біль**
zoobNIHY beel'
toothbrush - **зубна щітка**
zoobNAH SHCHEETkah
toothpaste - **зубна паста**
zoobNAH PAHStah
top - **верх** vehrkh
topaz - **топаз** tohPAHZ
torch - **ліхтар** leekhTAHR
torn; ripped (adj) - **рваний**
RVAHnihy
touch (to) - **торкатися**
tohrKAHtihsyah
tour - **екскурсія**
ehksKOORseeyah
tour guide - **екскурсовод**
ehkskoorsohVOHD
tourist - **турист** tooRIHST
towel - **рушник** rooshNIHK
tower - **башта** BAHSHtah
toy - **іграшка** EEGrahshkah
traffic light - **світлофор**
sveetlohFOHR

tragedy - **трагедія**
trahGEHdeeayh
train - **поїзд** POHyeezd
train compartment - **купе**
kooPEH
transfer; change (planes,
trains, buses etc)
пересадка
pehrehSAHDkah
translate (to) - **перекласти**
pehrehKLAHStih
translation - **переклад**
pehREHKlahd
translator - **перкладач**
pehrehklahDAHCH
trash - **сміття** smeetTYAH
traveler - **мандрівник**
mahndreevNIHK
travels; trip - **подорож**
POHdohrohzh
treatment - **лікування**
leekooVAHNnyah
tree - **дерево** DEHrehvoh
trip; flight - **рейс** reys
trip; way; path - **шлях**
shlyahkh
trolley bus - **тролейбус**
trohLEYboos
trout - **форель** fohREHL'
truck - **вантажний**
автомобіль
vahnTAHZHnihy
ahvtohmohBEEL'
true; faithful (adj) - **вірний**
VEERnihy
truth - **правда** PRAHVdah
tsar- **цар** tsahr
tuna - **тунець** tooNEHTS'
turkey - **індик** eenDIHK
turn on, switch on (to) -
включати
vklyooCHAHtih

turn out, switch off (to) -
виключати
vihklyooCHAHtih
turnip - **ріпа** REEpah
tweezers - **пинцет**
pihnTSEHT
typewriter - **друкарська**
машинка
drooKAHRS'kah
mahSHINkah

U

ugly (adj) - **потворний**
pohTVOHRnihy
Ukrainian (adj) -
український
ookrahYEENs'kihy
Ukrainian/(f) - **українець/**
ка ookrahYEEnehts'/-kah
ulcer - **виразка** VIHrahzkah
umbrella - **парасоля**
pahrahSOHlyah
unattainable (adj)
недосягаємий
nehdohsyahGAHyehmihy
uncle - **дядько** DYAHD'koh
unclean; dirty (adj) -
нечистий nehCHIHStihy
unclear (adj) - **неясний**
nehYAHSnihy
uncomfortable (adj) -
незручний
nehZROOCHnihy
unconscious (adj) -
несвідомий
nehsveeDOHmihy
under; beneath - **під** peed
underpants - **труси** trooSIH
undershirt - **майка** MAYkah
understand (to) - **розуміти**
rohzooMEEtih

201

understandable (adj)
зрозумілий
zrohzooMEElihy

undertaking; venture -
підприємство
peedprihYEHMstvoh

underwear - **нижня білизна**
NIHZHnyah beeLIHZnah

unfair; injust (adj) -
несправедливий
nehsprahvehdLIHvihy

unfamiliar (adj) -
незнайомий
nehznahYOHmihy

unfortunate; unhappy (adj)
нещасливий
nehshchahsLIHvihy

unhappy; unfortunate (adj) -
невдаха nehVDAHkhah

unimportant (adj) -
неважливий
nehvahzhLIHvihy

unintentional; involuntary (adj)
- **невільний**
nehVEEL'nihy

union - **союз** sohYOOZ

universal; general (adj) -
загальний
zahGAHL'nihy

university - **університет**
ooneevehrsihTEHT

unknown (adj) - **невідомий**
nehveeDOHmihy

unnatural (adj) -
ненатуральний
nehnahtooRAHL'nihy

unnoticable (adj) -
непомітний
nehpohMEETnihy

unpleasant; disagreeable (adj) -
неприємний
nehprihYEHMnihy

unprofitable; unfavorable (adj)
- **невигідний**
nehVIHgeednihy

unripe; not mature (adj) -
незрілий nehZREElihy

unsuccessful (adj) -
неуспішний
nehoosPEESHnihy

until - **до/поки** doh/POHkih

untruth; falsehood; lie -
неправда nehPRAHVdah

unusual; uncommon (adj)
незвичайний
nehzvihCHAYnihy

up, upwards (destination) -
вгору VGOHroo

up; upwards (location) -
нагорі nahgohREE

upper; top (adj) - **верхній**
VEHRKHneey

uprising; revolt - **повстання**
pohvsTAHNnyah

urgent; emergency (adj) -
негайний nehGAYnihy

urine - **сеча** sehCHAH

use; benefit - **користь**
KOHrihst'

useful; helpful (adj) -
корисний kohRIHSnihy

useless (adj) - **марний**
MAHRnihy

usually - **звичайно**
zvihCHAYnoh

V

vacation (from work) -
відпустка
veedPOOSTkah

vagina - **влагалище**
vlahgahlihSHCHEH

vaginal infection - **запалення**

202

влага́лища
zahPAHlehnnyah
vlahGAHlihshchah
vague; indefinite; uncertain
(adj) - неозна́чений
nehohzNAHchehnihy
valley - доли́на dohLIHnah
valuable (adj) - ці́нний
TSEENnihy
value; worth - ва́ртість
VAHRteest'
vanilla - ваніль vahNEEL'
vaseline - вазелі́н
vahzehLEEN
veal - теля́тина
tehLYAHtihnah
vegetable salad - вінігре́т
veeneeGREHT
vegetables - о́вочі OHvohchee
vegetarian - вегетаріа́нець
vehgehtahreeAHnehts'
vein - жи́ла ZHIHlah
vein - ве́на VEHnah
vending machine - автома́т
ahvtohMAHT
venison - олени́на
ohlehNIHnah
verb - дієсло́во
deeyehSLOHvoh
very - ду́же DOOzheh
vest - жиле́т zhihLYEHT
victory - перемо́га
pehrehMOHgah
village - село́ sehLOH
violence - наси́льство
nahSIHL'stvoh
virus - ві́рус VEEroos
visa - ві́за VEEzah
visible; clear; obvious - ви́дно
VIHDnoh
vitamins - вітамі́ни
veetahMEEnih

vodka - горі́лка
gohREELkah
voice - го́лос GOHlohs
voltage - вольта́ж
vohl'TAHZH
vote (to) - голосува́ти
gohlosooVAHtih

W

waist - та́лія TAHleeyah
wait (to) - чека́ти
chehKAHtih
waiter - офіціа́нт
ohfeetseeAHNT
waitress - офіціа́нтка
ohfeetseeAHNTkah
wall - стіна́ steeNAH
wallet; billfold - гамане́ць
gahmahNEHTS'
want (to) - хоті́ти khohTEEtih
war - війна́ veeyNAH
warm (adj) - те́плий
TEHPlihy
warning - попере́дження
pohpehREHDzhehnnyah
washing; laundry - пра́ння
prahnNYAH
wasp - оса́ ohSAH
watch - годи́нник
gohDIHNnihk
water - вода́ vohDAH
waterfall - водопа́д
vohdohPAHD
watermelon - каву́н
kahVOOH
wave - хви́ля KHVIHlyah
we - ми mih
weak (adj) - слабки́й
slahbKIHY
weather - пого́да pohGOHdah
wedding - весі́лля

203

vehSEELlyah

week - **тиждень**
TIHZHdehn'

weekday - **будній день**
BOODneey dehn'

weight - **вага** vahGAH

well; healthy (adj) -
здоровий zdohROHvihy

well; well then - **ну** noo

west - **захід** ZAHkheed

western (adj) - **західний**
ZAHkheednihy

wet (adj) - **мокрий**
MOHKrihy

what - **що** shchoh

wheat - **пшениця**
pshehNIHtsyah

wheel - **колесо** kohlehSOH

when - **коли** kohLIH

where - **де** deh

where to - **куди** kooDIH

which - **котрий** kohtRIHY

whisper - **шепіт** SHEHpeet

white (adj) - **білий** BEElihy

who - **хто** khtoh

whole; entire (adj) - **цілий**
TSEElihy

why - **чому** chohMOO

wide; broad (adj) - **широкий**
shihROHkihy

widow - **удова** oodohVAH

widower - **удівець**
oodeeVEHTS'

width - **ширина**
shihrihNAH

wife - **дружина**
drooZHIHnah

wild (adj) - **дикий** DIHkihy

wild game - **дичина**
dihchihNAH

wind - **вітер** VEEter

window - **вікно** veekNOH

windshield - **вітрове скло**
veetrohVEH skloh

windy (adj) - **вітряний**
VEETryahnihy

wine - **вино** vihNOH

winter - **зима** zihMAH

winter (adj) - **зимовий**
zihMOHvihy

wish; desire - **бажання**
bahZHAHNnyah

with; off; since - **з** z

without - **без** behz

without transfer -
безпересадочний
behzpehrehSAHdohchnihy

woman - **жінка** ZHEENkah

wonderful; miraculous (adj) -
чудовий chooDOHvihy

woodcock - **вальдшнеп**
vahl'dSHNEHP

wooden (adj) - **дерев'яний**
dehrehvYAHnihy

woolen (adj) - **шерстяний**
shehrstyahNIHY

word - **слово** SLOHvoh

work - **робота** rohBOHtah

work (to) - **працювати**
prahtsyooVAHtih

worker - **робітник**
rohbeetNIHK

workers' cooperative - **артіль**
ahrTEEL'

world - **світ** sveet

worried, agitated (to be) -
хвилюватися
khvihlyooVAHtihsyah

worried; troubled (adj) -
неспокійний
nehspohKEEYnihy

worry, trouble, bother, disturb
(to) - **турбувати**
toorbooVAHtih

worse - **гíрше** GEERsheh
worship service ;
 богослужíння
 bohgohslooZHEENnyah
wound - **páна** RAHnah
wounded (adj) - **поráнений**
 pohRAHnehnihy
wrapping for mailing printed
 matter - **бандерóль**
 bahndehROHL'
write (to) - **писáти** pihSAHtih
writer - **письмéнник**
 pihs'MEHNnihk
writing (in) - **письмóво**
 pihs'MOHvoh
wrong; incorrect (adj) -
 непрáвильний
 nehPRAHvihl'nihy

X

x-ray - **рентгéн** rehnGEHN

Y

year - **рíк** reek
years - **рóки** ROHkih

yearly; annual (adj) -
 щорíчний
 shchohREECHnihy
yellow (adj) - **жóвтий**
 ZHOHVtihy
yes - **так** tahk
yesterday - **вчóра** VCHOHrah
yesterday's (adj) -
 вчорáшнíй
 vchohRAHSHneey
yogurt-like drink - **кефíр**
 kehFEER
young (adj) - **молодúй**
 mohlohDIHY
young lady; waitress -
 дíвчина DEEVchihnah
young people - **мóлодь**
 MOHlohd'
younger (adj) - **молóдший**
 mohLOHDshihy
youth - **юнíсть** YOOneest'

Z

zero - **нуль** nool'
zipper - **змíйка** ZMEEYkah
zoo - **зоопáрк** zohohPAHRK

205

CPSIA information can be obtained
at www.ICGtesting.com
Printed in the USA
JSHW052006130723
44718JS00002B/34

9 780781 801881